The Exploratorium

SCIENCE SNACKBOOK

Cook Up Over 100 Hands-On Science Exhibits from Everyday Materials, Revised Edition

Exploratorium Teacher Institute

For the Exploratorium—www.exploratorium.edu

PUBLISHER: Robert J. Semper
BUSINESS MANAGER: Kurt Feichtmeir
CONTENT: Paul Doherty, Don Rathjen, and the staff of the Exploratorium Teacher Institute
PROJECT DIRECTOR/CONTRIBUTING EDITOR: Ruth Brown
PROJECT COORDINATOR: Laura Jacoby
PHOTOGRAPHY: Esther Kutnick, Susan Schwartzenberg, Amy Snyder
ILLUSTRATION: Larry Antila, David Barker, Gary Crounse, Jad King, Arthur Koch,
    Luisa Kolla, Alisa Lowden, Peter Olguin
RESOURCE EDITOR: Judith Brand
NATIONAL SCIENCE EDUCATION STANDARDS CONSULTANT: Rilla Chaney
COVER PHOTO: Amy Snyder
BOOK DESIGNER AND COMPOSITOR: Maureen Forys, Happenstance Type-O-Rama

All images copyright © 2009 Exploratorium

The original *Exploratorium Science Snackbook,* upon which this book is based, was made possible by a grant from The Pacific Telesis Foundation and funding for the Teacher Institute, a part of the Exploratorium Regional Science Resource Center, California Department of Education, National Science Foundation, and the Walter S. Johnson Foundation.

Exploratorium® is a registered trademark and service mark of the Exploratorium.

ISBN: 978-047-0-48186-8

Printed in the United States of America
FIRST EDITION

PB Printing   10 9 8 7 6 5 4 3 2 1

Welcome to the 2009 Edition of the
Exploratorium Science Snackbook

The Exploratorium turned forty in 2009, and this volume is just one of the many ways we're celebrating four decades of creativity, collaboration, and growth with the science-education community.

This book, originally published in 1991, began as a labor of love, as science teachers from the San Francisco Bay Area looked for innovative ways to bring the Exploratorium experience into their classrooms—all on a teacher's budget! Today, these explorations have been adapted for schoolrooms, universities, and educational enrichment programs all over the world.

We hope this new edition of the *Exploratorium Science Snackbook* continues to offer new insights and tools to inspire teaching and learning in the sciences and beyond.

Dennis Bartels
Executive Director, Exploratorium
San Francisco
July, 2009

Contents

Part Four: The Spinning Blackboard and Other Dynamic Explorations of Force and Motion

Part Five: The Wire-Hanger Concerto and Other Ear-Splitting Explorations of How We Hear the World

Introduction

This book is full of Snacks … but they're not the kind you eat. Exploratorium Science Snacks are miniature versions of some of the most popular exhibits, demonstrations, and activities at the Exploratorium, San Francisco's famed museum of science, art, and human perception.

For lack of a better description, the Exploratorium calls itself a museum. But the half-million visitors who come through the doors each year don't find hushed corridors, watchful guards, or "do not touch" signs. Instead, they walk into a cavernous space filled with whirring, buzzing, spinning things, where people of all ages are smiling and laughing and calling out to one another.

At the Exploratorium, you can touch a tornado, look inside an eye, or pull a giant bubble over your head. You can make your way through a pitch-dark labyrinth using only your sense of touch, participate in a lecture and discussion with some of the leading scientists of the day, or watch the production of a live Webcast. When you're done, you might find that you understand a little more about the world around you than you ever have before.

What is a science Snack?

Since the Exploratorium opened in 1969, teachers from the San Francisco Bay Area have brought their classes on field trips. As the popularity and reputation of the museum spread, teachers began to ask if there might be some way to bring the popular hands-on exhibits to their students. Our response was the creation of the *Snackbook*.

For three years, nearly a hundred teachers from the museum's Teacher Institute worked with staff members to create scaled-down versions of Exploratorium exhibits. The results were dozens of exciting "Snacks"—miniature science exhibits and investigations that teachers could make using familiar, inexpensive, easily available materials.

Why are they called Snacks?

At the Exploratorium, nobody thinks twice when someone says they're "building a Snack." People know they're a lot more likely to get instructions for creating a mini-exhibit than they are to get something to eat. Over the years, a community of teachers has spread the term to some far-flung places, but few know how it began. In fact, three books containing detailed instructions, or "recipes," for building exact full-sized replicas of Exploratorium exhibits were published in the 1980s. These publications, designed for other science museums engaged in building their own exhibit collections, were called *Cookbooks*. Need we say more?

What can you do with a Snack?

When this book was originally published, we knew teachers would be able to use Snacks as demonstrations, lessons, and labs, and that students could use Snacks for group and individual projects. But it wasn't long before we began to realize that Snacks were really getting around.

Within a week of publication, for example, we received a message from a teacher in the Australian Outback who needed help finding materials. We heard from elementary school teachers and university professors. Art teachers were using Snacks, as were shop teachers and math teachers. Sixth-graders at one school were building their own miniature science museum. At another school, an English as a Second Language (ESL) teacher found that building Snacks helped her students interact more: Those who understood science best were helping those more adept at building things, and all were getting better at communicating with each other. Teachers from all grade levels and many subject areas were finding useful ideas in the *Snackbook*.

And it wasn't just teachers who found Snacks useful: Children were bringing Snacks home to their families. Scouts were using Snacks to help get science badges. Snacks were making appearances at science fairs, birthday parties, and impromptu "magic" shows. In some cases, Snacks even found their way back to the Exploratorium as activities and demonstrations in museum events and programming.

Why republish the *Snackbook?*

The first edition of the *Snackbook*, which gathered together 107 science explorations based on Exploratorium exhibits, was published by the Exploratorium in 1991. In 1995, a revised and updated series of four books published by John Wiley & Sons offered many of the Snacks from the original book. Over time, however, the books went out of print and became more and more difficult to find. Materials once easily available were becoming scarce as well (record turntables, for instance, have become very hard to find, as have a variety of other handy toys and gadgets).

To commemorate the Exploratorium's fortieth anniversary, we decided to bring the *Snackbook* out of retirement and make it available once again. As a testament to the staff members and Teacher Institute teachers who worked so hard to make the first *Snackbook* a reality, we decided to update the activities, but keep the funky, fun flavor of the originals. So in this new edition, we've left the 1991 version much as it was—from the simple line drawings in the Snacks to the telltale fashions of our models.

On the surface, then, this book may look a bit retro, but there's nothing old about it. In addition to redeveloping the Snacks, we've included helpful information, updated the references and resources, added a new section of sound and hearing Snacks, and included charts identifying associated National Science Education Standards. There are helpful indexes, new time estimations, and suggestions for activity extensions.

With the growing importance of science and technology, and the unprecedented challenges being faced by science teachers today, this book offers the practical tools and information teachers need to transcend the limits of their textbooks and make science come alive in the classroom and beyond.

What's in a Snack?

Materials
A list of the materials you'll need to build the Snack; most include both English and metric units

Icons
Identify the major phenomena illustrated by this Snack

Snack Name
The name of an exhibit or activity created by Exploratorium staff

One-Liner
A one-line description of the Snack

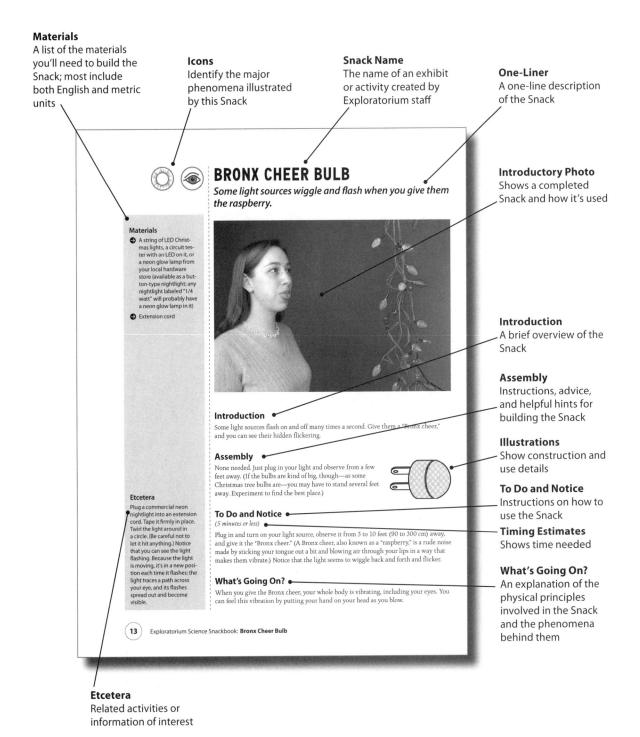

Introductory Photo
Shows a completed Snack and how it's used

BRONX CHEER BULB
Some light sources wiggle and flash when you give them the raspberry.

Materials
➔ A string of LED Christmas lights, a circuit tester with an LED on it, or a neon glow lamp from your local hardware store (available as a button-type nightlight; any nightlight labeled "1/4 watt" will probably have a neon glow lamp in it)
➔ Extension cord

Introduction
Some light sources flash on and off many times a second. Give them a "Bronx cheer," and you can see their hidden flickering.

Assembly
None needed. Just plug in your light and observe from a few feet away. (If the bulbs are kind of big, though—as some Christmas tree bulbs are—you may have to stand several feet away. Experiment to find the best place.)

To Do and Notice
(5 minutes or less)

Plug in and turn on your light source, observe it from 3 to 10 feet (90 to 300 cm) away, and give it the "Bronx cheer." (A Bronx cheer, also known as a "raspberry," is a rude noise made by sticking your tongue out a bit and blowing air through your lips in a way that makes them vibrate.) Notice that the light seems to wiggle back and forth and flicker.

What's Going On?
When you give the Bronx cheer, your whole body is vibrating, including your eyes. You can feel this vibration by putting your hand on your head as you blow.

Etcetera
Plug a commercial neon nightlight into an extension cord. Tape it firmly in place. Twirl the light around in a circle. (Be careful not to let it hit anything.) Notice that you can see the light flashing. Because the light is moving, it's in a new position each time it flashes: the light traces a path across your eye, and its flashes spread out and become visible.

13 Exploratorium Science Snackbook: **Bronx Cheer Bulb**

Introduction
A brief overview of the Snack

Assembly
Instructions, advice, and helpful hints for building the Snack

Illustrations
Show construction and use details

To Do and Notice
Instructions on how to use the Snack

Timing Estimates
Shows time needed

What's Going On?
An explanation of the physical principles involved in the Snack and the phenomena behind them

Etcetera
Related activities or information of interest

IMPORTANT SAFETY MESSAGE

(!) BE CAREFUL The experiments in this volume were designed with safety and success in mind. But even the simplest activity or the most common materials can be harmful when mishandled or misused. Use common sense whenever you're exploring or experimenting.

Icon Key

Chemistry

Color

Electricity

Fluids

Heat

Life Sciences

Light

Magnetism

Math

Mechanics

Perception

Polarization

Reflection

Refraction

Resonance

Sound

Waves

HOW TO USE CONTENT ICONS

Watch for the icons that accompany each Snack. Each icon represents a concept addressed, and/or the foundational ideas introduced or supported by the Snack. In addition to being a quick way to see how a Snack might be used for teaching and learning, icons can also offer ideas for extending and connecting concepts in the classroom.

Tips and Tales—By Teachers, for Teachers

The first *Snackbook* was published in 1991, and over the years, we've heard from hundreds of teachers and youth leaders who wanted to share their Snack-related ideas and experiences. Here are some helpful stories and suggestions—by teachers, for teachers.

Making Your Own Science Exhibits

In the years before the Snackbook *was published, teachers working with the Exploratorium Teacher Institute began experimenting with creating classroom-sized versions of museum exhibits. Erainya Neirro was so energized by the experience that she took it back to her classroom.*

Over the years, I've noticed that science becomes "real" for those students who can put something together and watch what it does. While looking for ways to expand my own repertoire of science activities for kids, I enrolled in a class offered by the Exploratorium Teacher Institute. I had such a great time! For six weeks, twelve teachers became inquisitive, involved students. We roamed the museum and played with exhibits. Our goal was to choose an exhibit and build a model that would somehow demonstrate the same scientific principle that the sophisticated Exploratorium exhibit illustrated.

During the class, I built four of my own original mini-exhibits and watched my colleagues construct and improve their own. I was more excited about hands-on science than ever. But most important, I really enjoyed and relied on the support of the other teachers as we all struggled together to perfect exhibits that sometimes worked—and sometimes didn't. I came away with innumerable projects for my classroom and the realization that this kind of approach didn't have to be just for teachers. My kids could do the same thing—learning about science, working with the support of their peers, doing things on their own, and having fun. I wanted my students to have this experience.

Since Presidio Hill School is close to the Exploratorium, most of my students were familiar with it. When I suggested the idea of an "Exploring Science" project based on my own experiences at the Exploratorium, the response was overwhelmingly enthusiastic. I brought in the four exhibit models I had built and let my students play with them. I told them that the Exploratorium exhibits I had replicated looked very different from my models, but both "said" the same thing about physics. Like me, the students wouldn't copy the construction of an exhibit; each student had to find some way to build a model that would show the same scientific principle that an Exploratorium exhibit demonstrated.

Finally, we were ready for our first visit to the Exploratorium. Once inside, the kids were given an hour to play with exhibits and pick one they wanted to replicate. This exploration time was essential, since each person was expected to build a different exhibit. As students made their decisions, they came right back to me: They knew that it was first come, first served.

Over the course of three visits to the museum, each student chose three different exhibits that demonstrated many different scientific principles, but several favorites came from sections of the Exploratorium that demonstrated perspective, vision, color, and light. Two favorites were Bird in the Cage and Blue Sky. If you look at the Bird in the Cage Snack (page 11), you can see its potential flexibility: A variety of colors and shapes can be used to demonstrate the concept of afterimages. The Blue Sky exhibit (page 123) is appealing because it's easy for the kids to figure out what they will need: essentially, water and some kind of light source. Besides this relatively simple assembly, Blue Sky answers a question that fascinates them: "Why is the sky blue?"

Once choices had been made, I asked students to tell me how they would design the exhibit for the classroom. It was important to assess whether their plans were feasible; occasionally, I had to make suggestions to help simplify the process. I also had to direct one or two students to do different, less complicated exhibits.

While at the museum, I left students alone so they could sketch preliminary designs and write notes from the information at each exhibit. I asked them to think about how other people would use their model and to consider the science their model would illustrate. Before we left the museum, I checked each student's designs and notes at least once. Many had to return to an exhibit to clarify some point or get more information. My class and I were at the Exploratorium approximately four hours during each of these three field trips.

Back at school, several class sessions were devoted to building science projects. We all brought in a variety of materials. Like most long-term science teachers, I have lots of stuff. I asked each child to get a sturdy shopping bag with handles so they could easily carry "in process" exhibits from school to home and back. Of course, this presented its own problems. Some of my students ended up misplacing their half-built exhibits; some left their projects on the bus. Other projects and materials just sort of "disappeared." None of the materials were expensive or irreplaceable, but it was no fun for those unfortunate students to start over again.

In the classroom, students selected the materials they needed and helped each other with the construction of the exhibits. I was amazed at how little they needed my help. These sessions were chaotic but wonderful. We had materials all over the room and at least three conversations going at once. We might start with a question like "What color should I make this part of my spinning disk?" and end up with a complex examination of how cones in the human eye actually work. Not everything went perfectly, of course. But, all in all, these sessions were very productive. The kids were committed to building with care. If something didn't work the first time, they pitched in to help each other.

Besides the time spent building the models, finishing details were sometimes done at home, and homework included doing a rough draft of a paper explaining each exhibit. As for the math part of the curriculum, it taught itself. The kids were so busy calculating, counting, and measuring, they hardly even noticed how much they were learning.

Finally, we had Evaluation Day. The students presented their projects and let their peers play with the finished exhibits. This display generated the kind of peer support I was hoping for. The majority of my kids were so invested in their work that each one came away with something they were proud of and thoroughly comprehended.

Their classmates were genuinely impressed. They had all seen the prototypes in various stages and now got to play with a finished model. I didn't have to use an inadequate textbook or workbook: I had a kid-directed course that was highly productive, encouraged peer support, and built the self-esteem of every student.

I encourage any teacher to give these hands-on experiments a try. Once you have a set of these demonstrations in your classroom—whether you do it by working with a local museum or by building the Snacks in the *Snackbook*—you'll have a student-built museum of your own.

Building a Mini-Exploratorium

Before he joined the Exploratorium's Teacher Institute staff, Modesto Tamez found a variety of unconventional ways to use Snacks—in the classroom and out.

One of the true joys of teaching is when you see the "lights go on" in a student's eyes: the lights of curiosity, wonder, and understanding. That's what I see when the tools for teaching are hands-on experiments that students choose and build themselves. With a little organization and effort, these projects can form the basis of a science museum in a classroom, a resource that can be shared with the entire school.

Creating a miniature science museum is easier and cheaper than you might think. I recently organized two science classes to build fifty-five exhibits. The exhibits took us a little over a month to complete and cost about $300. The rewards in student pride and knowledge—and the attention the mini-Exploratorium garnered for the school's science program—were well worth the time, effort, and expense. You can do it, too, with help from the *Exploratorium Science Snackbook*.

I start by building ten or twelve Snacks to demonstrate. I choose easy-to-handle projects and show them to my students, stressing how quick they were to assemble. On the first one or two Snacks, I go slowly through the demonstrations and spend some time helping students figure out the science behind what they're seeing.

For example, I recently used a modified version of the Fog Chamber Snack (page 97) to introduce the concept of air pressure. I stretched a rubber glove

TIP

It's great to have lots of Snack materials around, but don't forget the tools! Have simple tools available, and take the time to help students understand tool safety and use.

over the opening of a glass jar so the fingers of the glove dangled inside the jar. I chose one of the larger boys in the class to help demonstrate and asked him to put his hand all the way inside the glove. Much to the amusement of the rest of the class, he couldn't force his hand in. After they stopped giggling, I asked the students to guess why: What was already in the jar that might keep someone's hand from going in? They answered: "air." This is a very simple experiment, but with it I introduced a fundamental scientific principle to a class that had had no previous instruction in any of the physical sciences.

Sometimes I take a completely different approach to a Snack, as I did recently when I demonstrated the Doppler effect (page 249) to four separate science classes. The students assembled on a grassy knoll outside the classroom while I ran to get my car. For the next few minutes I zoomed past them—back and forth—blaring my horn as they cheered and waved. The students said they could clearly hear the Doppler effect: the pitch of the horn got higher when the car moved toward them and lower when it moved away. The experiment worked great until the fourth and final class. As I was cruising down the street with my hand jammed on the horn, I saw the flashing red lights of a police car in my rear-view mirror. The students, of course, were delighted. Peering into my car, a puzzled officer inquired, "What are you doing?" A school security guard, familiar with my antics, finally came to my rescue. "It's okay," he explained, "he's just a crazy science teacher."

After one or two demonstrations, I give my students some time to play with the completed Snacks. Don't worry if you can't answer all their questions or if some Snacks don't work the way they should. If something goes wrong, tell the class that trial and error is part of the scientific process. Tinker with the Snack and have the students help you figure out what's wrong. Pitching in and working together to solve a problem is a crucial part of doing hands-on science.

Once the students have been introduced to Snacks, it's time for them to build one of their own. I usually select a range of Snacks that I think are appropriate for my class level, pass them out, and have each student choose several favorites. If other students choose the same Snack, I may have to give some of them an alternate choice. Sometimes I opt for one of the harder Snacks if I want to challenge a student I know is capable of handling a more difficult assignment.

After the students know which Snacks they're building, I give them a week to gather materials. Some materials will be in the classroom; others they'll have to find for themselves. I also tell them it's okay if their Snack isn't exactly the same as the one in the book—it just has to make the same point. Then it usually takes three to four weeks for the students to assemble their Snacks and put on the finishing touches. If they run into problems or want to try a different approach, I talk it over with them. I'm always amazed at the creative solutions my students come up with; often, a modified Snack is an improvement over the original.

TIP

Snacks offer great team-building opportunities. Have groups help one another, and let the strengths of each student shine.

As the students experiment, they also work out the science behind their projects. The final step is writing and producing "graphics," the instructions and explanations that accompany each project.

Once the Snacks are built and the graphics completed, it's time to unveil the mini-Exploratorium. The Snacks are assembled on long tables in the classroom, and I assign four students at a time to be "Explainers," science guides who answer visitor questions. This means that students must be familiar with all the Snacks, not just their own. You can invite the whole school to the mini-Exploratorium. I'd also suggest a special parents' night exhibition. If you invite school administrators to the event they might be so impressed with the students' work that they loosen the purse strings for other innovative science programs!

Finding a New Approach to the Science Fair

Eric Kielich, science department head and teacher at the Mount Tamalpais School in Mill Valley, California, sees the creativity and ingenuity involved when his students build Snacks to be an important part of the learning experience.

As part of our curriculum, students present a mini-Exploratorium at our Middle School Science Night. Students select their projects from an Exploratorium activity publication, or from Snacks on the Exploratorium Web site, which is available on the computers in our school library. Students are made aware of the expectations and requirements of the assignment, are given a printed sheet that outlines the project for them, and are shown some of the past years' exhibits for ideas. The mini-Exploratorium projects are intended to be interactive and relatively easily constructed with a minimum of time and expense. Parents are encouraged to be supportive, but to keep their role to an advisory one.

Each Snack is to be accompanied by a self-standing display board that provides the necessary information for a person to interact independently with the activity. At the very least, it should include the title, the materials needed to assemble the Snack, and "To Do and Notice" and "What's Going On?" sections. Any additional information about the Snack that provides some insight for the participant is encouraged.

Since this assignment is one that students work on independently and mostly at home, it is important for them to have a definite plan for its completion. Students can ask for advice if they need help. Grades for the mini-Exploratorium Snacks are based on a number of considerations:

• Degree of challenge

• Innovation

• Classroom presentation

- Science night presentation

- Effectiveness of the exhibit and display board

- Meeting all due dates

These criteria are mostly subjective—and are intended to be. This assignment is not like taking a test—effort, ingenuity, and creativity are as much a part of this assignment as the completion of the display. If students challenge themselves and put in the necessary effort, they will do fine. The whole experience has proven to be a very positive one for all involved.

Placing Hands-On Materials Around Your Classroom

Before he "retired," longtime Exploratorium teacher and Snackbook *co-author Don Rathjen liked to leave intriguing tools and materials around his classroom and then watch as his students discovered them.*

Don Rathjen, known to other teachers as Mr. Snack, designs and builds hands-on exhibits, then uses them as demonstrations in his high school physics classroom in Pleasanton, California. Don knows how to grab his students' attention. He breaks a Pyrex stirring rod in half, drops both halves into a beaker filled with Karo syrup, and lets his students watch as they disappear in the fluid. Then he puts his hand in and pulls out a whole rod. Of course, the pieces of the broken rod are still in the beaker—and the unbroken rod was there all along. They just couldn't be seen.

This simple demonstration, called Disappearing Glass Rods (page 145), is one of Don's favorite Snacks. He leaves the beakers and rods and syrup lying around his classroom for months. The students who play with them get sucked into exploring and discovering science on their own.

When you enter Don's classroom, you may come face to face with a book-sized Fresnel lens hanging from the ceiling (see Giant Lens, page 149). Don tells of students who duck under the lens for months, and then suddenly discover it. When Don teaches optics, he uses the Giant Lens as a demonstration. By holding the lens at just the right distance in front of his face, his class sees his head replaced by a giant eye. The students laugh, but they want to try it, too.

Don always has his eyes open for interesting science materials. He find them at plastics stores, toy stores, even flea markets. A Fresnel lens that came from the back window of a delivery van looks just like the one Don has hanging in his class but produces the opposite visual effect. When Don holds it in front of his face, his head appears to shrink. The students love it.

Even if lenses are not a part of your curriculum, says Don, don't let that stop you from leaving them around for kids to experience. Don's classroom is filled with attention-getting materials: a gyroscope fashioned from a bicycle wheel, a pile of blocks used to demonstrate center of gravity, pendulums that swing

TIP
Make sure you know where students can obtain any specialized materials or equipment they might need. That way, their time is not spent in fruitless or frustrating searches. Instead, use even the search for materials as an educational opportunity—helping students with online research skills, for example, or introducing unfamiliar equipment or materials. Each step of building a Snack can be a learning experience.

Remind students that testing a Snack to make sure it works is part of the process—and be sure they know it's not a problem if things don't work perfectly the first time they're used. Reinforce the idea that science is trial and error, and that it's okay to make mistakes. Solving problems and fixing errors can lead to improvements and insights that might otherwise be missed!

in peculiar ways, and many, many more. These attention-grabbers motivate students. Try them yourself. You may be surprised at the discoveries both you and your students make.

Using Snacks as a Science Library

Teacher Judith Christensen finds a wealth of potential in Snackbook *activities, from helping kids understand science to helping them understand each other.*

In Judith Christensen's physics class, thirty-six high school sophomores are packed around six laboratory tables. The crowded class contains members from a variety of ethnic backgrounds: Asian, African American, white, Latino, and more. The class is popular, but students know they're expected to pitch in and work because, in Ms. Christensen's class, you learn science by doing science.

Judith organizes her class into six multiethnic groups. Each group builds its own equipment, does a scientific investigation using that equipment, and then presents oral and written reports based on its explorations. The students also evaluate each other's work. This day, the class is building the Electroscope Snack (page 95). Once the electroscopes have been constructed, the students will use them to investigate electrostatics.

For this lab, all the teams have successfully built electroscopes by draping charged strips of tape over bent soda straws stuck into film cans full of clay. Judith found the tape in administrative supplies; the straws were donated by a local fast-food restaurant; the film cans came from a neighborhood camera store; and the clay came from Judith's own collection of supplies. The resulting electroscopes are not black boxes made by some science supply house; there are no hidden or mysterious parts. The students have built them, and so "own" them. If an electroscope breaks, the students fix it or build a new one.

To build the exhibits, each team draws on the talents of all its members. Some students are better at figuring out how to build the equipment from the illustrations and photos, some are better at reading, others are better at making things work. If you listen carefully, you'll hear discussions in Cantonese, Vietnamese, and Spanish, but English is the *lingua franca* of this classroom. Students who are better at English become language teachers for the others in their group. Students who are better at science become science teachers, even if they're just learning English. The final result is a team effort.

In addition to science and English, students in this classroom are learning about different cultures. Judith finds that when students from different backgrounds work together, they become more understanding of each other. As a spur to participation, she requires that the groups give each member a group cooperation grade.

Judith doesn't have all the answers for her students' questions, but she admits when she doesn't know them and encourages her students to help her find the answers. Each year, she and her students learn more about science. And each year, the students guide Judith toward becoming more comfortable and adept at helping them to find their own answers.

Offering Hands-On Science in Nontraditional Classrooms

Snacks can be used in many different learning environments. Here, Vivian Altmann, director of the Exploratorium's Educational Outreach Department, takes one exploration to a community center and leads kids in a friendly competition that keeps them thinking and working together.

Vivian Altmann and her team regularly visit the Whitney-Young Community Center in Hunters Point, in San Francisco, with boxes of hands-on activities. The boxes contain parts for the Stripped-Down Motor Snack (page 117). The teenagers in the room are labeled at-risk and underserved, but once they get going, it's hard to tell them from any other group of energetic kids.

After the usual introductions, Vivian divides the kids into teams. She gives each group a length of insulated wire, a paper cup, twenty cents' worth of small magnets, two paper clips, a battery, and a rubber band.

The teams immediately initiate a friendly competition to see who can build the "best" motor. Soon, one team has its motor turning, then another team. The groups compare motors to see whose is fastest. When one group can't get their motor to run, Viv gets the "experts" from another team to help. The kids decide to swap parts between motors: the problem turns out to be a dead battery! The motor construction is just fine, after all. The kids razz the Exploratorium team for bringing them a dead battery, and then turn back to their motors. The room is buzzing.

Without even noticing it, these kids are learning about electricity, magnetism, and motors. When the kids make guesses about what will make their motors run better, and then test them, they are doing science. Will twice as many magnets make the motor turn twice as fast? Vivian answers by giving the team more magnets. The motor turns faster, but not twice as fast. What about using two batteries? The questions and suggestions come thick and fast, and the kids get the satisfaction of making discoveries on their own. They're learning important techniques for answering questions and solving problems; they're working cooperatively, making new friends, showing off their skills, and succeeding in science.

Building an Interactive Science Museum

Charles Reynes, a science teacher at Creekside Middle School in Castro Valley, California, takes a different approach to using Snacks. By adapting the instructions in the

TIP

Experiment with Snacks. Don't be afraid to make adjustments, changes, and alterations, and see what happens. Modify and improve Snack designs yourself, and encourage your students to do the same.

TIP

Encourage improvisation and innovation. Once students understand that they can find science-rich materials all around them, challenge them to design their own Snacks and devise their own experiments.

Snackbook, *he's built his own traveling museum, which he uses in demonstrations for students throughout the area.*

Using the *Exploratorium Science Snackbook* as a resource, I built twenty exhibits and set up a museum. Since durability was a concern, I beefed up each Snack whenever possible. My water spinner, with its acrylic tank and three-quarter-inch plywood turntable, has survived for more than twelve years. I used the write-ups in the *Snackbook* to create exhibit signs. The *Snackbook* also provided a template for me to use when I created my own Snacks. My museum currently has about forty exhibits.

Building the museum has not been easy. Most of my projects are built with scrap materials, so the size and shape depend on what's in my scrap pile. I collect and save lots of junk. I purposely keep the projects simple because I believe that a slick production sometimes hides the science. Whenever possible, I try to keep the projects small enough so they will fit into those red flip-top storage crates that are sold at Home Depot. In each case, I store the exhibit and the sign explaining it.

After a time, it can become difficult to maintain so many exhibits, so I have had to let some go. I have replaced some and added others. I have several groups that have reimbursed me for expenses or have paid to have me put on a science night for their school. These events energize me and help keep the museum going. I have also set up the museum at California State University Hayward, the lobby of the Tech Museum in San Jose, and at the Union City Science, Earth, and Health Festival. Often, my students serve as docents.

The *Snackbook* has been a valuable resource. As I built Snacks, I began to think more creatively, developing a taste for what motivates and inspires. I like to think of myself as a Snack chef!

Taking Snacks on Tour

Former Teacher Institute staff member Curt Gabrielson takes the idea of the mini-Exploratorium one step further. His classes not only build Snacks but also take them on tour!

When students get the opportunity to create work for an audience beyond the teacher and the classroom walls, the results are truly staggering. The satisfaction and confidence boost that students gain may even outshine the enormous amount of self-led learning that goes on.

Another dimension is added by going on tour. Instead of making arrangements for guests to come to us, we take our mini-Exploratorium to them. Our guests are primarily students at other schools. We go to at least one school and try to hit two or three classes at a minimum. When the introductions have been made, and the small groups of guests are moving from Snack to Snack, there is nothing to do but sit back, smile, and take some pictures. While it is

TIP
Be sure to build some Snacks yourself. Be flexible: Admit it when you don't have all the answers, and be open when your attempts fail. Share the process, not just the product, with your students.

advisable to have a small tool kit (hot glue, tape, wire, pliers, scissors, spare parts) on hand for emergency breakdowns, these presentations are often classes that run themselves.

This kind of "exhibit on tour" is a win-win-win-win situation. Both sets of students gain enormously, the teacher of the class where you are presenting sees that this is doable and may be inspired to do it in the future, and you have provided exceptional quality education while also getting considerable satisfaction.

Dealing with the logistics of the mini-Exploratorium can be frightening: finding materials, coordinating students and guests, ensuring correct understanding of concepts with each team and making sure everyone is done on time. But, taken a step at a time, it is manageable, and the results are well worth the effort.

The mini-Exploratorium can be a great way to wind up the year or an exciting ice-breaking project with a new class to start the year off right. It constitutes a fantastic science unit for students from elementary through high school and can be focused on any area of science. Of course, a great way to begin or end this unit is with a field trip to your local science museum.

PART ONE THE CHESHIRE CAT AND OTHER EYE-POPPING EXPLORATIONS OF HOW WE SEE THE WORLD

How do you see the world around you? You open your eyes and there it is: your room, your desk, the pictures on the walls, the trees outside your window.

When you take a look at the world, here's what's happening: Light is bouncing off the pictures, the trees, and all the things out there in the world. Some of that light gets into your eye. This light shines through the cornea, the tough, clear covering over the front of your eye, and then through the pupil, the dark hole in the center of your iris, the colored part of your eye. Your eye's lens focuses this light to make an image on your retina, a thin layer of light-sensitive cells that lines the back of your eyeball. The light-sensitive cells of the retina signal the brain, and the brain creates a mental image. Finally, you see the world "out there."

People have compared the eye to a film-loaded camera—and for good reason. Both your eye and a camera have adjustable openings that let in light: the pupil of your eye and the aperture of a camera. Both focus the light to make an image on a light-sensitive screen: the retina of your eye and the film of a camera.

But unlike a camera, your eye doesn't just passively record the image it receives. Working together, your eyes and brain decide what to see and how to see it. They fill in gaps in your visual field, taking limited information and creating a complete picture. They interpret the limited and distorted images that they receive and try to make sense of the world out there, often using past experience as a guide. They constantly filter out and ignore extraneous information.

You don't believe it? Then close one eye and take a look at the tip of your nose. You can see it clearly if you think about it. It's always in your view. Open both eyes and you can still see it, a shadowy protuberance in the center of your visual field. If you think about the tip of your nose, you can see it—but most of the time you don't notice it (even though it's as plain as the nose on your face).

The experiments in this section will show you some other sights you usually don't notice. Some experiments, such as Blind Spot, Pupil, and Afterimage, will help you understand more about how your eye works—its abilities and limitations. Others, like Vanna and Far-Out Corners, show how prior experience often influences perception: how what you "see" may not be what you "get." Still others, like Persistence of Vision and Jacques Cousteau in Seashells, demonstrate that your eyes and brain work together to make a picture of the world. Finally, some show how your eyes and brain can make mistakes in their interpretation of the world—mistakes that create optical illusions, deceptive pictures that fool your eyes.

Taken together, the experiments in this section let you explore visual perception, a fascinating interdisciplinary topic where biology and psychology overlap.

AFTERIMAGE
A flash of light prints a lingering image in your eye.

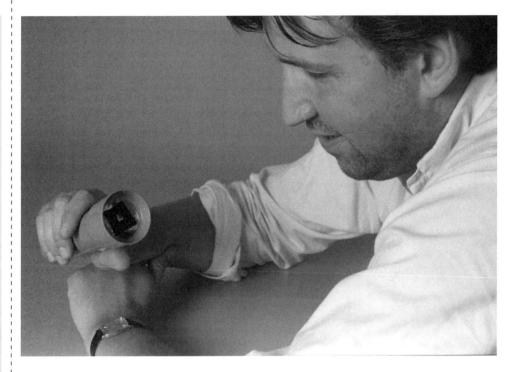

Introduction

After looking at something bright, such as a lamp or a camera's flash, you may continue to see an image of that object when you look away. This lingering visual impression is called an afterimage.

Assembly
(15 minutes or less)

1. Tape a piece of white paper over a flashlight lens.

2. Cover all but the center of the white paper with strips of opaque tape.

3. In the center of the paper, leave an area uncovered where the light can shine through the paper. This area should be a square, a triangle, or some other simple, recognizable shape.

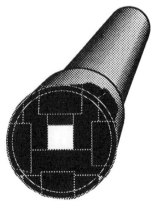

To Do and Notice
(15 minutes or more)

In a darkened room, turn on the flashlight, hold it at arm's length, and shine it into your eyes. Stare at one point of the brightly lit shape for about 30 seconds. Then stare at a blank wall and blink a few times. Notice the shape and color of the image you see.

For up to 30 minutes after you walk into a dark room, your eyes are adapting. At the end of this time, your eyes may be up to 10,000 times more sensitive to light than they were when you entered the room. We call this improved ability to see "night vision." It's caused by the chemical rhodopsin in the rods of your retina. Rhodopsin, popularly called visual purple, is a light-sensitive chemical composed of retinal (a derivative of vitamin A) and the protein opsin.

You can use the increased presence of rhodopsin to take "afterimage photographs" of the world. Here's how:

Cover your eyes to allow them to adapt to the dark. Be careful that you do not press on your eyeballs. It will take at least 10 minutes to store up enough visual purple to take a "snapshot." When enough time has elapsed, uncover your eyes. Open your eyes and look at a well-lit scene for half a second (just long enough to focus on the scene), then close and cover your eyes again. You should see a detailed picture of the scene in purple and black. After a while, the image will reverse to black and purple. You can take several "snapshots" after each 10-minute adaptation period.

Try again—first focusing on the palm of your hand and then focusing on a wall some distance from you. Compare the size of the image you see in your hand to the image you see on the wall.

Close your left eye and stare at the bright image with your right eye. Then close your right eye and look at the wall with your left eye. You will not see an afterimage.

What's Going On?

You see because light enters your eyes and produces chemical changes in the retina, the light-sensitive lining at the back of your eye. Prolonged stimulation by a bright image (here, the light source) desensitizes part of the retina. When you look at the blank wall, light reflecting from the wall shines onto your retina. The area of the retina that was desensitized by the bright image does not respond as well to this new light input as the rest of the retina. Instead, this area appears as a negative afterimage, a dark area that matches the original shape. The afterimage may remain for 30 seconds or longer.

The apparent size of the afterimage depends not only on the size of the image on your retina but also on how far away you perceive the image to be. When you look at your hand, you see the negative afterimage on your hand. Because your hand is near you, you see the image as relatively small—no bigger than your hand. When you look at a distant wall, you see the negative afterimage on the wall. But it's not the same size as the afterimage you saw on your hand. You see the afterimage on the wall as much bigger—large enough to cover a considerable area of the wall.

The afterimage is not actually on either surface—it's on your retina. The actual afterimage does not change size. The only thing changing is your interpretation of its size.

This helps explain a common illusion you may have noticed. The full moon often appears larger when it is on the horizon than when it is overhead. The disk of the moon is the exact same size in both cases, and its image on your retina is also the same size. So why does the moon look bigger in one position than in the other?

One explanation suggests that you perceive the horizon as farther away than the sky overhead. This perception might lead you to see the moon as being larger when it's near the horizon (just as the afterimage appeared larger when you thought it was on a distant wall), and smaller when it's overhead (just as the afterimage appeared smaller when you thought it was in the palm of your hand).

Negative afterimages do not transfer from one eye to the other. This indicates that they are produced on the retina and not in the visual cortex of the brain where the signals would have been fused together.

ANTI-GRAVITY MIRROR
It's all done with mirrors.

Materials

- A length of 2 × 4 inch wood and a router tool, or ring stands and clamps to make a stand to hold the mirror upright
- A good-quality flat plastic mirror, 2 × 3 feet (60 × 90 cm) or larger
- A partner

NOTE

It's important to get a good, flat mirror, because distortions will ruin the effect. Plastic mirrors are expensive, but glass mirrors can be dangerous. Look in your local yellow pages for a nearby plastics store.

⚠ CAUTION

Be careful with mirrors. Keep yourself and your kids safe by always using plastic mirrors instead of glass. If you must use a glass mirror, tape the edges to minimize the possibility of cuts, and glue one side to a suitable backing of cardboard or wood. Don't just spot-glue the mirror in a few places: The whole surface must be attached to the backing. That way, even if the mirror cracks or breaks, there will be no loose shards of glass.

Introduction

A reflection of your right side can appear to be your left side. With this Snack, you can appear to perform many gravity-defying stunts.

Assembly
(With stand, 15 minutes or less; without stand, 5 minutes or less)

You can make a stand for the mirror from a length of 2 × 4 inch wood. Use a router to cut a groove that is just wide enough to slip the mirror into. To help stabilize the mirror, nail some scrap wood to the ends of the board. You can also hold the mirror in a vertical position using ring stands and clamps, or just with your hands. An assistant might be of help here.

To Do and Notice
(15 minutes or less)

Stand the mirror on the floor. Put one leg on each side of the mirror. Shift your weight to the foot behind the mirror. Lift your other leg and move it repeatedly toward and away from the mirror. To an observer, you'll appear to be flying. If you use this Snack as a demonstration, you can make the effect more dramatic by covering the mirror with a cloth, straddling the mirror, and then dropping the cloth as you "take off."

Etcetera

The cars that seemed to float across the desert in the movie *Star Wars* each had a full-length mirror attached along its lower edge, hiding its wheels. The cars appeared to float above the sand because a camera pointing at a car saw a view of reflected sand and shadow in the mirror, rather than what was really there.

What's Going On?

If you stand with the edge of a large mirror bisecting your body, you will appear whole to a person who's watching. To the observer, the mirror image of the left half of your body looks exactly like the real right half. Or, if you are standing at the opposite edge of the mirror, your reflected right half looks like the real left half.

You look whole because the human body is symmetrical. The observer's brain is tricked into believing that an image of your right side is really your left side. So just straddle the mirror, raise one leg, and you'll fly!

Actually, you can try this out anyplace you find a good-sized mirror you can straddle or stand alongside of—at home, in a department store, or in a dance room with a doorway cut into a mirrored wall. Stand at the edge of the doorway so just half of your body is being reflected for a very convincing flight.

BENHAM'S DISK
A rotating black-and-white disk produces the illusion of color.

Materials
- → Access to a copy machine
- → Pattern disk (provided)
- → Poster board or cardboard
- → Scissors
- → Glue stick, tape, or other suitable adhesive
- → A black marking pen
- → Variable-speed electric drill (works well because it can be reversed) or record turntable
- → Double-sided tape, adhesive-backed Velcro, or some other way to attach your disk to your rotator (see Assembly)

BONUS!
You've just done most of the assembly for three other Snacks: Depth Spinner, Squirming Palm, and Whirling Watcher. Now all you need are the pattern disks for those Snacks, and you're good to go.

Introduction
When you rotate this black-and-white pattern at the right speed, the pattern appears to contain colored rings. You see color because different color receptors in your eyes respond at different rates.

Assembly
(30 minutes or less)

1. Make a copy of the pattern disk provided in this Snack.

2. Cut out the disk and mount it on a cardboard backing with the adhesive. If your copier does not make good solid blacks, fill in the black areas with a black marking pen. You can reduce or enlarge the pattern disk if you like.

3. Mount the pattern disk to a rotator and secure it in place with some double-sided tape or adhesive-backed Velcro. If you're using a drill with a chuck, a bolt can be used as a shaft, with two nuts to hold the disk. For something super-simple, you can reduce the size of the disk on a copy machine and then mount it on the flat upper surface of a suitable toy top, or try spinning the mounted disk on a pencil point, or on a pushpin stuck into a pencil eraser. Whatever you can devise to get the disk safely spinning should be fine.

To Do and Notice
(15 minutes or more)

Spin the disk under bright incandescent light or sunlight. Fluorescent light will work, but there's a strobe effect that gives the disk a pulsating appearance and makes it harder to look at. The brighter the light, the better the effect.

Etcetera

Like the cones of the eye, the three different color sensors in some color-television cameras also have different latency and persistence times. When a color-television camera sweeps across a bright white light in its field of view, it often produces a colored streak across the television screen.

Notice the colored bands that appear on the disk. Look at the order the colors are in. What color do you see at the center? What about the next few bands? Reverse the direction of rotation and compare the order of colors again, from the center of the disk to the rim.

Try varying the speed of rotation and the size of the pattern, and compare the results with your initial observations.

What's Going On?

Different people see different intensities of colors on this spinning disk. Just why people see color here is not fully understood, but the illusion involves color vision cells in your eyes called cones.

There are three types of cones. One is most sensitive to red light, one to green light, and one to blue light. Each type of cone has a different latency time (the time in which it takes to respond to a color), and a different persistence-of-response time (the time it keeps responding after the stimulus has been removed). Blue-sensitive cones, for example, are the slowest to respond (have the longest latency time), but they keep responding the longest (have the longest persistence time).

When you gaze at one place on the spinning disk, you are looking at alternating flashes of black and white. When a white flash goes by, all three types of cones respond. But your eyes and brain see the color white only when all three types of cones are responding equally. The fact that some types of cones respond more quickly than others—and that some types of cones keep responding longer than others—leads to an imbalance that partly explains why you see colors.

The colors vary across the disk because at different radial positions on the disk the black arcs have different lengths. As a result, the duration of the flash on the retina is also different.

A complete explanation of the colors produced by a Benham's disk is more complicated than the simple one outlined here (for example, the short black arcs on all Benham's disks must also be thin, or no colors will appear), but this is the basis of much of what you see.

Benham's disk was invented by Charles Benham, a nineteenth-century toymaker who noticed colors in a black-and-white pattern he had mounted on a top. Even now, tops with Benham's disks can occasionally be found in toy stores.

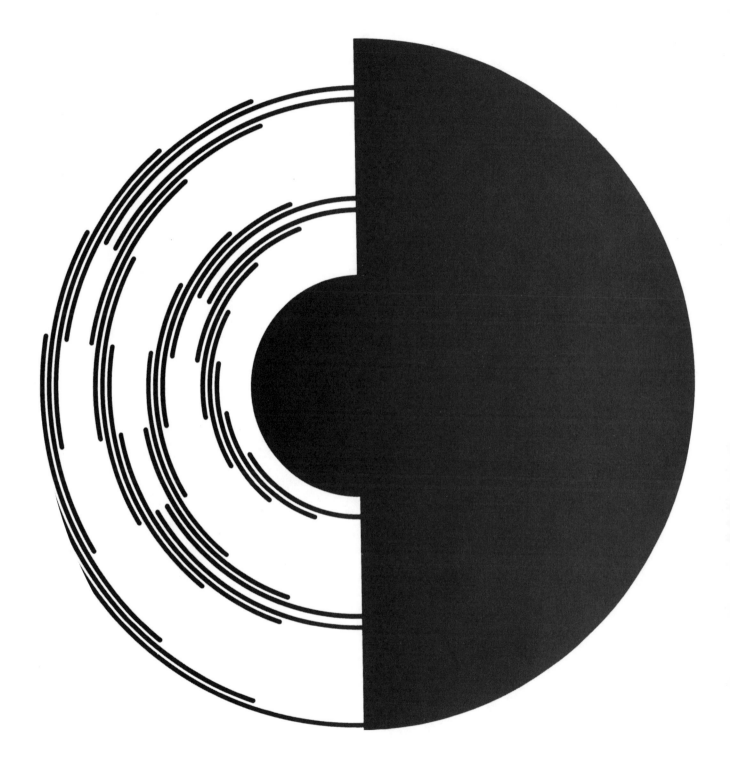

BIRD IN THE CAGE

Stare at one color—but see another.

Materials

→ Scissors

→ Bright red, green, and blue construction paper

→ Glue or glue stick

→ Four white poster boards or sheets of white paper

→ Black marking pen

Introduction

You see color when receptor cells (called cones) in your eye's retina are stimulated by light. There are three types of cones, and each is sensitive to a particular color range. If one or more of the three types of cones adapts to a stimulus because of long exposure, it responds less strongly than it normally would.

Assembly

(30 minutes or less)

1. Cut the same simple shape, such as a bird or a fish, from each of the three colored papers.

2. Glue each shape to its own white board.

3. Draw an eye for each bird or fish with the marking pen.

4. On the fourth white board, if you chose a bird as the shape, draw the outline of a birdcage; if you chose a fish, draw a fishbowl.

To Do and Notice

(15 minutes or less)

Place the boards in a well-lit area. (Bright lighting is a significant factor in making this Snack work well.)

Assuming you cut out birds, stare at the eye of the red bird for 15 to 20 seconds and then quickly stare at the white board with the cage you drew. You should see a

You can design other objects with different colored papers and predict the results. Try a blue banana! For smaller versions, you can use brightly colored stickers (from stationery, card, or gift stores) or drawings on index cards.

One classic variation of this investigation uses an afterimage to make the American flag. Draw a flag, but substitute alternating green and black stripes for the familiar red and white stripes, and black stars on a yellow field for the white stars on a blue field. For simplicity, you can reduce the flag to a few thick stripes and a few large stars. When you stare at the flag and then stare at a blank white background, the flag's afterimage will appear in the correct colors.

You may also want to experiment by changing your distance from the white board while observing the afterimage. Notice that the perceived size of the image changes, even though the size of the affected region of your retina remains the same. The perceived size of an image depends on both the size of the image on your retina and the perceived distance to the object.

bluish-green (cyan) bird in the cage. Now repeat the process, staring at the green bird. You should see a reddish-blue (magenta) bird in the cage. Finally, stare at the blue bird. You should see a yellow bird in the cage. If you used a fish, try the same procedure with the fish and the bowl.

What's Going On?

The ghostly images that you see here are called afterimages. An afterimage is an image that stays with you even after you have stopped looking at the object.

The lining at the back of your eye, called the retina, is covered with light-sensitive cells called rods and cones. Rods let you see in dim light, but only in shades of gray. Cones, however, detect color in bright light, and each of the three types of cones is sensitive to a particular range of color.

When you stare at the red bird, the image falls on one region of your retina. The red-sensitive cells in that region adapt to the exposure to red light and reduce their response.

The white board reflects red, blue, and green light to your eyes (because white light is made up of all these colors). When you suddenly shift your gaze to the white board with the bird cage, the adapted red-sensitive cells don't respond to the reflected red light, but the blue-sensitive and green-sensitive cones respond strongly to the reflected blue and green light. As a result, where the red-sensitive cells don't respond, you see a bluish-green bird. This bluish-green color is called cyan.

When you stare at the green bird, your green-sensitive cones become adapted to the unchanging stimulus. Then, when you look at the white board, your eyes respond only to the reflected red and blue light, and you see a red-blue, or magenta, bird. Similarly, when you stare at a blue object, the blue-sensitive cones adapt, and the reflected red and green light combine to form yellow.

BLIND SPOT
To see or not to see.

Materials

→ One 3 × 5 inch (8 × 13 cm) card or other stiff paper

→ Yardstick or meter stick

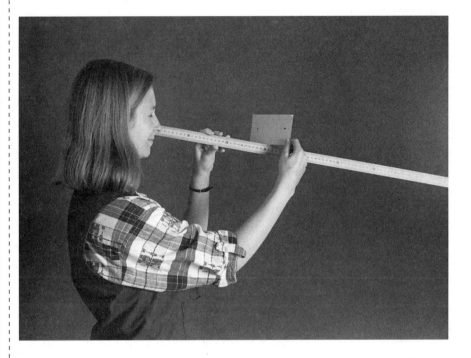

Introduction

The eye's retina receives and reacts to incoming light and sends signals to the brain, allowing you to see. There is one part of the retina, however, that does not give you visual information. This is your eye's "blind spot."

Assembly

Mark a dot and a cross on a card as shown.

To Do and Notice

(15 minutes or less)

Hold the card at eye level about an arm's length away. Make sure that the cross is on the right.

Close your right eye and look directly at the cross with your left eye. Notice that you can also see the dot.

Etcetera

If you want to try a variation of this activity, draw a straight line across the card, from one edge to the other, through the center of the cross and the dot, and try again. Notice that when the dot disappears, the line appears to be continuous, without a gap where the dot used to be. Your brain automatically "fills in" the blind spot with a simple extrapolation of the image surrounding the blind spot. This is why you don't notice the blind spot in your day-to-day observations of the world.

Focus on the cross, but be aware of the dot as you slowly bring the card toward your face. The dot will disappear, and then reappear, as you bring the card toward your face.

Now close your left eye and look directly at the dot with your right eye. This time the cross will disappear and reappear as you bring the card slowly toward your face.

Try the activity again, this time rotating the card so that the dot and cross are not directly across from each other. Are the results the same?

Using a simple model for the eye, you can find the approximate size of the blind spot on your retina.

First, mark a cross on the left edge of a 3 × 5 inch (8 × 13 cm) card. Hold the card 10 inches (25 cm) from your eye. (You will need to measure this distance: it's important in determining the size of your blind spot.)

Close your left eye and look directly at the cross with your right eye. Move a pen across the card until the point of the pen disappears in your blind spot. Mark the places where the pen point disappears. Use the pen to trace the shape and size of your blind spot on the card. Then you can measure the diameter of the blind spot on the card.

In our simple model, we are assuming that the eye behaves like a pinhole camera, with the pupil as the pinhole. In such a model, the pupil is 0.78 inches (2 cm) from the retina. Light travels in a straight line through the pupil to the retina. Similar triangles can then be used to calculate the size of the blind spot on your retina. The simple equation for this calculation is

$$s/2 = d/D$$

where s is the diameter of the blind spot on your retina, d is the size of the blind spot on the card, and D is the distance from your eye to the card (in this case, 10 inches [25 cm]).

$$s/2 = d/D$$

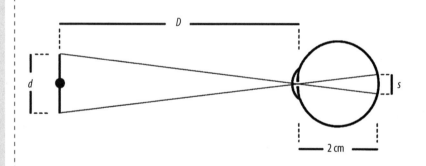

What's Going On?

The optic nerve—a bundle of nerve fibers that carries messages from your eye to your brain—passes through one spot on the light-sensitive lining, or retina, of your eye. In this spot, your eye's retina has no light receptors. When you hold the card so the light from the dot falls on this spot, you cannot see the dot.

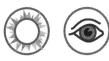

BRONX CHEER BULB

Some light sources wiggle and flash when you give them the raspberry.

Introduction

Some light sources flash on and off many times a second. Give them a "Bronx cheer," and you can see their hidden flickering.

Assembly

None needed. Just plug in your light and observe from a few feet away. (If the bulbs are kind of big, though—as some Christmas tree bulbs are—you may have to stand several feet away. Experiment to find the best place.)

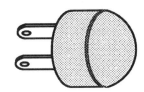

To Do and Notice

(5 minutes or less)

Plug in and turn on your light source, observe it from 3 to 10 feet (1 to 3 m) away, and give it the "Bronx cheer." (A Bronx cheer, also known as a "raspberry," is a rude noise made by sticking your tongue out a bit and blowing air through your lips in a way that makes them vibrate.) Notice that the light seems to wiggle back and forth and flicker.

Try shaking your head rapidly and notice whether the light still flickers. See if you can find other body motions that make the light flicker. Try the Bronx cheer on other light sources, such as incandescent lightbulbs and car taillights. Notice whether the light flickers.

Etcetera

Plug a commercial neon nightlight into an extension cord. Tape it firmly in place. Twirl the light around in a circle. (Be careful not to let it hit anything.) Notice that you can see the light flashing. Because the light is moving, it's in a new position each time it flashes: the light traces a path across your eye, and its flashes spread out and become visible.

Find an oscilloscope and set it up so that the beam goes straight across the middle of the screen in about 1/100 of a second. Ask a couple of friends to stand back a few yards from the scope. Tell them that the oscilloscope is an eating detector. With your friends both watching the scope at the same time, ask just one to eat a peanut. The person eating the peanut will see the beam jump up and down. Eating causes vibrations of your skull, including your eyes. If your eyes are moving, the dot of light scanning across the oscilloscope shines on different parts of your eyes and appears to jump around.

What's Going On?

When you give the Bronx cheer, your whole body is vibrating, including your eyes. You can feel this vibration by putting your hand on your head as you blow.

LEDs flash on and off 60 times a second, and neon glow tubes go on and off 120 times a second. This flashing is so fast that your eyes normally can't separate the "blinks." But when your body is vibrating, your eyes are in a different position each time the bulb flashes. As the image of the bulb traces a path across your eyes, it looks like the bulb is moving and flickering. An incandescent bulb won't flicker when you give it the Bronx cheer because the bulb doesn't flash on and off. Incandescent bulbs give a steady glow.

CARDBOARD TUBE SYLLABUS
Your brain combines information from your eyes in surprising ways.

Materials
- Several sheets of white paper
- Transparent tape
- A well-lit white screen, wall, or sheet of paper

Introduction

You have two eyes, yet you see only one image of your environment. If your eyes receive conflicting information, what does your brain do? Do receptors in the eye act independently, or do they influence each other? By looking through some simple tubes made from rolled-up pieces of paper, you can explore how your two eyes influence each other.

Assembly
(15 minutes or less)

1. Roll three of the sheets of paper into tubes 11 inches (28 cm) long and about 1/2 inch (1.25 cm) in diameter. Use tape to keep the tubes from unrolling.

2. Squash one of the tubes so that its cross-section is a very flat oval.

3. Cut one piece of paper into a strip that's about 2½ inches (6.4 cm) wide and 11 inches (28 cm) long.

4. Roll this strip into a tube that's about 1/2 inch (1.25 cm) in diameter and 11 inches (28 cm) long.

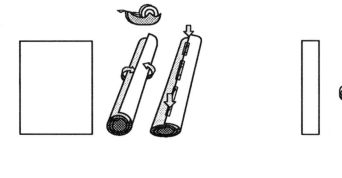
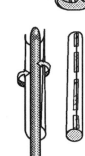

With these tubes, you can perform a variety of experiments. Try all four!

1. Hole in Your Hand

To Do and Notice

(5 minutes or more)

Take a full-sized tube in your right hand. Hold it up to your right eye and look through the tube, keeping both eyes open.

Now put your left hand, fingers up, palm toward your face, against the left side of the tube, about halfway down. Notice that you see a hole in your hand.

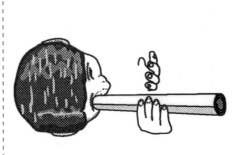 

What's Going On?

One eye sees a hole, the other sees a hand. Your eyes and brain add the two images together, creating a hand with a hole in it!

2. Overlapping Spots

To Do and Notice

(5 minutes or more)

Take two round tubes that you made from full sheets of paper. Put the tubes up to your eyes and look through them at the white screen, wall, or sheet of paper. First close one eye, and then open it and close the other. Does the brightness of the spot appear the same for each eye?

Move the tubes to overlap the two spots. Notice that there is a brighter area where the two spots overlap.

Overlap the spots completely. Does the combined spot look brighter than either spot alone? Find out by closing one eye.

What's Going On?

When you partly overlap the two spots, your open eye and brain conclude that the sum of the two spots of light should be brighter than one spot alone. If the spots overlap completely, it's more difficult to perceive the brightening.

Etcetera

You probably know your dominant hand (are you right- or left-handed?), but do you know which eye is your dominant eye? To find out, cut or tear a coin-sized hole in a piece of paper, pick a distant object, and look through the hole at that object. Slowly bring the piece of paper toward your face, keeping the object in view through the hole. At some point, the piece of paper will be right up against your face—and you will have found your dominant eye.

3. Circles or Ovals?

To Do and Notice

(5 minutes or more)

Hold one of the round tubes up to one eye and hold the tube that you flattened up to the other eye. Look through the tubes at the white screen, wall, or paper. Overlap the spots. Do you see the circle or the oval?

Switch the tubes and repeat. If you saw only the circle before, you may see the oval now.

What's Going On?

Your eyes and brain have trouble merging the different shapes. Most people have a dominant eye. The brain will choose to see the image that is coming from the dominant eye. Some people do not have a dominant eye and therefore see the two shapes overlapped. The best baseball hitters do not have a dominant eye.

4. Lateral Inhibition

To Do and Notice

(5 minutes or more)

With both eyes open, look at the white screen, wall, or paper through one of the full-sized paper tubes. Notice that the spot of light you see through the tube appears brighter than the wall of the tube.

Now do the same thing using the tube you made from the narrow strip of paper. Notice that the spot appears darker than the wall of the tube.

What's Going On?

When light receptors in your eyes receive light, they send a signal to your brain. A receptor receiving light also sends signals to neighboring receptors, telling them to turn down their own sensitivity to light. When you look at the white wall without a tube, you see a uniform field of brightness because all the receptors are equally inhibited. When you look through the tube that you made from a full sheet of paper, the spot of light is surrounded by the dark ring of the tube. The spot appears brighter because the receptors in the center of your retina are not inhibited by signals from the surrounding dark ring.

In contrast, light shines through the walls of the tube that you made from the thin strip of paper. When you look through this thin-walled tube, the spot appears darker because light comes through the wall of the tube, causing the receptors at the center of your retina to be inhibited. This is known as lateral inhibition.

CHESHIRE CAT
Make a friend disappear, leaving only a smile behind.

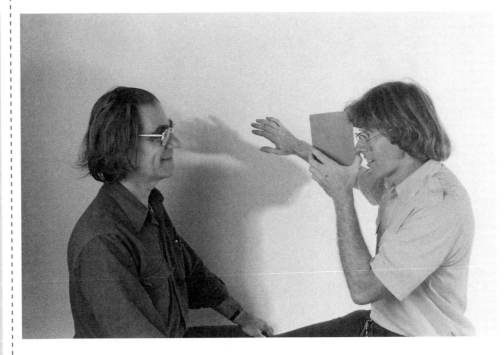

Introduction

Under most circumstances, both of your eyes receive fairly similar views of the world around you. You fuse these views into a single three-dimensional picture. This Snack lets you explore what happens when your eyes receive different images.

Assembly

None needed.

To Do and Notice
(15 minutes or more)

Sit so that the white surface or wall is on your right. Hold the bottom of the mirror with your left hand, and put the mirror edge against your nose so that the reflecting surface of the mirror faces sideways, toward the white surface.

While keeping the mirror edge against your nose, rotate the mirror so that your right eye sees just the reflection of the white wall, while your left eye looks forward at the face of a friend who is sitting a couple of feet away (see diagram). Move your hand in front of the

Etcetera

The name for this exhibit comes from the Cheshire Cat in Lewis Carroll's story *Alice's Adventures in Wonderland*. The cat disappears, leaving behind only its smile.

white surface as if passing a blackboard eraser over the surface. Watch as parts of your friend's face disappear.

It will help if your friend is sitting very still against a plain, light-colored background. You should also try to keep your own head as still as possible.

If you have trouble seeing your friend's face disappear, one of your eyes might be stronger than the other. Try the experiment again, but this time switch the eye you use to look at the person and the eye you use to look at the wall.

Individuals vary greatly in their ability to perceive this effect. You may have to try this several times, and a few people may never succeed in observing it. Don't give up too soon! Give yourself time to see the effect.

What's Going On?

Normally, your two eyes see very slightly different pictures of the world around you. Your brain analyzes these two pictures and then combines them to create a single, three-dimensional image.

In this Snack, the mirror lets your eyes see two very different views. One eye looks straight ahead at another person, while the other eye looks at the white wall or screen and your moving hand. Your brain tries to put together a picture that makes sense by selecting bits and pieces from both views.

Your brain is very sensitive to changes and motion. Because the other person is sitting very still, your brain emphasizes the information coming from your moving hand, rather than the unmoving face. As a result, parts of the person's face disappear. No one knows how or why some parts of the face may remain, but the eyes and mouth seem to be the last features to disappear. The lingering mouth gives rise to the name of this exhibit.

COLOR CONTRAST

A colored object may look different against different-colored backgrounds.

Materials

➔ Scissors

➔ Construction or origami paper in yellow, purple, green, blue (two shades), and orange (two shades); select pieces of paper of the same size

➔ Glue

➔ Paint-sample cards (from paint or hardware stores) that show gradations of one color

Introduction

From this investigation, you can see how colors seem to change when you place them against different-colored backgrounds. You need to consider this phenomenon when you pick out colors for carpeting or walls or when you are painting a picture.

Assembly

(15 minutes or more)

1. Cut one sheet of orange paper in half lengthwise and glue it to cover up half of a blue sheet. This will give you a large sheet of paper that's half blue and half orange. This large piece of paper will be your background for other colors.

2. Cut two small squares from each of the colors you have, including squares of blue or orange of a different shade from that of the large sheets.

3. Glue these squares across from each other, one on the blue background and one on the orange background.

4. From the same colors as the small squares, cut strips of each color as wide as the sides of the square to use for comparison.

Etcetera

When nineteenth-century astronomers observed Mars through telescopes, they saw a wave of green spread down from the planet's north pole as the polar cap disappeared each spring. Modern astronomers know that this wave of green is actually gray volcanic dust spread by carbon dioxide expanding from the dry ice of the polar cap. A red background makes gray spots look greenish. The gray dust of Mars appeared green to human eyes when it was viewed against the planet's red background.

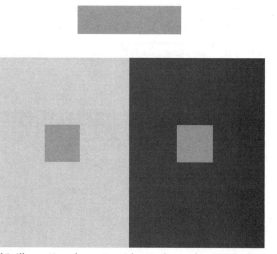

This illustration shows two identical sample squares on two different backgrounds, and a comparison bar.

To Do and Notice

(15 minutes or more)

Notice that two small squares of the same color may appear to be different shades when mounted on different-colored backgrounds. Place the comparison strip so that it touches both small squares of color at the same time to verify that the squares are actually the same color. Experiment with different colors to see which background colors make foreground colors appear lighter and which make them appear darker.

Color contrast also works in reverse: Against certain backgrounds, different colors can look the same. From the paint samples, choose two shades that are very similar but are clearly distinguishable when placed right next to each other. Put the paint samples on different backgrounds. The slightly different colors may then appear to be the same. You will have to experiment with different backgrounds to get the desired effect.

What's Going On?

The back of your eye is lined with light-sensitive cells, including color-sensitive cone cells. Your cones affect each other in complex ways. These connections give you good color vision, but they can also fool your eye.

When cones in one part of your eye see blue light, they make nearby cones less sensitive to blue. Because of this, you see a colored spot on a blue background as less blue than it really is. If you put a purple spot on a blue background, for instance, the spot looks a little less blue than it otherwise would. Similarly, a red spot on an orange background looks less orange than it otherwise would.

DEPTH SPINNER
What happens when you get off the merry-go-round?

Materials

- Access to a copy machine
- Pattern disk (provided)
- Scissors
- Poster board or cardboard
- Glue stick, tape, or other suitable adhesive
- A black marking pen
- Variable-speed electric drill (works well because it can be reversed) or record turntable
- Double-sided tape, adhesive-backed Velcro, or some other way to attach your disk to your rotator (see Assembly)

BONUS!

You've just done most of the assembly for three other Snacks: Benham's Disk, Squirming Palm, and Whirling Watcher. Now all you need are the pattern disks for those Snacks, and you're good to go.

Introduction

When you watch a continuously rotating spiral, the motion detectors in your eyes become adapted to that motion. Then, when you look away, the world seems to move toward or away from you.

Assembly
(15 minutes or less)

1. Make a copy of the pattern disk provided in this Snack.

2. Cut out the disk and mount it on a cardboard backing with the adhesive. If your copier does not make good solid blacks, fill in the black areas with a black marking pen. You can reduce or enlarge the pattern disk if you like.

3. Mount the pattern disk to a rotator and secure it in place with some double-sided tape or adhesive-backed Velcro. For something super-simple, you can reduce the size of the disk on a copy machine and then mount it on the flat upper surface of a suitable toy top, or try spinning the mounted disk on a pencil point or on a pushpin stuck into a pencil eraser. If you're using a drill with a chuck, a bolt can be used as a shaft, with two nuts to hold the disk. Whatever you can devise to get the disk safely spinning should be fine.

To Do and Notice
(15 minutes or less)

Start the spiral rotating and stare at its center for about 15 seconds.

Look away from the disk and stare at a nearby person. Notice that the person will seem to be expanding or contracting, as though he or she is rushing toward you or away from you.

If you can, try rotating the spiral in the opposite direction. Now what happens when you look up from the spinning pattern?

What's Going On?

Your visual system is sensitive to inward and outward motion. Nerve cells in the visual cortex fire more when objects move outward from the center of your field of view, and others fire more when objects move inward. When you're looking at something that's standing still, the inward and outward channels are in balance with one another; they send equally strong signals to your brain. When you stare at this moving pattern, however, one detector channel adapts, and its response is reduced. Then, when you stare at the person, the detector that hasn't been working sends a stronger signal to your brain than the adapted one does.

If, for example, the spiral seemed to be moving away from you, the person will seem to be moving toward you when you look up. If you rotate the spiral in the other direction, so that it seems to be moving toward you, the person will then seem to be moving away when you look up.

DISAPPEARING ACT
If you want to stay hidden, you'd better stay still.

Materials

- Scissors
- Two pieces of dark blue or black construction paper
- Liquid correction fluid or silver or gold marking pens
- A piece of clear plastic the same size as the construction paper
- A partner

Introduction

Some animals blend in with their surroundings so well that they're nearly impossible to see. Only when these animals move can you detect their presence and shape. With this Snack, you can compare what you see when a camouflaged figure remains still to what you see when the figure is moving.

Assembly
(30 minutes or less)

1. Cut out an animal shape from one of the pieces of construction paper.

2. Leave a projecting rectangle of paper to serve as a handle (see photo).

3. Use correction fluid or metallic marking pens to make a random pattern of dots on both the animal figure and the second piece of construction paper. The second piece of paper will act as the background for the figure.

4. Place the figure on the background and cover both pieces of paper with the plastic. The transparent covering keeps the edges of the animal flat against the background.

To Do and Notice
(5 minutes or more)

View the animal cutout against the background from an arm's length away. It should be very difficult, if not impossible, to detect the shape of the animal. If you can see the edges, move about 6 feet (2 m) away and have a friend hold the animal and the background.

Etcetera

What animals can you think of that use camouflage to blend into their environment?

Place the cutout so you can use the handle to move the animal while it is under the glass or plastic. Notice that this movement makes it easy to detect the presence of the animal and to identify its shape.

What's Going On?

Many animals have patterns of color on their bodies that allow them to blend into the background. These animals are hard to detect when they're still, but when they move, you can easily pick them out. That's because humans—as well as many other animals—have specialized brain cells that detect motion. These cells receive information from the light-sensitive cells at the back of the eye.

EVERYONE IS YOU AND ME
See yourself become someone else!

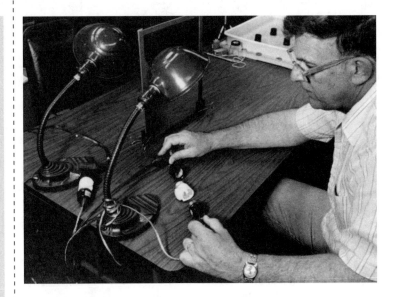

Introduction

You and a partner sit on opposite sides of a "two-way" mirror. Each of you varies the amount of light illuminating your own face. As you adjust the light, you will see yourself gradually assume aspects of your partner's features, so that your image becomes a "composite" person.

Dimmer Switch Assembly

Assembly
(1 hour or less)

You can make a two-way mirror from inexpensive Mylar reflecting film and ordinary window glass. The variable illumination is accomplished with dimmers commonly available at hardware stores.

To make a two-way mirror:

1. Put the reflecting film on one side of the glass, following the instructions for the particular brand of film used.

2. Cover the edges of the glass with cloth tape to prevent the film from peeling and to avoid cuts from any sharp edges on the glass.

Etcetera

Next time you go shopping, take a look at the store windows as you pass by. Depending on the lighting levels inside and out, you may see through into the shop, you may see a reflection of yourself, or—as in this Snack—you may be able to see both at the same time!

3. Place the lamps as shown in the diagram.

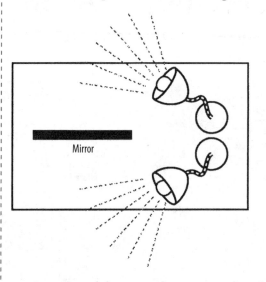

4. Connect each lamp to a dimmer switch and an extension cord.

5. Stand the mirror on a table. This may be done by standing the mirror between two heavy masses (such as 2-pound [1-kg] lab masses), or by making a wooden stand of some sort. A "sandwich" of two pieces of wood with the mirror in the middle, all rubber-banded together, will work. If you have a table saw or a router, cut a slot for the mirror in a piece of wood. Anything that works will do.

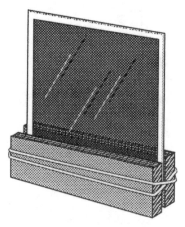

To Do and Notice
(15 minutes or more)

Sit across the table from your partner with the two-way mirror in between. The room should be dimly lit or dark. Be sure that you and your partner are the same distance from the mirror. You should be able to see both your partner's face through the mirror and your own face reflected in the mirror.

Point one lamp directly at your face and have your partner do the same, so you each have the same amount of light on your face. Line up your reflected eyes and nose so that they coincide with your partner's. (You'll probably have to adjust your distance from the mirror a bit as you do this.)

Adjust both lamps so they are initially very dim. Now use the dimmer to vary the amount of light reaching your face. Have your partner adjust the other dimmer. Watch your features blend with your partner's features.

What's Going On?

The mirror reflects about half of the light that hits it and transmits the other half. If your lamp is dim, there's not much light to bounce off your face and reach the two-way mirror, and your reflection will be dim. If your lamp is dim at the same time your partner's is brightly illuminated, then light will be transmitted through the two-way mirror and you will see your partner's features clearly. As you make your lamp brighter and your partner dims the other lamp, you will see more of your own features and less of your partner's. Your brain combines the two images into one perceived face.

FADING DOT

Now you see it; now you don't: An object without a sharp edge can fade from your view.

Materials

- Blue paper (just enough to cut a dot about 1 inch [2.5 cm] in diameter)
- Scissors
- Pink paper (1 sheet)
- Waxed paper
- Optional: Glue stick or tape

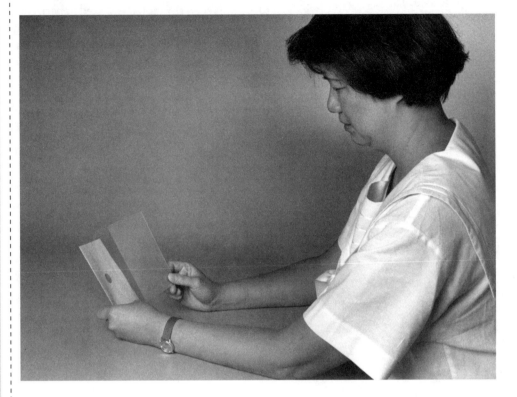

Introduction

A fuzzy colored dot that has no distinct edges seems to disappear. As you stare at the dot, its color appears to blend with the colors surrounding it.

Assembly

(5 minutes or less)

1. Cut the blue paper to make a 1-inch (2.5-cm) dot.

2. Place the dot in the center of the pink paper (you may want to stick it on with a dab of glue or piece of tape).

3. Cover the paper with a sheet of waxed paper.

To Do and Notice

(15 minutes or less)

Look through the waxed paper at the colored papers below. Lift the waxed paper upward, away from the pink paper and toward your face, until you see very faint blue color in a field of pale pink.

Stare at a point next to the fuzzy dot for a while without moving your eyes or your head. The blue will gradually fade into the field of pink. As soon as you move your head or eyes, notice that the dot reappears. Experiment with other color combinations.

Etcetera

Low contrast can affect your vision in a number of unexpected ways. In 2003, an article in the *Proceedings of the International Joint Conference on Neural Networks* reported that moving cars seem to slow down in foggy conditions because low contrast reduces perceived speed!

What's Going On?

Even though you're not aware of it, your eyes are always making tiny jittering movements. Each time your eyes move, they receive new information and send it to your brain. You need this constant new information to see images.

Your eyes also jitter around when you look at this blue dot. But because the edge of the dot looks fuzzy (as seen through the waxed paper), the color changes are so gradual that your eyes can't tell the difference between one point on the dot and a point right next to it. Your eyes receive no new information, and the image seems to fade away. If the dot had a distinct border, your eyes would immediately detect the change when they jittered, and you would continue to see the dot.

You may have noticed that, although the dot fades, just about everything else in your field of vision remains clear. That's because everything else you see has distinct edges.

FAR-OUT CORNERS
Your experience of the world influences what you see.

Materials

- Flat-black spray paint
- A large cardboard box measuring about 19 × 15 inches (48 × 38 cm)
- Thick, white, nonflexible poster board measuring at least 15 × 15 inches (38 × 38 cm) or several empty tissue boxes or clean milk cartons (see Assembly)
- X-Acto knife or utility knife
- Masking tape or transparent tape
- A bright freestanding lamp

Introduction

When they first glance at this exhibit, many people say, "What's the big deal? It's just a bunch of boxes." But there are no boxes at all. A closer look reveals that the Far-Out Corners exhibit is a cluster of corners lit from below. When you walk past the exhibit with one eye closed, the cubes seem to turn mysteriously so that they follow your movement.

Assembly
(1 hour or less)

You can cut the inside corners from square-cornered containers, such as clean milk cartons or tissue boxes, or you can make your own corners from poster board.

To make your own:

1. Spray-paint the inside of the large cardboard box black.

2. Use an X-Acto or utility knife to cut the poster board into nine squares, each of which measures 5 × 5 inches (13 × 13 cm).

3. Use three of the squares to construct a partial cube or corner in the following fashion:

   (a) Tape two squares together at one edge. Open the two squares into a right angle, and then tape the third square on top of the first two squares.

(b) Make three of these partial cubes, or corners.

(c) When the spray-painted box is dry, arrange the corners so that two are side by side on the bottom of the box, as shown below. Make sure the hollow open sides of each corner are facing out toward you and down.

(d) Tape the two corners so they are tilted up at a small angle. Place the third corner as far forward as possible on top of the original two, also tilted upward.

(e) Tape all three corners in place. Now position the light so it shines directly into the box.

To Do and Notice
(15 minutes or more)

Stand back 10 feet (3 m) and close one eye. With a little mental effort, you can see the corners that you have constructed as three-dimensional cubes, rather than as the hollow corners that they are.

Walk back and forth parallel to the box. Notice that the cube on top seems to be following you as you move.

What's Going On?

The first step to successfully seeing the top partial cube turn with you lies in your ability to perceive it as a complete six-sided figure. This perception has a lot to do with being raised in a society that recognizes cubes as a common shape. Your brain is used to seeing cubes, so it fills in the rest of the cube shape, even though this partial cube only has three sides.

As you move past the exhibit, your view of the corners changes in a way that would not make any sense if the corners were stationary cubes. Your eye-brain system is accustomed to seeing things that are near you move faster than things that are farther away. When you're riding in a car, for example, nearby objects seem to whiz by, whereas distant objects seem to follow you at a slower pace. Because you perceive this inside corner to be the outside of a solid cube, your brain "sees" the corner farthest from you as being the closest. To maintain this misconception, your brain perceives a rapid rotation of the cube as your angle to the corner changes.

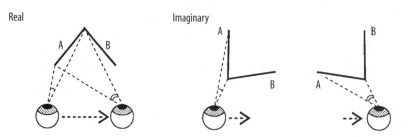

The diagram above shows how this illusion works. In the real situation, as your eye moves to the right, it sees more of side A. In order to see more of side A of the imagined corner, the perceived cube must be seen to rotate as you move.

GRAY STEP

Without a boundary, it's hard to distinguish different shades of gray.

Materials

- A copy of the full-page Gray Step master supplied here
- Stiff cardboard or other backing
- Glue or tape
- Scissors
- Yarn or twine to make a fuzzy "horse tail"

Introduction

Two slightly different shades of the same color may look different when there's a sharp boundary between them. But if the boundary is obscured, the two shades may be indistinguishable.

Assembly

(15 minutes or less)

1. Copy the full-page Gray Step master supplied here and glue or tape it to your cardboard (or other) backing.

2. Make a "horse tail" by knotting together several lengths of yarn or twine.

3. Attach the horse tail with tape or glue so it hangs down from above to cover the central boundary.

To Do and Notice

(5 minutes or more)

If you are looking at the image in this book, just place a pencil or your finger over the boundary between the gray halves. What do you see? If you are using your own construction, position the "horse tail" so that it covers the boundary and ask your friends what they see. Most people will see a uniformly gray piece of paper with a rope hanging down the middle.

Lift the tail and ask again. Most people will see two uniform areas, each a different shade of gray.

Etcetera

If you want to prove that the two sides of the Gray Step are identically shaded from one side to the other, you can make a simple mask from a piece of white paper and a single-hole punch. Punch two holes in the plain paper so they're spaced just far enough apart to show a bit of the far right (or left) side of each gray rectangle. When you put this sheet of paper over the master, a small gray circle from each side will show through the holes. Push the white paper back and forth across the Gray Step master and notice that, no matter where you move it, the two areas viewed through the punches are always matching shades of gray.

Another easy Gray Step demonstration can be constructed out of paint-sample pieces from a hardware store. Some paint brands provide good-sized individual color chips. Experiment with how different two colors can be and yet appear the same when the boundary between them is obscured.

In this Snack, a fuzzy cord (the "horse tail") obscures the boundary between two gray areas. You see one uniform gray area when the horse tail is in place, and two different gray areas when the horse tail is removed. But you never see the truth: Both gray areas are actually identical to one another, grading from lighter gray at one edge to darker gray at the other.

What's Going On?

Without the horse tail in place, the right and left sides of the rectangle will look different. Actually, they're the same, but graduated in color. At the right edge, both rectangles are light gray. Both become darker toward the left. Where the rectangles meet, the darkest part of one rectangle contrasts sharply with the lightest part of the other, so you see a distinct edge. When the edge is covered, however, the two regions look the same uniform shade of gray (in general, your brain ignores slight gradations in gray levels).

It's often difficult to distinguish between different shades of gray or shades of the same color when no sharp edge divides them. This is true even though a sensitive light meter would show that the different shades are reflecting different amounts of light to your eyes. Your eyes do not lack the necessary sensitivity to detect the difference: with an edge between the two shades, the difference is obvious.

Your eye-brain system, however, condenses the information it obtains from more than a hundred million light-detecting rods and cones in the retina in order to send the information to over a million neurons to your brain. Your eye-brain system enhances the ratio of reflected light at edges. If one region of the retina is stimulated by light, lateral connections turn down the sensitivity of adjacent regions. This effect is called lateral inhibition. Conversely, if one region is in the dark, the sensitivity of adjacent regions is increased. This means that a dark region next to a light region looks even darker, and vice versa. As a result, your visual system is most sensitive to changes in brightness and color.

When the horse tail is absent and the normal boundary is visible, lateral inhibition enhances the contrast between the two shades of gray. The bright side appears brighter and the dark side darker. When the tail is in place, the boundary between the two different grays is spread apart across the retina so that it no longer falls on adjacent regions. Lateral inhibition then does not help distinguish between the different shades, and the eye-brain system judges them to be the same.

JACQUES COUSTEAU IN SEASHELLS
There's more to seeing than meets the eye.

Materials

- ➡ A black-and-white picture
- ➡ Graph paper with 1/4-inch (6 mm) squares
- ➡ Paper clips
- ➡ A pencil

Introduction

Seeing is a cooperative effort involving your eyes and your brain. Your eyes may perceive a group of dots, but it's your brain that has to decide whether or not the dots form a pattern that means something. In the exhibit Jacques Cousteau in Seashells, created for the Exploratorium by artist Ken Knowlton, a framed collection of seashells seems to be a random pattern when viewed up close. At a distance, however, the pattern is seen to be a likeness of well-known oceanographer Jacques Cousteau.

Assembly

(30 minutes or less)

You can use the pattern of dots supplied here for the "To Do and Notice" section, or you can make your own dot pattern. If you choose to make your own, you will need a black-and-white photograph of a simple, easily recognizable scene or person. Then you can translate this photo into a pattern of dots by following these steps:

1. Place graph paper on top of the photo.

2. Clip the picture to the graph paper so it doesn't move while you're drawing.

3. Pick a square to start with.

4. Notice that dark portions of the photo show through the graph paper. Estimate what portion of your chosen square is black.

25%

50%

75%

100%

5. Draw a dot whose size corresponds to the percentage of black you estimate is in the square: The more black in the square, the bigger your dot. (See the sample above.) If the square is not black but rather some shade of gray, the size of the dot will depend on how dark the gray is. In a square filled with pale gray, put a small dot; in a square filled with dark gray, put a bigger dot.

6. Repeat the process with each square in the picture until you are finished.

To Do and Notice
(5 minutes or more)

When you're done with your dot picture, hold it at arm's length. If the dot picture is of a familiar object, it should be easily recognizable at this distance. See if other people can identify the object in the picture.

For simplicity, we've used a picture of an eye as a sample here. Unfamiliar or complicated objects may be more difficult to recognize at close range.

Place the picture across the room, and you'll notice that it becomes much easier to recognize. The dots will seem to disappear, with only the pattern remaining. The picture may appear slightly fuzzy, but it certainly doesn't appear to be made of dots!

Pictures made of dots are easily recognized by the brain because the brain is always attempting to interpret what it sees. Even though our sample picture is made up of different-sized dots, the brain recognizes the overall shape as that of an eye, since it is very familiar with that shape. This is the same reason you may see shapes in clouds, inkblots, or even pieces of toast. Your brain does not merely register these shapes as abstract patterns, it attempts to interpret them based on previous experience.

The dots disappear when you view the picture from a distance because of the limited resolving power of your eyes. You see the dot picture because light reflecting from the page makes an image on the retina of your eye. This image stimulates the light-sensitive cells in the retina and your brain interprets the result. When you move the dot picture farther away from your eye, the image the picture makes on your retina becomes smaller. The images of the dots overlap on the light-sensitive cells. Unable to distinguish between adjacent dots, your eye perceives shades of gray, rather than black dots and white spaces.

Etcetera

To print shades of gray using black ink on white paper, printers use "halftone" reproduction. The phenomenon of the "disappearing" dots is the basis of these halftones. A magnifying glass will show you that printed photos in newspapers, books, and magazines are actually composed of thousands of tiny dots, often too small for the eye to separate.

Artists in the late nineteenth century, taking advantage of this phenomenon, created a style called Pointillism. Paintings in this style—most notably those by Georges Seurat (1859–1891)—are made up of thousands of tiny dots of brilliant color that, at a distance, merge in the beholder's eye.

The picture on a color TV set is also made up of dots. Your eye blends these dots to make a picture.

If the picture looks like this. . . → . . .your dot would look like this

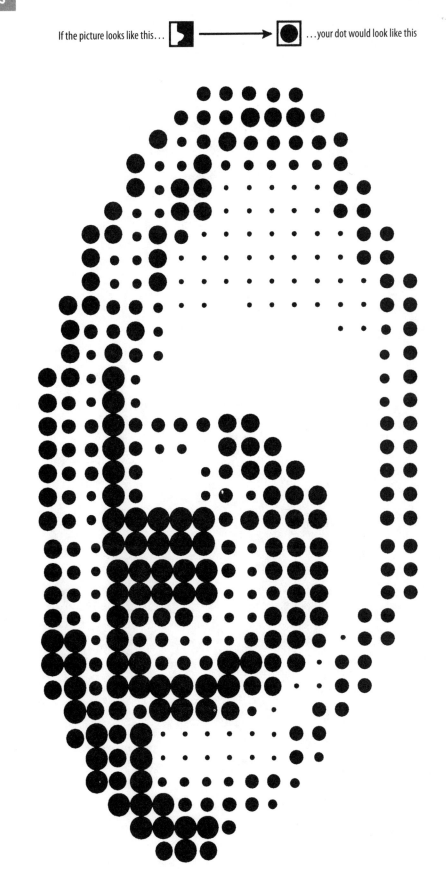

MIRRORLY A WINDOW

What you see is often affected by what you expect to see.

Materials

- ➡ Epoxy glue
- ➡ Two mirrors, 12 × 12 inches (30 × 30 cm), either glass mirror tiles or plastic mirrors
- ➡ Duct tape
- ➡ Two wooden dowels, 1 inch (2.5 cm) in diameter × 1 foot (30 cm) long
- ➡ Optional: Dowel screw

⚠ CAUTION

Be careful with mirrors! Keep yourself and your kids safe by always using plastic mirrors instead of glass. If you must use a glass mirror, tape the edges to minimize the possibility of cuts, and glue one side to a suitable backing of cardboard or wood. Don't just spot-glue the mirror in a few places: The whole surface must be attached to the backing. That way, even if the mirror cracks or breaks, there will be no loose shards of glass.

Introduction

When your brain expects to see one thing and is presented with something quite different, you may feel some peculiar sensations.

Assembly

(15 minutes, plus time for glue to dry)

1. Glue the mirrors together, back to back.

2. If you are using glass mirror tiles, tape the sharp edges—and be careful! Broken glass and unprotected edges can be dangerous!

3. Glue a wooden dowel to each mirror. The dowel should be positioned so that it sticks straight out of the middle of the mirror. (For a more durable assembly, you can use plastic mirrors and a dowel screw. This is a double-ended screw used to join two dowels. Drill a hole in the mirror and a hole in the end of each dowel. Insert the dowel in the mirror hole and screw on the dowels until tight.)

To Do and Notice

(5 minutes or less)

Grab a dowel with each hand. While looking at one side of the mirror, move the hand on the other side of the mirror.

Etcetera

A simpler version of this experiment uses a single 12 × 12 inch (30 cm) mirror with no epoxied handles. Prop the mirror up on a table. Hold one of your arms on each side of the mirror so that you see the reflection of one arm as the continuation of the other arm. Snap the fingers on both your hands simultaneously, then stop snapping the fingers on only one hand. Or have someone drop an object (such as a set of keys) into the hand behind the mirror.

What's Going On?

Here, your brain is fooled into thinking that the image it sees in the mirror is actually your other hand. When you move that hand, your brain naturally expects to see the hand move. After all, messages from the nerves in that hand tell your brain that the hand is moving. The hand's apparent failure to move can be profoundly disturbing to your brain, which doesn't enjoy having its assumptions trifled with!

MOIRÉ PATTERNS

When you overlap materials with repetitive lines, you create moiré patterns.

Materials

- Two identical pocket combs, or a pocket comb and a mirror
- Two pieces of window screen, or a window screen, a sheet of white cardboard, and a bright light
- Two transparencies made from the pattern provided in this Snack (see "Etcetera" for other suggestions)

Introduction

When you look through one chain-link fence at another, you sometimes see a pattern of light and dark lines that shifts as you move. This pattern, called a moiré pattern, appears when two repetitive patterns overlap. Moiré patterns are created whenever one semitransparent object with a repetitive pattern is placed over another. A slight motion of one of the objects creates large-scale changes in the moiré pattern. These patterns can be used to demonstrate wave interference.

Assembly

None needed.

To Do and Notice

(15 minutes or more)

Hold two identical combs so that one is directly in front of the other and they are about a finger-width apart. Look through the teeth and notice the patterns of light and dark that appear. This is a moiré pattern. Slide the combs from side to side and watch the moiré pattern move. Now rotate one comb relative to the other and notice how the pattern changes.

If you only have one comb, hold it at arm's length, about 1 inch (2.5 cm) from a mirror. Look through the comb at its reflection in the mirror. Notice how the moiré pattern moves when you move the comb to the side or slowly tip one end away from the mirror.

Once you've learned to see moiré patterns, you'll begin to see them practically everywhere. Look through two chain-link fences and notice the pattern. Watch it shift as you drive by. Look through a thin, finely woven fabric, such as a thin curtain or some pantyhose material. Now fold the fabric over and look again through two layers. You'll see moiré patterns. Slide the fabric around and watch the patterns dance and change.

Look through two layers of window screen. Observe the moiré patterns as you slide one layer from side to side across the other, or when you rotate one layer. You can also create interesting patterns by flexing one of the screens.

If you only have one piece of screen, you can still make moiré patterns—even if the screen is still mounted in a window or a door. Have a friend hold a sheet of white cardboard behind the screen, and shine a single bright light onto the screen. (On a sunny day, sunshine can serve as your light source.) Start with the cardboard touching the screen, then move it away, tilting the cardboard a little as you go. The screen will form a moiré pattern with its own shadow. Replace the cardboard with flexible white paper and bend the paper. Notice how the pattern changes.

Use a copier to make two transparencies from the pattern of concentric circles provided on the next page. Look through these two patterns as you move them apart and then together. The moiré pattern consists of radiating dark and light lines.

You can project moiré patterns so that a large group can see them. Just make two transparencies of a repetitive pattern and overlap them on an overhead projector. Moiré patterns from books may be enlarged or reduced and made into transparencies on a copy machine.

What's Going On?

When two identical repetitive patterns of lines, circles, or arrays of dots are overlapped with imperfect alignment, the light and dark lines that we call a moiré pattern appears. The moiré pattern is not a pattern in the screens themselves; rather, it is a pattern in the image formed in your eye. In some places, black lines on the front screen hide the clear lines on the rear screen, creating a dark area. Where the black lines on the front screen align with black lines on the rear, the neighboring clear areas show through, leaving a light region. The patterns formed by the regions of dark and light are moiré patterns.

In the case of the two sets of concentric circular lines, the dark lines are like the nodal lines of a two-source interference pattern. A typical two-source interference pattern is created when light passes through two slits. Along lines known as nodal lines, the peaks of the light waves from one slit and the valleys of the light waves from the other slit overlap and cancel each other. No light is detected along a nodal line.

In the black radiating lines of the moiré pattern, the black lines of one moiré pattern fill the transparent lines of the other. Note that as the patterns are moved apart, the dark nodal lines move together. This is the same thing that happens when light passes through two slits and the slits are moved farther apart.

Moiré patterns magnify differences between two repetitive patterns. If two patterns are exactly lined up, then no moiré pattern appears. The slightest misalignment of two patterns will create a large-scale, easily visible moiré pattern. As the misalignment increases, the lines of the moiré pattern will appear thinner and closer together.

PERIPHERAL VISION

We're not usually aware of our eyes' limitations.

Materials

→ A pushpin to use initially in drawing a circle, and finally as a point of reference

→ Poster board, cardboard, foamcore, or other stiff material, 1 × 2 feet (30 × 60 cm)

→ A piece of string about 2 feet (60 cm) long

→ A pencil

→ Scissors

→ Glue

→ Small plastic cup

→ Marking pens in different colors

→ A few 3 × 5 inch (8 × 13-cm) file cards or a tall, thin piece of wood

→ A partner

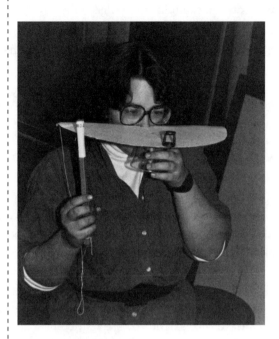

Introduction

This Snack is basically a large protractor that lets you test the limits of your peripheral vision. With the help of a friend, you can measure how much you can see out of the corner of your eye. You'll find that you can detect motion at a wide angle, colors at a narrow angle, and detailed shapes at a surprisingly narrow angle.

Assembly

(30 minutes or less)

1. Stick the pushpin, point down, halfway along the 2-foot (60 cm) edge of the poster board (or whatever board you use as a base).

2. Tie the pencil to one end of the string, and wrap the other end of the string around the pushpin to improvise a compass.

3. Draw a half-circle with a 1-foot (30 cm) radius.

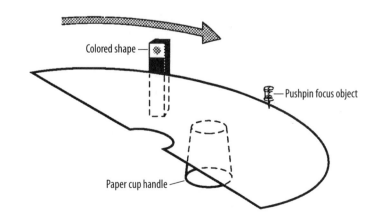

Colored shape

Pushpin focus object

Paper cup handle

You almost always need an assistant to do this Snack. As the colored shape approaches the center of your field of view, the temptation to cheat and move your eyes to look at the object becomes nearly irresistible. An assistant can watch you and stop the experiment when you give in to temptation and move your eyes to look.

4. Now shorten the string and draw another, smaller half-circle, about 3/4 inch (2 cm) in diameter.

5. Cut these both out (see the diagram). The small circle should be just big enough for your nose.

6. Now stick the pushpin in at the edge of the half-circle, directly across from the nose hole. This will be your focus object.

7. Use glue to attach the plastic cup to the bottom of the poster board. The cup will serve as a handle.

8. Use the marking pens to draw simple shapes (such as rectangles, squares, and triangles), each in a different color, on the faces at one end of the length of wood or on the file cards. This will allow you to reveal only one shape at a time.

To Do and Notice
(15 minutes or more)

Using the cup as a handle, hold the poster-board base up to your face and put your nose in the center hole. Have your partner hold the wood or file card so that it is against the curved side of the base, as far from the focus object as possible. Keep your eyes on the focus object while your partner moves the colored shape around the outside edge until you can see it. Note the angle.

Have your partner keep moving the colored shape toward the focus object. Note the angle at which you first detect color. Then note the angle at which you first discern the shape itself. Have your partner expose a different shape and repeat the experiment. You'll probably find that your partner has to move the wood surprisingly close to the focus object before you can make out color or shape.

What's Going On?

Your retina—the light-sensitive lining at the back of your eye—is packed with light-receiving cells called rods and cones. Only the cones are sensitive to color. These cells are clustered mainly in the central region of the retina.

When you see something out of the corner of your eye, its image focuses on the periphery of your retina, where there are few cones. Thus, it isn't surprising that you can't distinguish the color of something you see out of the corner of your eye.

The rods are more evenly spread across the retina, but they also become less densely packed toward the outer regions of the retina. Because there are fewer rods, you have a limited ability to resolve the shapes of objects at the periphery of your vision.

In the center of your field of view is a region in which the cones are packed tightly together. This region is called the fovea. This region, which is surprisingly small, gives you the sharpest view of an object. The fraction of your eye covered by the fovea is about the same as the fraction of the night sky covered by the moon.

You can demonstrate this effect more simply by focusing on one of the words on this page while at the same time trying to make out other words to the right or left. You may be able to make out a word or two, depending on how far the page is from your eyes. But the area that you can see clearly is the area imaged on the fovea of your eye.

Generally, you are not aware of the limitations of your peripheral vision. You think that you have a clear view of the world because your eyes are always in motion. Wherever you look, you see a sharp, clear image.

Interestingly, your peripheral vision is very sensitive to motion—a characteristic that probably had strong adaptive value during the earlier stages of human evolution.

PERSISTENCE OF VISION

Your eye and brain hold on to a series of images to form a single complete picture.

Materials

→ Utility knife

→ Cardboard mailing tube about 3 inches (8 cm) in diameter and 2 to 3 feet (60 to 90 cm) long, with a cap over one end

Introduction

When you look through a narrow slit, you can see only a thin strip of the world around you. But if you move the slit around rapidly, your eye and brain combine these thin strips to make a single complete picture.

Assembly

(5 minutes or more)

1. With your knife, cut a slit in the cap of the mailing tube. The slit should be about 1 inch (2.5 cm) long and 1/8 inch (3 mm) wide.

2. Replace the cap on the end of the tube.

To Do and Notice

(5 minutes or more)

Close one eye. Put the other eye to the open end of the tube. Cup your hand around the tube to make a cushion between the tube and your eye. Hold the tube so that the slit is vertical.

When the slit is stationary, you can't see much. Keep your head and body still and sweep the far end of the tube back and forth slowly while you look through it. Increase the scanning speed and compare the views. Notice that when you sweep the tube quickly from side to side, you can see a remarkably clear view of your surroundings.

Etcetera

The *Viking 1* and *2* landers photographed the surface of Mars by recording narrow-slit images that were transmitted to earth and assembled by computer to make the final surface photographs. As this demonstration shows, your eye and brain can "take a photograph" in the same way.

What's Going On?

Your eye and brain retain a visual impression for about 1/30 of a second. (The exact time depends on the brightness of the image.) This ability to retain an image is known as persistence of vision.

As you swing the tube from side to side, the eye is presented with a succession of narrow, slit-shaped images. When you move the tube fast enough, your brain retains the images long enough to build up a complete image of your surroundings.

Persistence of vision accounts for our failure to notice that a motion picture screen is dark about half the time, and that a television image is just one bright, fast, little dot sweeping the screen. Motion pictures show one new frame every 1/24 of a second. Each frame is shown three times during this period. The eye retains the image of each frame long enough to give us the illusion of smooth motion.

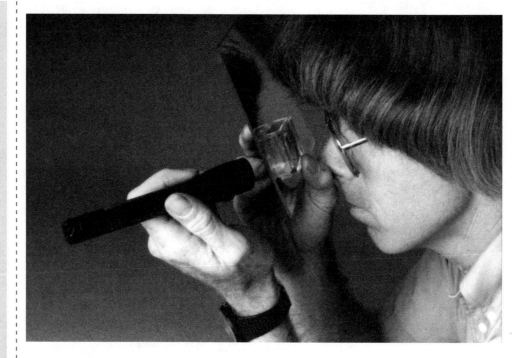

PUPIL

Your pupil changes size to control how much light enters your eye.

Materials

- Magnifying glass at least 1 inch (2.5 cm) in diameter
- Any size handheld or wall mirror (note that plastic mirrors are safer than glass)
- Flashlight

Introduction

You can watch the pupil of your eye change size in response to changes in lighting. You can also experiment to determine how light shining in one eye affects the size of the pupil in your other eye.

Assembly

None needed.

To Do and Notice

(15 minutes or more)

Place the magnifying glass on the surface of the mirror. Look into the center of the magnifying glass with one eye. If you wear contact lenses or glasses, you may either leave them on or remove them.

Adjust your distance from the mirror until you see a sharply focused and enlarged image of your eye. Notice the white of your eye, the colored disk of your iris, and your pupil, the black hole in the center of your iris.

Shine a light into the pupil of one eye. If you are using a small mirror, hold the flashlight behind the mirror and shine the light around the edge of the mirror into your eye. If you are using a large mirror, bounce the flashlight beam off the mirror into your eye. Observe how your pupil changes size.

Etcetera

The size of your pupils actually reflects the state of your body and mind. Pupil size can change because you are fearful, angry, in pain, in love, or under the influence of drugs. Not only does the pupil react to emotional stimuli, it is itself an emotional stimulus. The size of a person's pupils can give another person a strong impression of sympathy or hostility.

The response of the pupil is an involuntary reflex. Like the knee-jerk reflex, the pupillary response is used to test the functions of people who might be ill or injured.

The pupil of your eye is also the source of the red eyes you sometimes see in flash photographs. When the bright light of a camera flash shines directly through the pupil, it can reflect off the red blood of the retina (the light-sensitive lining at the back of your eye), and bounce right back out through the pupil. If this happens, the person in the photograph will appear to have glowing red eyes. To avoid this, photographers move the flash away from the camera lens. With this arrangement, the light from the flash goes through the pupil at an angle, illuminating a part of the retina not captured by the camera lens.

Notice that it takes longer for your pupil to dilate than it does to contract. Notice also that the pupil sometimes overshoots its mark. You can see it shrink down too far, and then reopen slightly.

Observe changes in the size of one pupil while you, or an assistant, shine a light into and away from the other eye.

In a dimly lit room, open and close one eye while observing the pupil of the other eye in the mirror.

What's Going On?

The pupil is an opening that lets light into your eye. Since most of the light entering your eye does not escape, your pupil appears black. In dim light, your pupil expands to allow more light to enter your eye. In bright light, it contracts. Your pupil can range in diameter from 1/16 of an inch (1.5 mm) to more than 1/3 of an inch (8 mm).

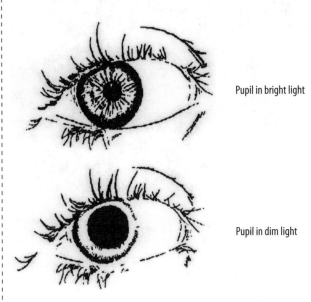

Pupil in bright light

Pupil in dim light

Light detected by the retina of your eye is converted to nerve impulses that travel down the optic nerve. Some of these nerve impulses go from the optic nerve to the muscles that control the size of the pupil. More light creates more impulses, causing the muscles to close the pupil. Part of the optic nerve from one eye crosses over and couples to the muscles that control the pupil size of the other eye. That's why the pupil of one eye can change when you shine the light into your other eye.

In this experiment, the light reflecting from your eye passes through the magnifying lens twice—once on its way to the mirror and once on its way back. Therefore, the image of your eye is magnified twice by the magnifying glass.

SIZE AND DISTANCE
A clueless way to determine the size of an object.

Introduction

By removing clues to the actual size and distance of an object, you can trick your brain into thinking that two similar objects of different sizes are really the same size. You can then compare what you see when you limit your information to what you see when you have complete information.

Assembly
(30 minutes or less)

1. Remove the box lid.

2. At the center of one end-panel of the shoebox, cut a hole large enough for one-eyed viewing—approximately 1/2 inch (1.25 cm) in diameter.

3. Then cut out a window, approximately 3 × 5 inches (8 × 13 cm), with the viewing hole in the center.

4. Replace the cardboard in the window from which it was cut, and tape it in place along its bottom edge to form a hinge inside the box (see diagram).

5. At the other end of the box, make a hole for each straw approximately 1/2 inch (1.25 cm) to each side of the center of the panel.

6. Cut the piece of poster board so it's the same height as the box and about 2 inches (5 cm) wider than the box.

7. Fold back 1 inch (2.5 cm) on each side of the poster board panel to make two flaps. Then make two holes in the panels so that they coincide exactly with the two holes in the end of the box.

8. Tape or glue the flaps of the posterboard to the inside sides of the box, using them as spacers to position this piece 1 inch (2.5 cm) from the end with the holes (see diagram).

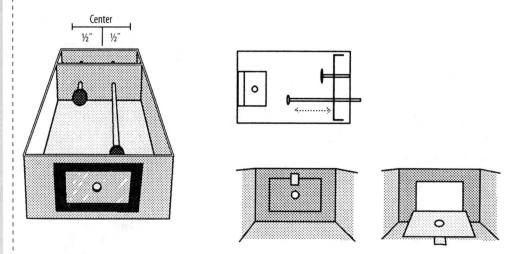

9. Insert the straws into the holes. The double set of holes will keep the straws properly aligned.

10. Using the quarter and dime as templates, cut one circle of each size from the construction paper. Make sure the color of the construction paper contrasts strongly with the color of the inside of the box.

11. Use clay to mount the circles on the ends of the straws inside the box.

To Do and Notice

(15 minutes or more)

With the cover on the box and the hinged window closed, close one eye and look through the viewing hole at the circles. Lift the end of the box cover closest to you and slide it away from you until adequate viewing light reaches the inside of the box. Push or pull on the straws from the outside rear of the box until the mounted circles appear to be the same size. Note that your depth perception is almost nonexistent: both circles look essentially the same distance away, and it's very difficult to judge which circle is closest to you.

Fold down the window and look with both eyes to see the actual positions of the circles. (You may have to move your head back a little from the box to get both circles focused.) Note that depth perception is now a factor and the circles no longer look the same size or the same distance away.

Position the small disk a couple of inches closer to you than the large disk. With both eyes open, look through the window at the disks. Notice that you have no trouble establishing their size and distance.

Now close one eye and notice that it may be much more difficult to tell whether the small disk is now actually a small disk that's close to you, or a large disk that's far away. You can also use the dime and quarter by themselves, without building the box, to illustrate the same principle. Close one eye. Holding one coin in each hand, move them toward or away from your viewing eye until they appear to be the same size. A solid-colored background gives less distraction than an irregular background. A very bright,

Etcetera

There is a pattern on the pupa of the *Spalgis epius* butterfly that looks like the face of a rhesus macaque monkey. Even though the pupa is only half as wide as a human fingernail, it still seems to scare away predatory birds who mistake it for a more distant, and therefore larger, monkey.

solid-colored background works best, so that the coins appear essentially in silhouette, and their features cannot easily be distinguished.

What's Going On?

Large, distant objects can appear to be the same size as small, nearby objects. Under normal viewing conditions, with both eyes open, you have the ability to perceive depth. If two objects appear to be the same size, but you know that one is farther away than the other, your brain tells you that the distant object is larger.

When one eye is closed, your depth perception is impaired. In the case of the circles, you can't tell how far away either of the circles really is. Since they are not actually the same size, this means that, for the smaller one to look the same size as the larger one, it will have to be closer to you than the larger one.

With both eyes open, you can gather more information and more points of view, and so you can make more accurate judgments about an object's size, shape, and distance from you.

SQUIRMING PALM

This visual illusion makes the palm of your hand appear to squirm and twist.

Materials

- Access to a copy machine
- Pattern disk (provided)
- Poster board or cardboard
- Scissors
- Glue stick, tape, or other suitable adhesive
- A black marking pen
- Variable-speed electric drill (works well because it can be reversed) or record turntable
- Double-sided tape, adhesive-backed Velcro, or some other way to attach your disk to your rotator (see Assembly)

BONUS!

You've just done most of the assembly for three other Snacks: Depth Spinner, Squirming Palm, and Whirling Watcher. Now all you need are the pattern disks for those Snacks, and you're good to go.

Introduction

If you stare at a waterfall for some time, and then stare at the rocks nearby, the rocks will appear to be moving upward. This illusion is known as the waterfall effect. Using the pattern provided here, you can create the waterfall effect—without getting wet.

Assembly

(15 minutes or less)

1. Make a copy of the pattern disk provided in this Snack.

2. Cut out the disk and mount it on a cardboard backing with the adhesive. If your copier does not make good solid blacks, fill in the black areas with a black marking pen. You can reduce or enlarge the pattern disk if you like.

3. Mount the disk to a rotator and secure it in place with some double-sided tape or adhesive-backed Velcro. If you're using a drill with a chuck, a bolt can be used as a shaft, with two nuts to hold the disk. For something super-simple, you can reduce the size of the disk on a copy machine and then mount it on the flat upper surface of a suitable toy top, or try spinning the mounted disk on a pencil point, or on a push-pin stuck into a pencil eraser. Whatever you can devise to get the disk safely spinning should be fine.

Etcetera

Try this effect on pictures in magazines or books. Stare at the spinning pattern disk, and then look right at the image. It will seem to pulse and squirm as if it were animated. This is especially fun to do if you have art books that show paintings (try a Picasso or something by Dali!).

To Do and Notice

(5 minutes or more)

Rotate the disk slowly (1 or 2 seconds per revolution) and stare at its center for about 15 seconds. Now look at the palm of your hand. Notice that your palm seems to be turning. Your palm will turn in the opposite direction from the way the disk was turning.

What's Going On?

Mechanisms in your eye and brain detect motion in various directions. For example, regions of your brain fire nerve impulses when your eye forms images that are rotating in a clockwise direction. Other regions respond to counterclockwise rotation. When something is stationary, both of these motion detectors still fire, but their firing rates are equal. The two signals balance each other out, and you see no motion.

As you stare at the spinning disk, the set of motion detectors that respond to its rotation adapts to the motion of the pattern. These motion detectors start out firing rapidly, and then slowly decrease their firing rate. When you look away from the rotating pattern and stare at a stationary object (such as your palm), the motion detectors that have been firing fire less rapidly than the ones that have not been stimulated. As a result, you see motion in the opposite direction.

You also have sets of motion detectors that respond to upward and downward motion. Adaptation of these upward and downward motion detectors causes the version of the waterfall effect that you notice when you watch a waterfall.

THREAD THE NEEDLE
Using two eyes gives you depth perception.

Materials

- A dowel (a pencil will also work)
- A washer with a hole that's a little larger than the dowel's diameter
- A lump of modeling clay to hold the washer on its edge

Etcetera

Stretch a string from just under your nose to the end of your outstretched arm. You will see two strings stretching out in front of you. Look at the string with just your left eye, and then with just your right eye. Notice that the two strings are separate images—one from each eye. The two strings cross at the point on which your eyes are focused. Try looking at different points on the string and notice how the crossover point moves.

Introduction

Close one eye and you eliminate one of the clues your brain uses to judge depth. Trying to perform a simple task with one eye closed demonstrates how much you rely on your depth perception.

Assembly

Stand the washer on its edge, using the lump of clay to support it so that the edge of the washer—not the hole—is facing you.

To Do and Notice

(5 minutes or more)

Stand far enough from the washer so that you must extend your arm to reach it. Now close one eye and try to put the dowel through the hole in the washer.

Open both eyes and try again.

What's Going On?

One of the clues your brain uses to judge distance and depth is the very slight difference between what your left eye sees and what your right eye sees. Your brain combines these two views to make a three-dimensional picture of the world.

Try this experiment again with one eye closed. But this time, move your head from side to side as you "thread the needle." People who have lost an eye can learn to perceive depth by comparing the different views they obtain from one eye at two separate times.

VANNA

A face seen upside down may hold some surprises.

Materials

- Three identical full-page (or at least fairly large) pictures of a familiar face from a magazine (try cover photos from popular magazines suitable to your audience—pictures of a smiling person work exceptionally well; avoid photos with shadows around the mouth area)
- Scissors
- Poster board or cardboard for backing
- Glue stick or other adhesive

Introduction

Your brain gets used to seeing familiar things in certain ways. When the brain receives a strange view of a familiar object, the consequences can be intriguing. In the Exploratorium exhibit called Vanna, two pictures of the face of TV personality Vanna White seem identical when viewed upside down, but exhibit a bizarre difference when viewed right side up.

Assembly

(30 minutes or less)

1. Cut two pieces of poster board to the size of the pictures you cut out. If you're using a magazine cover, you can use the whole cover or you can trim off the title. It's not necessary to trim the picture to the outline of the person.

2. Glue the first picture to a piece of poster board.

3. Cut the eyes and mouth from the second picture. Turn them upside down and glue them over the eyes and mouth of the third picture. (Note that you'll probably need to cut out slightly larger rectangular areas so they neatly cover the features on the third picture.)

4. Glue this picture to a piece of poster board.

To Do and Notice

(5 minutes or more)

Place both pictures upside down before letting anyone see them. Then have viewers look at the two upside-down pictures. Finally, turn both pictures around, and have viewers look at them right side up.

Etcetera

Can people recognize familiar upside-down faces? Find digital images showing faces of familiar personalities online or use digital images of family members and friends. Make copies of these images, turn one copy upside down using a simple photo-editing program, and then ask people to identify the person.

Your viewers may or may not recognize the personality in your picture when the picture is upside down. The two upside-down views may look strange (one perhaps stranger than the other), but turn them right side up and one looks normal, while the other may look grotesque.

Since an upside-down face is not a familiar point of view, your viewers may not have noticed that one of the pictures has been altered. It's only when the photos are turned right side up, and the view is more familiar, that you notice the real difference.

WHIRLING WATCHER
When you view short bursts of moving images, you see some interesting effects.

Materials

- Access to a copy machine
- Pattern disk (provided)
- Scissors
- Poster board or cardboard
- Glue stick, tape, or other suitable adhesive
- Black marking pen
- Variable-speed electric drill (works well because it can be reversed) or a record turntable
- Double-sided tape, adhesive-backed Velcro, or some other way to attach your disk to your rotator (see Assembly)
- A large mirror
- Running (or siphoned) water
- Black poster board to use as a background for the water
- A partner
- Optional: Adhesive-backed Velcro

Introduction

A series of slits moving rapidly past your eye allows you to see images in short bursts. Such rapid but fragmented views of moving objects can make the objects appear to jerk along, change speed, or even move backward.

Assembly
(30 minutes or less)

1. Make a copy of the stroboscope pattern provided here. Enlarge it if you wish. Cut out the pattern and glue it to the poster board.

2. Cut the poster board to the same shape as the stroboscope, including the slits. You can cut with a good pair of scissors alone, or use scissors in combination with a utility knife.

3. Mount the stroboscope disk to a rotator and secure it in place with some double-sided tape or adhesive-backed Velcro. If you're using a drill with a chuck, a bolt can be used as a shaft, with two nuts to hold the disk. Whatever you can devise to get the disk safely spinning should be fine.

To Do and Notice

(15 minutes or more)

Close one eye. Hold the stroboscope so that the side with the horses is facing away from you, and so that you can see through a slit with your open eye. Spin the disk and look through the slits at your surroundings. Notice that you can see the entire scene on the other side of the disk, not just one small strip of it.

Try spinning the disk faster, then slower, and compare the results.

Have a friend hold out a hand so you can see it through the spinning disk. Ask your friend to move the hand from side to side. Notice that the movement you see is jerky rather than smooth. Have your friend move rapidly, and then slowly. Notice that the amount of jerkiness changes as the speed of the hand movement changes.

Stand facing a mirror, and hold the disk and rotator in front of you. Be sure the disk is mounted on the rotator so that the horses are facing the mirror. Spin the disk and watch its reflection in the mirror through one of the slits. Concentrate your attention on one of the horses, and you will see it gallop!

Let water run slowly enough to produce a stream that breaks up into separate droplets as it falls. Place a black background behind the well-illuminated drops of water. Look through the spinning stroboscope and watch the water droplets fall in slow motion. Vary the stroboscope's speed and see if you can make the water droplets stand still or even look as if they are moving upward.

What's Going On?

As the strobe disk rotates, a series of open slits moves rapidly past your eye. Each time a slit passes your eye, you see a glimpse of the scene on the far side of the disk. Each open-slit image lingers in your eye and brain long enough to merge with the next image. This phenomenon, called persistence of vision, can combine the glimpses in such a way that your brain sees continuous motion.

If an object in the scene moves, your eye and brain can draw incorrect conclusions about that object's motion. When you look at the stream of water, for example, one slit allows you to view a droplet in a particular position. Depending on how fast your strobe is turning, the next slit might let you see a different droplet just slightly below the position of the one previously viewed. Your eye-brain system interprets the combined views as the slow motion of a single droplet. If the second view catches the droplet in a position just above that of the previous view, the droplet will seem to rise.

PART TWO THE COOL HOT ROD AND OTHER ELECTRIFYING EXPLORATIONS OF ENERGY AND MATTER

As you read this sentence, your body is busily transforming energy from one form to another. In your cells, chemical energy in the form of sugar is changing into a variety of other forms. Some of this chemical energy becomes the energy of motion, as your muscles flex and move your body. Some becomes electrical energy, as your nervous system sends out electrical signals that carry information throughout your body. And some becomes heat, a metabolic by-product that flows from your body into the environment around you.

Just about everything you do involves changing energy from one form to another. Flip a switch to turn on the light, and the bulb in your lamp changes electrical energy into heat and light. Go for a drive, and your car engine transforms the chemical energy contained in gasoline into the kinetic energy of motion.

Most of us are quite comfortable ignoring the energy transformations that take place in our bodies and in the world around us. Most of the time, it's easy not to think of energy. After all, you can't see it. You only worry about it when you don't have enough of it—when you're tired and you don't have the energy to finish a task; when your car's out of gas and there's a line at the gas pump. But the study of energy and energy transformations is a cornerstone of physics. You can't really understand how the universe works without paying attention to energy.

The experiments in this section are designed to call your attention to energy transformations and how they affect the world around you. Some of these experiments dramatically demonstrate how one form of energy can become another.

In Stripped-Down Motor, for example, the energy of an electric current is transformed into movement. This very simple motor relies on the same principles as the electric motors that power fans, blenders, washing machines, and other electrical appliances.

In Short Circuit, a flow of electrical energy is transformed into heat energy, which melts a wire. The same thing happens when you blow a fuse. A larger surge of electric current melts a thin wire in the fuse, thus shutting off the current.

Other experiments consider the flow of heat, a form of energy produced in machines that convert energy from one form to another. Cool Hot Rod, for example, demonstrates that changes in temperature can make a copper tube shrink or expand. Cold Metal makes heat-flow a phenomenon you can feel because the metal conducts heat away from your skin more readily than the Styrofoam does.

Taken together, the experiments in this section will help you understand some basic physical principles related to heat and other forms of energy. They give you ways to see the effects of some of the energy transformations that are happening all around you and inside you.

CHARGE AND CARRY

Store up an electric charge, and then make sparks.

Materials

For the Electrophorus:

- Hot glue gun or masking tape
- Plastic foam cup
- Disposable aluminum pie pan
- A plastic foam dinner plate or flat sheet of plastic foam packing material (the kind used to pack electronic devices)—the thicker, the better
- A piece of wool or acrylic cloth (other fabrics may work, but wool and acrylic will definitely work)

For the Leyden jar:

- A plastic 35 mm film can or similar-sized plastic container, such as a pill bottle
- A nail slightly longer than the film can
- Some aluminum foil
- Tap water

Introduction

Are you tired of electrostatic experiments that just won't work? This experiment will produce a spark that you can feel, see, and hear. You rub a foam plate with wool to give it a large electric charge. Then you use the charged foam to charge an aluminum pie pan. The entire apparatus for charging the aluminum plate is called an electrophorus, which is Greek for charge carrier. An even larger charge can be stored up in a device called a Leyden jar, made from a plastic bottle.

Assembly

(15 minutes or less)

Electrophorus:

1. Tape or hot-glue the foam cup to the middle of the inside of the pie pan. (Note that most household glues won't work for this because they dissolve the foam.)

2. Place the pie pan on top of the upside-down foam plate or on a piece of acrylic plastic (see photo).

Leyden Jar:

1. Push the nail through the center of the lid of the film can.

2. Wrap aluminum foil around the bottom two-thirds of the outside of the film can. You may tape the aluminum foil in place.

3. Fill the film can almost full with water, and then snap on the lid. The nail should touch the water.

To Do and Notice

(30 minutes or more)

Rub the foam plate with the wool cloth. If this is your first time using the foam in an electrostatic experiment, rub it for a full minute. Then charge the pie plan by following the next steps exactly:

1. Use the foam-cup handle to place the pie pan on top of the charged foam plate.

2. Briefly touch the pie pan with your finger. You may hear a snap and feel a shock.

3. Remove the pie pan by holding only the insulating foam cup (see photo). You may have to hold the foam plate down with your other hand.

The pan is now charged. You can discharge it by touching it with your finger. You'll hear a snap, feel a shock, and if the room is dark, see a spark.

To make the largest spark, have the pie plate at least one foot (25 cm) away from the foam plate. After charging the foam plate once, you can charge the pie pan several times. The pie pan is portable and can be used for many electrostatic experiments.

Charge the Leyden jar by touching the charged pie pan to the nail while holding the Leyden jar by its aluminum-foil covering. You can make several charge deliveries by recharging the pan before touching it to the nail. Discharge the jar by touching the aluminum foil with one finger and the nail with another. Watch for a spark.

What's Going On?

When you rub the foam plate with a wool cloth, you charge it negatively. That's because the foam attracts electrons from the cloth. Often, a plate fresh from the package will start with a positive charge. If it does, you will have to rub the plate long enough to cancel this initial charge before you can begin building a sizable negative charge. By using an electroscope (such as the one you can build with the Electroscope Snack), you can determine whether the foam is positively or negatively charged. Plastic foam or Styrofoam is an insulator; it will hold its charge until it is discharged by current leaking into the air or along a moisture film on its surface.

When you place the pie pan on the foam plate, the electrons on the foam repel the electrons on the pan. Since the electrons can't leave the pie pan because it is completely surrounded by insulating air and foam, the pan remains neutral. If you touch the pie pan while it is near the foam plate, the mobile electrons will be pushed off the pan and onto you. The electrons make a spark as they jump a few millimeters through the air to reach your finger. The air in the spark is ionized as the moving electrons knock other

Etcetera

To give the foam plate a positive charge, try rubbing it with a plastic bread bag. Try rubbing it with other materials, too. Try charging the Leyden jar in reverse. That is, while holding the nail, touch the aluminum foil with the pan.

Tie a piece of Christmas tinsel into a loop (tinsel is aluminum-coated Mylar), then charge the pie pan and hold it with its bottom upward. Toss the tinsel loop onto the pie pan. Electric charge will flow between the tinsel and the pie pan, making both of them positive. The electrostatic repulsion will allow you to fly the tinsel loop.

The Leyden jar is the forerunner of the modern-day capacitor. It was invented in 1745 at the University of Leyden by Pieter Van Musschenbroek. Early Leyden jars were larger than a plastic film can and could hold more charge. The inventor discharged one through himself and wrote, "My whole body was shaken as though by a thunderbolt." At another time, a Leyden jar was discharged through 700 monks who were holding hands. The charge caused them to simultaneously jump slightly off the ground.

electrons off air molecules. The ionized air emits light and sound. You can also feel the flow of electrons though your finger.

After the electrons leap to your finger, the pan has a positive charge. Physicists say the pan has been charged by induction. You can carry the positively charged pan around by its handle and carry the positive charge to other objects. For example, if you bring the positively charged pan near your finger again, or near any object that can be a source of electrons, the pan will attract electrons, creating a second spark.

When you touch a positively charged pie pan to the nail on the Leyden jar, electrons from the nail flow onto the pie pan. The resulting positive charge on the nail attracts electrons from your body through your hand onto the aluminum foil of the jar. The Leyden jar will then have a positive center separated from a negative foil outside by the insulating plastic of the film can. If you touch one finger to the foil and bring another finger near the nail at the center of the Leyden jar, a spark will jump as the negative charges are attracted through you to the positive nail.

The beauty of the Leyden jar is that it can store charges from several charged pie pans, thus building up to a larger, more visible, more powerful (and more painful) spark.

CIRCLES OF MAGNETISM I
You can make a magnetic field that's stronger than the earth's!

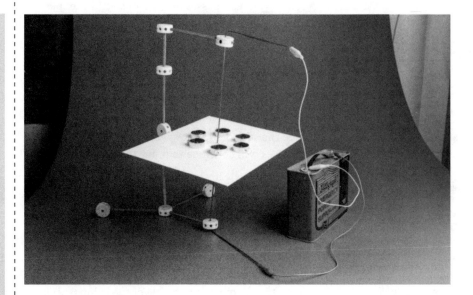

Introduction

A compass allows us to observe the direction of a magnetic field: compass needles are just little magnets that are free to rotate. Normally, compasses respond to the earth's magnetic field, orienting themselves parallel to magnetic field lines. If we create a magnetic field that is stronger than the field of the earth—for example, by using electric currents—a compass needle will orient itself parallel to the new field.

Assembly
(30 minutes or less)

1. Construct a Tinkertoy stand (or the equivalent), and lay the flat support surface in position on the stand, as shown in the figure.

2. If the coat-hanger wire is painted or varnished, scrape the coating off to expose about 1 inch (2.5 cm) of bare metal at each end.

3. Insert the wire through the hole in the flat support surface, and support the wire vertically in the stand, as shown.

4. Arrange the compasses in a circle on the support surface, as shown.

5. Attach one clip lead to each battery terminal, but do not attach the other ends of the lead wires to the coat hanger wire yet.

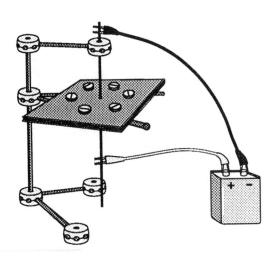

Etcetera

To find the direction of the magnetic field made by an electrical current, you can use a technique called the right-hand rule.

Place your right hand with the thumb parallel to the wire carrying the current. Point your thumb in the direction of the electrical current in the wire. (Remember: The electric current flows from the plus side of the battery through the wire to the minus side.) Wrap your fingers around the wire. Your fingers will now point in the direction of the magnetic field around the wire. If there are compasses near the wire, they will point in the same direction as your fingers.

Note that what actually moves in the wire are electrons flowing from the negative side of the battery to the positive side. Electrical engineers and scientists think of "current" as a flow of positive charges that produces the same effect as that produced by the flow of negative charges in the opposite direction.

To Do and Notice

(15 minutes or more)

Observe the compass needles when there is no current passing through the wire. Rotate the support surface. What happens to the compass needles? They will point north, orienting themselves so that they are parallel to the earth's magnetic field. (*Note:* A few of your compasses may point south! Inexpensive compasses that are exposed to a strong magnet will sometimes become magnetized in the reverse direction. It's nothing to worry about, though—just keep in mind which end of each compass points north.)

Attach the clip leads to the ends of the coat hanger wire where it has been scraped. Watch what happens to the compass needles as current passes through the wire. If the electrical current is large enough, each compass will point in a direction tangent to a circle centered on the wire.

Rotate the support surface again. What happens to the compass needles this time? The compasses will continue to point in a direction tangent to a circle centered on the wire.

Switch the clip leads to the other terminals of the battery. What happens? The compass needles will reverse direction when the electrical current reverses direction.

What's Going On?

Compass needles line up with magnetic fields. Since the earth is a magnet, a compass will normally line up with the earth's magnetic field. Because opposite magnetic poles attract, the magnetic north pole of the compass points toward the magnetic south pole of the earth. (The magnetic south pole of the earth is located in northern Canada! That is not a misprint. The magnetic south pole of the earth magnet is near the geographic north pole. To make things even more confusing, mapmakers call this the north magnetic pole.)

The electric current passing through the wire creates a magnetic field that is stronger than the earth's field (in a region close to the wire). You can visualize the shape of this new field as a set of circles surrounding the wire. These are concentric circles—each of them has its center at the wire.

The closer to the wire you are, the stronger the magnetic field. The compass needles align themselves with the total magnetic field at each point, the sum of the earth's field and that of the wire. Since the magnetic field from the wire is significantly larger than that from the earth, each needle ends up pointing essentially in the direction of the magnetic field of the wire.

When you reverse the current, the direction of the magnetic field also reverses, and the needles dutifully follow it.

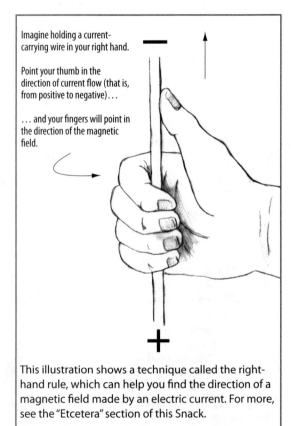

Imagine holding a current-carrying wire in your right hand.

Point your thumb in the direction of current flow (that is, from positive to negative)...

... and your fingers will point in the direction of the magnetic field.

This illustration shows a technique called the right-hand rule, which can help you find the direction of a magnetic field made by an electric current. For more, see the "Etcetera" section of this Snack.

CIRCLES OF MAGNETISM II

Two parallel, current-carrying wires exert forces on each other.

Materials

- A Tinkertoy set for building a stand (or another improvised stand)
- Light aluminum foil
- Masking tape or transparent tape
- Two electrical lead wires with alligator clips at both ends (available at RadioShack)
- A 6- or 12-volt lantern battery (you can also use two alkaline D cells in a battery holder, but be careful not to leave the circuit on too long!)

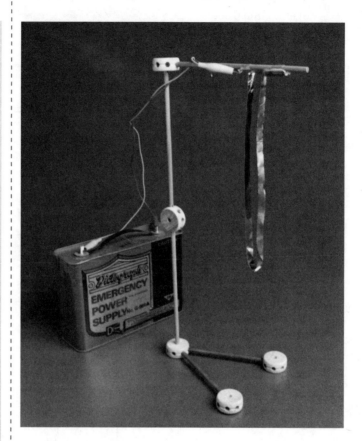

Introduction

When an electric current flows through a wire, a magnetic field is created around the wire. If you place two current-carrying wires near each other, the magnetic field around each wire exerts a force on the current flowing in the other wire. These forces can push two current-carrying wires apart or pull them together.

Assembly

(15 minutes or less)

1. Make a stand from wood or Tinkertoys, or build a stand of your own design from available materials.

2. Cut a strip of aluminum foil measuring about 2 feet (60 cm) long and 1/2 inch (1.25 cm) wide.

3. Tape one end of the foil strip to your support.

4. Run the strip down and back up to the support, making a loop, then tape the other end in place. Be sure the ends of the strip do not touch.

5. Attach one clip lead to each battery terminal, but do not attach the other ends of the lead wires to the strip yet.

Etcetera

The ampere, the fundamental unit of electrical current, is defined by the force exerted by one wire on another. The definition of the ampere is as follows: A current of 1 ampere flowing in each of two infinitely long parallel wires separated by 1 meter will produce an attractive force of 2×10^{-7} newton on each 1-meter length of wire. To get a sense of a force of 1 newton, bounce a quarter-pound stick of butter or margarine in your hand.

To Do and Notice

(15 minutes or more)

Touch the two clip leads to the ends of the foil strip. The descending and ascending portions of the loop will repel each other. The closer you can hang the descending and ascending portions of the loop to each other—without allowing them to touch—the larger the repulsion.

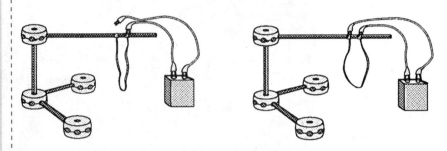

Now hang the foil strip from the support with the two ends overlapping, so they make a good electrical contact. Connect one of the clip leads to these overlapping ends. Separate the two sides of the loop and briefly touch the other clip to the bottom of the loop. Notice that the sides of the loop are attracted to each other when the current flows. (*Note:* This step requires a little coordination and a delicate touch to clearly demonstrate that it is the current flow in the strips that makes them move together and not forces that you create when you touch the clip to the bottom of the loop.)

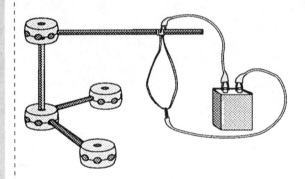

What's Going On?

A current-carrying wire generates a magnetic field that circles the wire. (See Circles of Magnetism I.)

When a current flows in a magnetic field, the field exerts forces on that current. So each current-carrying wire in this Snack generates a magnetic field at the position of the other wire and thus exerts a force on the current in the other wire. Two parallel wires will either attract or repel each other, depending on the direction of current flow in each wire. If both currents flow in the same direction, the wires will attract; if they flow in opposite directions, the wires will repel.

The forces produced on the aluminum foil are small. This is because the electrical current flowing through the foil is small, only a couple of amperes. Larger currents produce larger forces.

COLD METAL

"Cold" metal and "warm" wood may be the same temperature.

Materials

- Various materials (metal, wood, Styrofoam, glass, plastic, cardboard, and anything else that comes to mind) with one flat surface larger than the size of your hand
- A thermometer (liquid crystal thermometer cards or strips work well)

Introduction

Your hand is not always a good thermometer. When you touch a variety of materials, some will seem warmer or colder than others, even when they are at the same temperature.

Assembly

None needed. Be sure that you have many different surfaces and that they are large enough for you to touch easily. Allow an hour or so for all the materials to come to room temperature before you begin.

To Do and Notice

(15 minutes or more)

Place your palms flat on the various surfaces and compare how cold they feel. Arrange the materials in order from cold to warm. Then place a thermometer on each surface. Notice that all the materials are at the same temperature.

Etcetera

You probably have experienced this many times without thinking very much about it. Walk around barefoot in your house and see how warm or cold different surfaces feel, even though they're all at "room temperature." Put one bare foot on a carpet or wooden floor and the other on the tile floor of your bathroom, for instance, to feel the difference.

NOTE

Metals will warm to above room temperature after just a few rounds of being touched. The surfaces should be allowed to cool for a few moments after each person's turn. It might be useful to have multiple metal samples. While you are using one sample, the extras have time to cool back to room temperature.

What's Going On?

The temperature-sensitive nerve endings in your skin detect the difference between your inside body temperature and your outside skin temperature. When your skin cools down, your temperature-sensitive nerves tell you that the object you are touching is cold. An object that feels cold must be colder than your hand, and it must carry your body heat away so that your skin cools down.

Styrofoam (or plastic foam) and metal are two materials that work well for this Snack. They both start at room temperature and are both colder than your hand. They do not feel equally cold because they carry heat away from your hand at different rates.

Styrofoam is an insulator, a very poor conductor of heat. When your hand touches the Styrofoam, heat flows from your hand to the Styrofoam and warms the Styrofoam surface. Because this heat is not conducted away quickly, the surface of the Styrofoam soon becomes as warm as your hand, so little or no additional heat leaves your hand. There is no difference in temperature between the inside of your body and the outside of your skin, so the temperature-sensitive nerves detect no difference in temperature. The Styrofoam feels warm.

The metal, in contrast, carries heat away quickly. Metal is a good conductor of heat. Heat flows from your hand into the metal and then is conducted rapidly away into the bulk of the metal, leaving the metal surface and your skin surface relatively cool. That's why metal feels cool.

CONVECTION CURRENTS
Make your own heat waves in an aquarium.

Materials

- Two electrical lead wires with alligator clips at both ends (available at RadioShack)
- A 6- or 12-volt lantern battery or a suitable low-voltage battery eliminator or power supply
- A pencil lead
- A clear plastic or glass container with rectangular flat sides (a small aquarium works fine)
- Tap water
- A light source, such as a flashlight (a point-source, such as a Mini Maglite flashlight with the reflector removed will produce sharp images)
- A projection screen or white poster board
- Food coloring (in a small dropper bottle or an eyedropper)
- Optional: Switch or dimmer switch (both available at hardware stores) or any sort of rheostat or variable resistor

Introduction

This demonstration gives you a simple and visually appealing way to show convection currents in water. Warmer water rising through cooler water creates turbulence effects that bend light, allowing you to project swirling shadows onto a screen.

Assembly

(15 minutes or more)

1. Use one alligator clip to attach the positive terminal of the battery to one end of the pencil lead, and the second clip to attach the negative terminal to the other end of the pencil lead. If you like, you may connect a simple switch, or a dimmer switch, in series. The switch makes using the device more convenient; the dimmer switch lets you vary the amount of current going through the carbon rod.

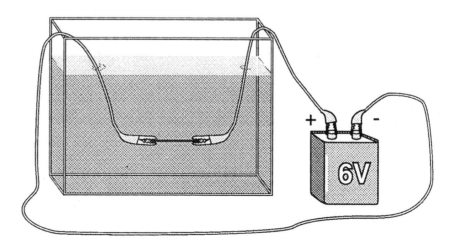

Etcetera

A simple method of doing this Snack is to place a candle on a table and project its image onto a screen or wall with a flashlight. The point source of a Mini Maglite projects clear images of convection when used on a small-scale desktop experiment like this. Changing the distance from the point light source to the candle will change the magnification of the image of the convection currents projected.

2. Fill the container with water and place the wires and pencil lead in it so that the pencil lead is positioned horizontally.

3. Connect the two wires to the terminals of the battery, and allow the heating to start.

4. Shine the light source through the liquid, projecting the light onto the screen or white poster board.

To Do and Notice

(15 minutes or more)

Observe the convection currents. If you have a dimmer switch, vary the current and observe the effects of the different settings. If you are using a rheostat or variable resistor, you may have to try several settings to find which one works best. You can also vary the orientation of the pencil lead to see if this has any significant effect on the convection pattern. Add a few drops of food coloring and observe the effects.

What's Going On?

Like air, water expands as it gets warmer and so becomes less dense. Because the water warmed by the current flowing through the carbon rod is less dense than the surrounding colder water, the warm water rises through the colder water to the surface, causing the food coloring to move along with it.

Because the cold and warm water have different densities, they have different indices of refraction. Light bends (refracts) as it passes from warmer to colder or colder to warmer. When light is bent onto an area of the screen, that area becomes brighter. When light is bent away from an area of the screen, that area becomes darker. The positions of warm and cold water are constantly changing, so the images projected on the screen shimmer and flow like heat waves in air.

COOL HOT ROD

Objects change size when heated or cooled.

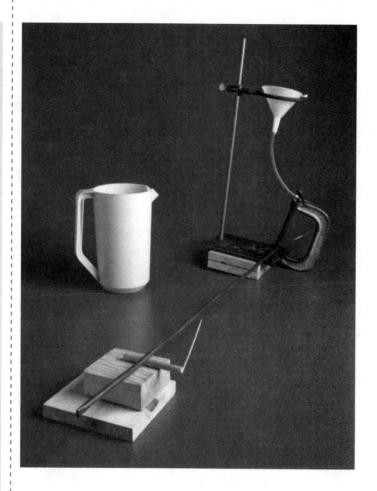

Introduction

Changes in temperature cause objects to expand or contract. This Snack allows you to directly observe the expansion and contraction of a metal tube.

Assembly

(30 minutes or more)

1. Insert one end of the copper tubing into the plastic tubing.

2. Slip the plastic tubing over the end of the funnel. Make sure that the tubes all fit snugly together.

3. Place the ring stand near the edge of a table, positioning the ring so that it supports the funnel a few inches above the tabletop.

4. Position the copper tubing so that the end farthest from the funnel sticks out beyond the edge of the table by a few inches.

5. Place a small block under the copper tubing at the end near the funnel.

6. Clamp the tubing and block to the table so that they can't move.

NOTE

If the needle slips instead of rotating, try placing a microscope slide between the wood and the needle. You can also increase the friction by wrapping a rubber band around the wood and the tubing to hold them together more tightly.

7. Place the second block under the other end of the tubing.

8. Put the needle between the copper tubing and the second block, positioned perpendicular to the tubing. Make sure that the eye of the needle extends past the block.

9. Stick the toothpick through the eye of the needle. As the tubing expands and contracts, the needle will rotate, rolled along by the movement of the tubing. The toothpick will shift from an upright position to a slanted position as the needle rotates, making the rotation more evident.

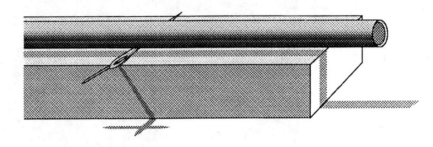

10. Put the bucket under the end of the copper tubing that sticks out beyond the edge of the table. The bucket will catch the water that you will pour through the copper tubing.

To Do and Notice

(*15 minutes or more*)

Pour hot water into the funnel to heat the tubing. For best results, heat the water to near boiling. When you do this, remember to keep your hands away from the copper tubing: It will become very hot!

When you pour the hot water into the funnel, notice the direction in which the needle rotates. Immediately pour cold water through the funnel, and watch the needle again. Notice the direction in which it rotates.

What's Going On?

The copper tubing, like everything else in the world, is made of atoms that are constantly vibrating. The higher the temperature, the faster the atoms vibrate. When you pour hot water into the tubing, heat flows from the water to the copper, giving energy to the copper atoms, which vibrate faster. This increase in vibration causes the atoms to collide with each other more often and more violently, so the space between the atoms increases. As a result, the whole tube gets longer and thicker. The needle turns as the tube expands.

When you pour cold water into the tube, the copper atoms give up some of their heat energy to the water, vibrate less violently, and move closer together. The tube shrinks and the needle turns in the opposite direction as the tube contracts.

The copper tube expands by 1.7×10^{-5} of its length for every 1.8 degrees Fahrenheit (1 degree Celsius) of temperature increase. So a copper tube that is 3.3 feet (1 meter) long will expand by 5.6×10^{-3} feet (1.7×10^{-3} m) over a 180-degree Fahrenheit (100-degree Celsius) temperature change, lengthening by almost 0.06 inch (1.7 mm).

As the copper tube expands, it will make the needle roll over this distance of 0.06 inch (1.7 mm). When an average-sized needle rolls 0.06 inch (1.7 mm), it makes more than two complete revolutions. The toothpick in the eye of the needle dramatically amplifies the motion of the expanding or contracting rod.

CURIE POINT

When a piece of iron gets too hot, it is no longer attracted to a magnet.

Materials

- ➡ A small magnet (RadioShack's disk magnets work fine)
- ➡ String, about 1 foot (30 cm) long
- ➡ One 3-inch (8 cm) length of thin steel wire, obtained by separating one strand from ordinary braided galvanized picture-hanging wire
- ➡ A stand to hold the magnet pendulum and wire (can be easily made from Tinkertoys or pieces of wood)
- ➡ Two electrical lead wires with alligator clips at both ends (available at RadioShack)
- ➡ One 6-volt lantern battery (or other 6-volt power supply)

NOTE

Braided copper wire and aluminum wire are available, but will not work here; iron wire can work, but is not commonly available. Whatever you use, be sure to stay away from plastic-coated wire, which can burn if it gets hot.

⚠ CAUTION

Electricity can really heat things up!
The wires can get really hot when you're doing this Snack. Be careful.

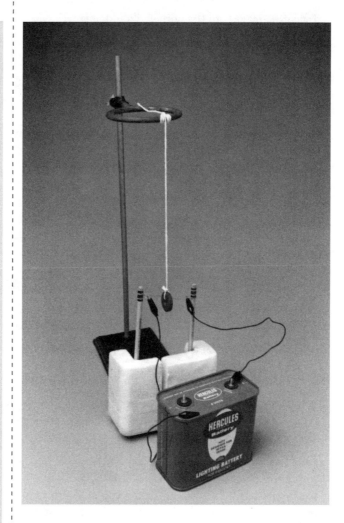

Introduction

A piece of iron will ordinarily be attracted to a magnet, but when you heat the iron to a high enough temperature (called the Curie point), it loses its ability to be magnetized. Heat energy scrambles the iron atoms so they can't line up and create a magnetic field. Here is a simple demonstration of this effect.

Assembly

(15 minutes or less)

1. Make a stand from Tinkertoys or other suitable materials as shown in the diagrams.

2. Suspend the magnet from the top of the stand with a string. Make the pendulum at least 4 inches (10 cm) long.

3. Stretch the wire between two posts so that, at its closest, the wire is 1 inch (2.5 cm) from the magnet.

To Do and Notice

(15 minutes or more)

Touch the magnet to the wire. It should magnetically attract and stick to the wire.

Connect the clip leads to the terminals of the lantern battery. Connect one clip lead to one side of the wire, and touch the other clip lead to the wire on the opposite side of the magnet. Current will flow through the wire, causing it to heat up. (Be careful! The wire will get hot!) As the wire heats up and begins to glow, the magnet will fall away from the wire.

Take a clip lead away from the wire and let the wire cool. When the wire is cool, notice that the magnet will stick to it once again.

If the wire does not heat up enough to glow red, move the clip leads closer together.

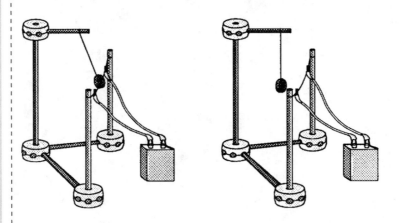

What's Going On?

Steel wire is made of atoms that act like tiny magnets, each of which has a north and south pole of its own. These atoms usually point in all different directions, so the steel has no net magnetic field. But when you hold a magnet up to the wire, the magnet makes the steel atoms line up. These lined-up atomic magnets turn the steel wire into a magnet. The steel is then attracted to the original magnet.

High temperatures can disturb this process of magnetization. Thermal energy makes the steel atoms jiggle back and forth, disturbing their magnetic alignment. When the vibration of the atoms becomes too great, the atomic magnets do not line up as well, and the steel loses its magnetism. The temperature at which this occurs is called the Curie point.

EDDY CURRENTS

A magnet falls more slowly through a metallic tube than it does through a nonmetallic tube.

Materials

- One 3-foot (1 m) length of aluminum, copper, or brass tubing (do not use iron!) with an inner diameter larger than the magnet and with walls as thick as possible

- A neodymium disk magnet at least 1/2 inch (1.25 cm) in diameter and longer than its diameter: you can stack several magnets together to get the right length

- A nonmagnetic object, such as a plastic-barreled pen or a wooden pencil

- One 3-foot (1 m) length of PVC or other nonmetallic tubing

- Optional: Two thick, flat pieces of aluminum (available at hardware and home-improvement stores); cardboard; masking tape; rubber bands or cord

Introduction

When a magnet is dropped down a metallic tube, the changing magnetic field created by the falling magnet pushes electrons around in circular, eddy-like currents. These eddy currents have their own magnetic field that opposes the fall of the magnet. The magnet falls dramatically slower than it does in ordinary free fall in a nonmetallic tube.

Assembly

None required.

To Do and Notice

(15 minutes or less)

Hold the metal tube vertically and drop the magnet through the tube. Then drop a non-magnetic object, such as a pen or pencil, through the tube. Notice that the magnet takes noticeably more time to fall. Now try dropping both magnetic and nonmagnetic objects through the PVC tube.

In addition to dropping these objects through the tubes, a simple, visible, and dramatic demonstration can be done by merely dropping the magnet between two thick, flat

Etcetera

Eddy currents are often generated in transformers, leading to power losses. To combat this, thin laminated strips of metal are used in the construction of power transformers, rather than making the transformer out of one solid piece of metal. The thin strips are separated by insulating glue, which confines the eddy currents to the strips. This reduces the eddy currents, thus reducing the power loss.

With the new high-strength neodymium magnets, the effects of eddy currents become even more dramatic. These magnets are now available from many scientific supply companies, and the price has become relatively affordable.

Eddy currents are also used to dampen unwanted oscillations in many mechanical balances. Examine your school's balances to see whether they have a thin metal strip that moves between two magnets.

pieces of aluminum. The aluminum pieces should be spaced just slightly farther apart than the thickness of the magnet. A permanent spacer can easily be made with cardboard and masking tape if you don't want to hold the pieces apart each time. Rubber bands or cord can hold the pieces all together. The flat surfaces need to be only slightly wider than the width of the magnet itself. Thickness, however, is important. The effect will be seen even with thin pieces of aluminum, but a thickness of about 1/4 inch (6 mm) will produce a remarkably slow rate of fall. Allow at least a 6-inch (15 cm) fall.

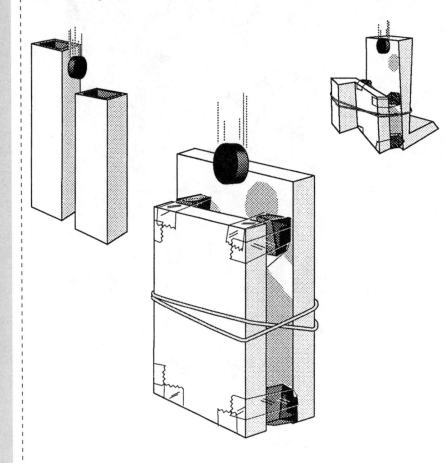

What's Going On?

As the magnet falls, the magnetic field around it constantly changes position. As the magnet passes through a given portion of the metal tube, this portion of the tube experiences a changing magnetic field, which induces the flow of eddy currents in an electrical conductor, such as the copper or aluminum tubing. The eddy currents create a magnetic field that exerts a force on the falling magnet. The force opposes the magnet's fall. As a result of this magnetic repulsion, the magnet falls much more slowly.

⚡ ELECTRICAL FLEAS
Start your own electric flea circus!

Materials

- → A large sheet of paper, 11 × 17 inches (28 × 43 cm)
- → Four supports about 1 to 2 inches (2.5 to 5 cm) high (tuna cans work nicely)
- → A sheet of acrylic plastic or other clear plastic (about 1 foot [30 cm] square and 1/8-inch [3 mm] thick)
- → Tiny bits of "stuff": aluminized ceiling glitter works well, as do grains of rice, puffed rice cereal, spices (dried dill weed or basil, ground cloves, ground nutmeg), or bits of Styrofoam
- → A piece of wool cloth or fur

Introduction

You're probably familiar with some of the effects of static electricity: It makes the sparks when you comb your hair on a cold day, and it makes balloons stick to the wall at a birthday party. In this Snack, static electricity makes electric "fleas" jump up and down.

Assembly

(15 minutes or less)

1. Put the piece of paper on the table.

2. Place the supports on the paper beneath the four corners of the plastic.

3. Scatter the tiny bits of Styrofoam, spices, ceiling glitter, or rice under the plastic. (You can set up this assembly on any tabletop.)

To Do and Notice

(15 minutes or more)

Charge the plastic by rubbing it vigorously with the piece of wool cloth or fur. Watch the "fleas" dance!

Try different types of material for charging the plastic, including your hand, and experiment with other materials for fleas. Also, try the plastic at different heights.

What's Going On?

Both the plastic and the "fleas" start out electrically neutral: That is, they have an equal number of positive and negative charges. When you rub the plastic with the wool cloth, the cloth transfers negative charges to the plastic. These negative charges polarize the fleas, attracting the positive charges to the tops of the fleas and pushing the negative

Etcetera

While the "fleas" are dancing, put your ear on the plastic plate. Listen to the tapping of the fleas as they hit the plastic. The tapping rate slowly decreases as the charge on the plastic is depleted. The dance of the fleas sounds like the clicking of a Geiger counter measuring a radioactive source that is decaying.

charges to the bottoms of the fleas. The attraction between the negative plastic and the positive charge concentrated on the tops of the fleas makes the fleas jump up to the underside of the plastic.

When a flea actually touches the plastic, some of the plastic's negative charge flows to the flea. The top of the flea becomes electrically neutral. But since the whole flea was originally neutral, the flea now has some excess negative charge. The negatively charged flea and the negatively charged plastic repel each other strongly, which causes the flea to jump quickly back to the table. As the flea's excess negative charge slowly drains away to the tabletop, or to the air, the flea again becomes neutral and is ready to jump up to the plastic once more.

ELECTROSCOPE
What's your (electrical) sign?

Materials
- → Two plastic 35 mm film cans or small, bathroom-sized paper cups
- → Enough modeling clay to fill the cans or cups halfway
- → Four plastic drinking straws with flexible ends
- → A roll of 3M Scotch® Magic™ Tape, 3/4-inch (2 cm) width (don't sub-stitute other brands of tape the first time you try this Snack; once you know what to expect, you can experiment with other tapes)
- → A plastic comb and someone with a full head of hair, or a piece of wool cloth

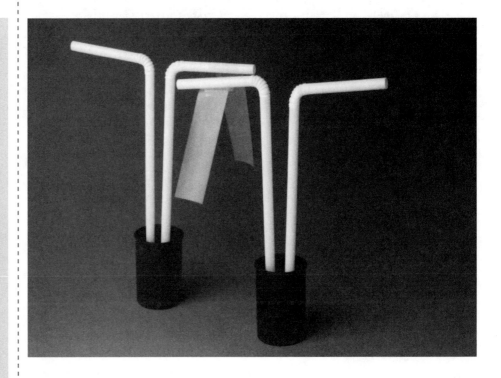

Introduction

By suspending pieces of tape from a straw, you can build an electroscope, a device that detects electrical charge. A commonly available brand of plastic tape can gain or lose negatively charged electrons when you stick it to a surface and rip it off. A plastic comb will enable you to identify whether the pieces of tape are positively or negatively charged.

Assembly
(5 minutes or less)

1. Press enough modeling clay into each film can or paper cup to fill them both half-way to the top.
2. Press the inflexible ends of two drinking straws into the clay in each can, and bend the flexible ends to form horizontal arms that extend in opposite directions. The heights of the straws should be the same.

To Do and Notice
(15 minutes or more)

Tear off two 4-inch (10 cm) pieces of tape. Press each piece firmly to a tabletop or other flat surface, leaving one end of each tape sticking up (or out over the table's edge) as a handle. Quickly pull the tapes from the table and stick one piece on an arm of a straw in one film can, and the other piece on an arm of a straw in the other film can.

Etcetera

You can use your electroscope to test whether an object is electrically charged. First, use the comb to determine the charge on a piece of tape, and then see whether an object whose charge is unknown repels the tape. If the tape is negatively charged and an object repels it, then the object is negatively charged.

Don't use attraction to judge whether an object is charged: A charged object may attract an uncharged one. If tape is attracted to an object, the tape and the object may have opposite charges, or the tape may be charged and the object uncharged, or the object may be charged and the tape uncharged. But if the tape is repelled by the object, the tape and the object must have the same charge. The only way that tape and an object will neither repel nor attract is if both are uncharged.

Move the cans so the two tapes are face to face, about 6 inches (15 cm) apart. Then move the cans closer together. Notice that the two tapes repel each other.

Tear off two more pieces of tape and press the sticky side of one against the smooth side of the other, leaving one end of each tape sticking out as a handle. Quickly pull the tapes apart and stick them to the two remaining arms. Bring the arms close together. Notice that these two tapes attract each other.

Run the comb through your hair, or rub the comb with the wool cloth. Then hold the comb near the dangling tapes. Notice that the comb repels the piece of tape with its smooth side in the middle of the "sandwich" and attracts the tape with its sticky side in the middle. When you hold the comb near the tapes pulled from the flat surface, the comb will repel both tapes if they were pulled from a Formica surface; the comb may attract tapes pulled from other surfaces.

Note that some table surfaces will not charge the tape, so be sure to test yours before trying this Snack. You can also put a few pieces of tape onto a piece of cardboard, leave the tape there, and put a second strip of tape on top of the first. Then, when you pull off the top piece of tape, it will always be charged.

Try pulling other kinds of tape from various surfaces, or rubbing various objects together, and then bringing the tape or objects near the tapes on the arms. Bring your hand near the tapes and notice what happens.

What's Going On?

When you rip the two pieces of tape off the table, there is a tug-of-war for electric charges between tape and table. The tape either steals negative charges (electrons) from the table or leaves some of its own negative charges behind, depending on what the table is made of (a positive charge doesn't move in this situation). In any case, both pieces of tape end up with the same kind of charge, either positive or negative. Since like charges repel, the pieces of tape repel each other.

When the tape sandwich is pulled apart, one piece rips negative charges from the other. One piece of tape therefore has extra negative charges. The other piece, which has lost some negative charge, now has an overall positive charge. Because opposite charges attract, the two tapes attract each other.

When you run a plastic comb through your hair, the comb becomes negatively charged. Tapes repelled by the comb have a net negative charge, and tapes attracted by the comb either have a net positive charge or are uncharged.

You may have found that your hand attracts both positively and negatively charged tapes. Your body is usually uncharged, unless you have acquired a charge—by walking across a carpet, for example.

An uncharged object attracts charged objects. When you hold your hand near a positively charged tape, the tape attracts electrons in your body. The part of your body nearest the tape becomes negatively charged, while a positive charge remains behind on the rest of your body. The positive tape is attracted to the nearby negative charges more strongly than it is repelled by the more distant positive charges, and the tape moves toward your hand.

Note that charge leaks slowly off the tape into the air or along the surface of the tape, so you may have to recharge your tapes after a few minutes of use.

FOG CHAMBER
Make a portable cloud in a bottle: Now you see it; now you don't!

Materials

- A 1-gallon (3.5 L) clear glass or plastic jar with a wide mouth (a pickle jar works well)
- Tap water
- A rubber glove (Playtex brand works well)
- Matches

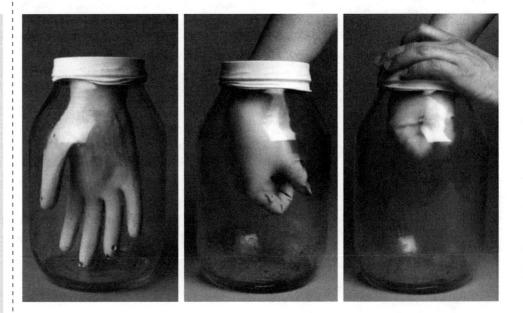

Introduction

Clouds form when invisible water vapor in the air cools enough to form tiny droplets of liquid water. In the atmosphere, this usually happens when moist air cools as it rises to higher altitudes. At higher altitudes the pressure is lower, so the gas expands, loses internal energy, and cools. You can create the same effect by rapidly expanding the air in a jar.

Assembly

(5 minutes or more)

1. Barely cover the bottom of the jar with water.

2. Hang the glove inside the jar with its fingers pointing down

3. Stretch the glove's open end over the mouth of the jar to seal it.

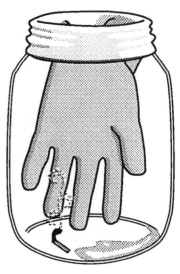

To Do and Notice

(15 minutes or more)

Insert your hand partway into the glove and pull it quickly outward without disturbing the jar's seal. Nothing will happen.

Next, remove the glove, drop a lit match into the jar, and replace the glove. Pull outward on the glove once more. This time, notice that fog forms inside

Etcetera

For an added treat, shine the beam of a flashlight through the cloud you make in the jar. When the smoke is fresh, the droplets will be large compared to all wavelengths of visible light, and the light they scatter will be white. As the smoke dissipates, the water drops will become smaller, and the light scattered will create beautiful pastel colors at some viewing angles. Light of different colors diffracts around the small droplets, going off in different directions. If you look at clouds near the sun, you can often see bands of these pastel colors. (Just remember to never look directly at the sun!)

the jar when you pull the glove outward and disappears when the glove snaps back. The fog will form for 5 to 10 minutes before the smoke particles settle and have to be replenished.

What's Going On?

Water molecules are present in the air inside the jar, but they're in the form of an invisible gas, or vapor, flying around individually and not sticking to one another. When you pull the glove outward, you allow the air in the jar to expand. In expanding, the air must do work, which means that it loses some of its thermal energy, which in turn means that its molecules (including those of the water vapor), slow down slightly. This is a roundabout way of saying that the air becomes cooler!

When the water molecules slow down, they can stick to each other more easily, so they begin to bunch up in tiny droplets. The particles of smoke in the jar help this process along: The water molecules bunch together more easily when they find a solid particle to act as a nucleus. When you push the glove back in, you warm the air in the jar slightly, which causes the tiny droplets to evaporate and again become invisible.

In the atmosphere, air expands as it rises to regions of lower pressure and cools off, forming clouds. This is why clouds often obscure mountaintops. Dust, smoke, and salt particles in the air all provide nuclei that help the droplets condense.

Meteorologists consider a falling barometer reading (low air pressure) to be a sign of an approaching storm, whereas high pressure is usually a sign of clear weather. The temperature at which water vapor begins to form droplets on a surface is called the dew point.

GAS MODEL
Caged molecules do their thing.

Materials

- Latex paint
- A paintbrush
- Twelve or more Styrofoam balls, approximately 1¼ inches (3 cm) in diameter (available in craft or fabric stores), or table tennis balls
- A small rodent cage with wire mesh on all sides, or two plastic strawberry or utility baskets with open-grid sides put together to form a cage
- Short pieces of wire or twist ties
- A hair dryer, fan, or other blower

⚠ CAUTION
Be careful with metal!
The sharp ends of a wire can give you a very nasty cut.

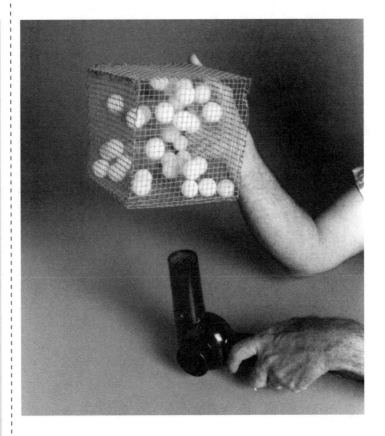

Introduction

The atomic theory of matter tells us that a gas is made up of tiny particles called atoms (or molecules, which are combinations of atoms), which are constantly in motion, smashing into each other and the walls of whatever container they might be in. Here is a highly visual model of this idea.

Assembly
(15 minutes or less)

1. Paint one of the balls a bright color, using latex paint (because oil-based paint dissolves Styrofoam).

2. Place the balls in the cage and secure the door of the cage with short pieces of wire or twist ties.

To Do and Notice
(15 minutes or more)

Hold the blower under the cage and blow air up through it. The moving air will agitate the balls, simulating the kinetic behavior of a gas. Watching the colored ball will allow you to follow the motion of a single "molecule."

Etcetera

If you blow air on one side of the bottom of the cage and not the other, the balls will eventually "condense out." That is, they will form a pile on the side away from the blower, where it is "cooler."

By adjusting the speed of the blower through the cage, you can simulate heating and cooling a gas. The faster the balls are moving, the hotter the gas.

Listen for the clicking of the balls against the walls of the cage. At lower "temperatures," the clicking is quieter and occurs at a slower rate.

You may also want to try this using cages of different volumes—or try nesting baskets to change their volume. In this way, you can model the ideal gas law by changing temperature, pressure, and volume.

What's Going On?

Adding heat (simulated by the blower) to a gas increases its internal energy. The molecules of the gas move faster and strike the walls of their container more often, yielding an increase in pressure (force per area). This increased pressure is simulated by the faster motion of the balls, which strike the sides of the cage harder and more often. Cooling the gas (moving the blower farther from the cage) lowers the internal energy, slowing the motion of the molecules and thus lowering the pressure.

GIVE AND TAKE

Dark-colored materials both absorb and emit energy more readily than light-colored materials.

Materials

- A black marking pen
- A metallic silver marking pen
- Temperature-sensitive liquid crystal material strip or card
- Desk lamp or sunlight

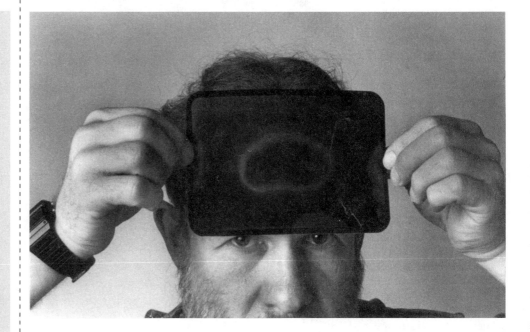

Introduction

Using a card or strip made of temperature-sensitive liquid crystal material, you can monitor temperature changes. By observing these changes, you can show that dark-colored materials absorb and re-emit the energy contained in light more readily than light-colored materials.

Assembly

(15 minutes or less)

Use the marking pens to color one half of the back of the liquid crystal card black (if it isn't already black) and the other half silver.

To Do and Notice

(15 minutes or more)

Hold the silver-and-black side of the card that you colored with the marking pens toward the light source. Hold the card a few inches away from the lamp. Or, if the sun is your light source, just hold the card in the sunlight.

Watch the liquid crystal side of the card. Notice that the side with black on the back changes color faster than the side with silver on the back. This color change indicates that the blackened side is changing temperature faster than the silvered side.

Let the card cool until the liquid crystal is black again. Then heat up the card by touching it to your hand or by shining light onto the liquid crystal side. Remove the card from the heat and watch the liquid crystal as it cools. The black side should cool faster than the silver side.

Etcetera

The term liquid crystal sounds like an oxymoron. However, if you examine molecules of a liquid crystal that are close to one another, they will be arranged in an orderly structure, like a crystal. If you examine molecules that are separated by longer distances, the molecules will be disordered, as they would be in a liquid. Liquid crystals, therefore, have a short-range order, like a crystal, and a long-range disorder, like a liquid.

Temperature-sensitive liquid crystal material is cholesteric—that is, arranged so that the long, rod-shaped molecules sit side by side in layers, with each layer at a slight angle from the layer above and below it. You could picture this arrangement as a spiral staircase, with the molecules as the risers in the stairs.

When the liquid crystal is heated, two things happen. First, the layers move farther apart. Second, the angle between the molecules in each layer increases. These two changes combine to cause the spiral staircase of molecules to wind up tighter as the crystal heats up. As a result, at lower temperatures, the spiral matches and reflects visible light with longer wavelengths—red light. At higher temperatures, the spiral matches and reflects light with shorter wavelengths—blue light.

What's Going On?

Dark-colored materials absorb visible light better than light-colored materials. That's why the dark side of the card heats up first. The lighter side absorbs less of the incident light, reflecting some of the energy. Darker materials also emit radiation more readily than light-colored materials, and so they cool faster.

You may be tempted to skip coating half of the card with the silver marker. After all, that half is probably white, which indicates that it reflects light in the visible portion of the electromagnetic spectrum. But, although the white paper reflects visible light, it also absorbs infrared light. If you could see infrared light, the white paper would look black when illuminated with infrared.

Unlike plain white paper, silver paint reflects infrared light as well as visible light. The white paper is an infrared absorber, and so it is also a good infrared emitter: It will cool almost as fast as the blackened paper. The silver is a good infrared reflector and a poor infrared emitter: It will cool more slowly than the blackened side. Therefore, the heating experiment with visible light will work with black-and-white halves of the card, but the cooling experiment will not!

Even with the silvered coating, the cooling effect is harder to observe because the card is cooled by conduction and convection in addition to radiation. This is in contrast to the heating experiment, where the only heating is from radiation.

HAND BATTERY
Your skin and two different metals create a battery.

Materials

- An aluminum plate and a copper plate, each about the size of your hand
- Flat wood surface or nonmetallic surface
- Two clamps
- Two wires with alligator clips at both ends (available at RadioShack)
- A digital multimeter (inexpensive models are available online)

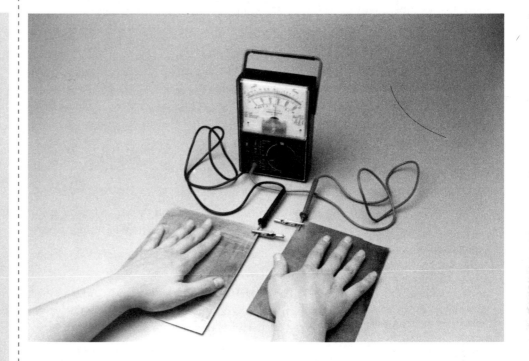

Introduction

When you place your hands on metal plates, you and the plates form a battery.

Assembly
(15 minutes or less)

1. Mount both metal plates on a piece of wood or simply clamp them to a nonmetallic surface. (If you prefer, you don't even have to mount the two plates. You can attach the wires as described below and then simply hold one plate in each hand. This has the benefit of allowing you to easily substitute other metals.)

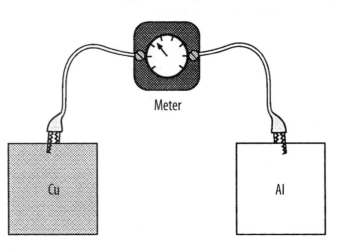

Etcetera

You can use other pairs of different metals in a circuit to produce a current. The success you have using various metals will depend on a metal's electrode potential, that is, its ability to gain or lose charges. Try various metals to see which produces the highest current reading. An electromotive series table shows the electrode potentials of metals and allows you to predict which metals will work well in making a hand battery.

You can sometimes get a small current even between two plates made of the same metal. Each plate has a slightly different coating of oxides, salts, and oils on its surface. These coatings create slight differences in the surfaces of the metals, and these differences can produce an electrical current.

The slightly painful sensation of a fork tine touching a metal filling, the process of plating metals, sacrificial anodes used to preserve ship hulls and iron bridges, potato clocks, and dielectric unions to prevent deterioration of copper and iron plumbing are all everyday examples of metals transferring charges.

2. Using the clip leads, connect one plate to one of the multimeter's test probes and connect the other plate to the other probe. At this point it doesn't matter which plate attaches to which probe.

3. Set the multimeter to measure current in milliamps.

To Do and Notice

(15 minutes or more)

Place one hand on each plate. You should notice a reading on the meter. If the meter shows a negative current, simply reverse your connections, attaching the copper plate to the probe that the aluminum was connected to and vice versa. If the meter shows no current, check the connections and the wiring. If that doesn't produce current, try cleaning the plates with a pencil eraser or steel wool to remove oxidation.

Experiment with different metals to find out what combination produces the most current. Try pressing harder on the plates. Get your hands wet and try again.

Switch the multimeter to measure voltage, and repeat the above experiments.

Have one person put a hand on the copper plate and another person put a hand on the aluminum plate, and then have them join their free hands.

What's Going On?

Most batteries use two different materials and an electrolyte solution to create an imbalance of charge and thus a voltage. When the terminals of the battery are connected with a wire, this voltage produces a current.

In this Snack, the thin film of sweat on your hands acts like an electrolyte solution and reacts with the copper and aluminum plates. When you touch the copper plate, the copper gives up negatively charged electrons and acquires a positive charge. When you touch the aluminum plate, it takes electrons and becomes negatively charged.

This difference in charge between the two plates creates a flow of electrical charge, or electrical current. Because electrons can move freely through metals, the excess electrons on the aluminum plate flow through the meter on their way to the copper plate. In addition, negative electrons move through your body from the hand touching the copper to the hand touching the aluminum. As long as the reactions continue, the charges will continue to flow and the meter will show a small current.

Your body resists the flow of current. Most of this resistance is in your skin. By wetting your skin you can decrease your resistance and increase the current through the meter. Since two people holding hands have more resistance than one person, the flow of current should be less. If you like, you can use the multimeter to measure resistance directly in these situations.

When you do the experiments while measuring voltage, you may see a slight change, but it will be much less than the change you saw when you measured the current.

HOT SPOT
You can focus the invisible light from an electric heater.

Materials

● A small electric heater

● A large concave mirror, about 16 inches (40 cm) in diameter (of the type sometimes called "spherical mirrors" or "demonstration mirrors"—or you can use the bottom mirror from a commercially made Mirage Maker or Mind Boggling Optic Mirage, available from various online vendors)

NOTE

If you're using the bottom mirror from a Mirage Maker or Mind Boggling Optic Mirage (both of which are smaller than a full-sized concave "spherical" or "demonstration" mirror), you'll need to find this hot spot by focusing the orange glow from the coil on two fingers stuck out close to the mirror.

Introduction

Infrared radiation from an electric heater is just another "color" of light. Though you can't see this light with your eyes, you can focus it with a mirror or a lens and feel the warmth it produces. From this Snack, you can also learn how parabolic shapes concentrate energy.

Assembly

(5 minutes or less)

Place the heater many focal lengths away from the mirror. (The focal length for the recommended mirror is about 1 foot [30 cm], so place the heater about 10 feet [3 m] away.)

To Do and Notice

(15 minutes or more)

Move your hand around in front of the mirror until you can feel the hot spot. This spot will be close to the mirror's focal point. Look into the mirror and find the visible image of the heater: This image of the heater is also near the focal point.

Look into the mirror and move around, observing your reflection. Move toward and away from the mirror, and see how your image and the images of the objects around you change.

Etcetera

Satellite dishes for TV reception operate on this same principle, except they focus radio waves instead of light waves. The surface of such a reflector doesn't need to be polished like the parabolic mirror because radio waves are much longer than light waves. To a radio wave, the surface of the dish looks very smooth: Small irregularities don't affect the long radio waves. The very short light waves, on the other hand, are bounced off in all directions by the radio dish's surface roughness, so light waves are not focused. For reasons of economy and weight, the large dishes used to focus the even longer radio waves from astronomical objects (stars, quasars, and so on) sometimes are constructed out of a rather large mesh screen, which appears smooth to the very long waves.

A family of snakes called pit vipers (which includes rattlesnakes) takes advantage of this effect to locate its prey. These snakes have two or more sensory "pits," which they use like pinhole cameras to image infrared light. The snake can locate a warm-blooded creature, such as a mouse, by imaging the infrared heat radiated by the mouse. With two pits, the snake even has some depth perception in the infrared.

Move the heater off the axis of the mirror or closer to the mirror. Search around, using the back of one hand as an infrared-radiation detector. Find where the infrared radiation from the heater is concentrated. This will be the position of the infrared image of the heater. Locate the visible-light image of the heater with your eyes. Notice that the infrared energy from the heater comes back together at the visible-light image position. Notice also that the image point is not the focal point.

Place your face close to the mirror and talk into the mirror. Keep talking as you move away from the mirror. At one point, your voice will sound much louder. At this point, the sound waves radiating from your mouth bounce off the mirror and are concentrated at your ear. When this happens, the mirror is making a sound image of your voice at the position of your ear.

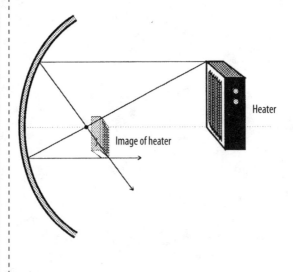

Heater

Image of heater

What's Going On?

Every parabolic mirror has a focal point, a place where all parallel light waves, sound waves, or any other form of radiation directed at the mirror along its axis will be concentrated. Infrared radiation is simply light with a wavelength too long for your eyes to see. But your skin can feel infrared radiation as heat. The skin of your cheek and on the back of each of your hands is particularly sensitive to warming by infrared radiation. The parabolic mirror concentrates the infrared radiation coming from a distant heater at its focal point. That's why you feel a hot spot when you put your hand at the mirror's focal point.

When the heater is moved closer to the mirror, the point where its radiation is concentrated—the infrared image of the heater—moves away from the focal point.

MAGNETIC LINES OF FORCE

Iron filings will trace out the lines of a magnetic field in three dimensions.

Materials

- A plastic water or soda bottle, 16 oz. (0.5 L) size
- Iron filings (available at science museums or from scientific suppliers, or you can use magnetic sand—black sand— collected by dragging a magnet through iron-rich beach sand)
- A plastic test tube that fits into the mouth of the bottle and is about 75 percent as long as the bottle is tall
- Masking tape
- A cow magnet or other cylindrical magnet that fits into the plastic tube (a stack of button magnets from RadioShack works fine)

 CAUTION

Be careful with iron filings! Iron filings may seem harmless, but they can really give you nasty cuts and splinters.

Introduction

Iron filings will line up parallel to a magnetic field, making the pattern of the field visible. This is a simple Snack to build—and because the filings are trapped in a bottle, they don't make a mess.

Assembly

(15 minutes or less)

1. Remove the label from the plastic bottle.
2. Fill the bottle about one-fifth full of iron filings. (See diagram.)
3. Wrap the top of the test tube with masking tape so the tube fits snugly into the mouth of the bottle, plugging the opening completely.
4. Jam the tube into the mouth of the bottle.
5. Slide the cylindrical magnet into the test tube and put the bottle cap back on.

To Do and Notice

(5 minutes or more)

Turn the bottle on its side and rotate it. Watch what happens to the iron filings. They will form a three-dimensional pattern that traces out the magnetic field of the magnet.

Etcetera

Cow magnets are strong, permanent magnets made out of alnico, an iron alloy containing aluminum, nickel, and cobalt. These magnets are available at most feed stores. Ranchers feed these magnets to their cows. The magnet settles in the cow's first stomach. When the cow eats bits of steel or iron, the magnet attracts the metal bits and holds them in its first stomach. If the sharp pieces of metal were to pass through the cow, the animal would suffer what ranchers call "hardware disease."

Pay particular attention to what happens at the end of the magnet. Here, the iron filings stand out like a punk haircut.

Shake the magnet out of the tube, and watch the filings collapse.

What's Going On?

Each atom in a piece of iron is a magnet, with a north pole and a south pole. Most pieces of iron are not magnetic, because the atomic magnets all point in different directions.

When you bring a magnet near a piece of iron, the iron-atom magnets line up with the applied magnetic field: The north poles of the iron atoms all point in the same direction. Because the iron atoms line up, the piece of iron becomes a magnet and is attracted to the original magnet.

In a rod-shaped piece of iron, the atoms will tend to line up so that all the north poles face one end of the rod and all the south poles face the other end. Since iron filings are rod-shaped, the atoms line up pointing along the length of the rod, and the rods line up parallel to the direction of the applied magnetic field. The field of a cylindrical magnet comes out of the end of the magnet and then loops around next to the side. The iron filings stick out like a crew cut on the ends of the magnet but lie flat on the sides.

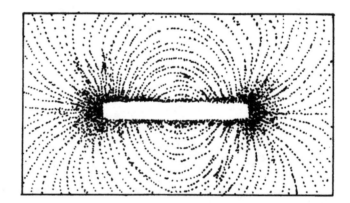

Because the iron filings become magnets themselves, their presence slightly changes the shape of the magnetic field. Even so, this Snack gives an indication of the shape of the magnetic field in three dimensions.

Note that if you've sealed the plastic bottle really well by jamming the test tube into its mouth, the sides of the bottle will begin to collapse inward after a few hours—particularly if the inside of the bottle is damp. This happens because the iron filings are rusting. As the iron rusts, it combines with and removes oxygen from the air trapped in the bottle. To prevent the bottle's collapse, simply punch a small hole in the plastic with a pushpin.

MAGNETIC SUCTION

This investigation shows how your doorbell works.

Materials

- ➔ Forty feet (12 m) of insulated bell wire
- ➔ A plastic or cardboard tube 4 to 6 inches (10 to 15 cm) long and about 1/4 inch (6 mm) in diameter
- ➔ A large battery, 6 volts or more, or use a battery holder with two alkaline D cells for power (an ordinary 1.5-volt D battery will work, but may go dead quickly and will require more coils to get the same effect)
- ➔ The largest iron nail that will fit in the tube loosely

⚠ CAUTION

Electricity can really heat things up!
The wires in this Snack can get hot, so be careful.

Don't hang on too long!
Leaving the wires connected too long will result in death for your battery and perhaps a burn for you from the hot wires, so be careful!

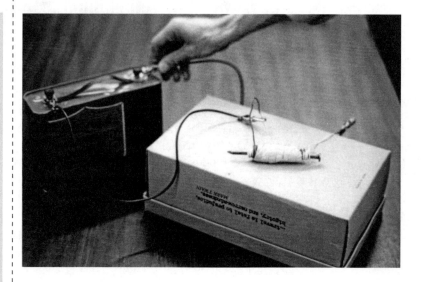

Introduction

A coil of wire with current flowing through it forms an electromagnet that acts very much like a bar magnet. The coil will magnetize an iron nail and attract it in a remarkably vigorous way.

Assembly

(15 minutes or less)

Tightly wrap as many coils of wire as possible around the tube, leaving the two ends free so you can strip the insulation off them and connect them to a battery.

To Do and Notice

(15 minutes or more)

Insert the nail partway into the coil and briefly connect the ends of the wires to the battery. The nail should be sucked into the coil. Reverse the leads to the battery and repeat the experiment, after predicting what will happen.

Any moving electric charge creates a magnetic field around it. A loop of wire with a current creates a magnetic field through the loop. You can increase the strength of this field by piling up a lot of loops. The more loops, the stronger the magnet. Like a bar magnet, this coil of wire now has a north pole and a south pole.

Because of the spin of the electrons, which can be thought of as rotating balls of charge, each atom acts like a small magnet. Ordinarily, all these "loops" point in different directions, so the iron has no overall magnetism. But suppose you bring a nail near the south pole of your electromagnet. The north poles of the iron atoms will be attracted to the south pole of the electromagnet and will all line up pointing in the same direction. The nail is now magnetized, with its north poles facing the south pole of the electromagnet. The opposite poles attract each other, and the nail is sucked into the electromagnet.

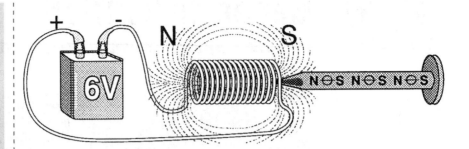

Etcetera

To extend this activity, hold the coil vertically and repeat the experiment. Try smaller nails and straightened paper clips in the coil. Remove the nail from the coil and test its magnetic properties by seeing if you can pick up some paper clips with it. If the electromagnet is not strong enough, the nail will not stay magnetized after the battery is disconnected, so to see this effect use as large a current source as possible. If the electromagnet is strong enough, the nail may stay magnetized for a while, until the random jiggling of the iron atoms eventually moves them out of alignment again. To demagnetize the nail rapidly, drop it several times onto a solid surface, such as a cement floor. This knocks the iron atoms out of alignment. Try to pick up paper clips with the demagnetized nail.

The principle of magnetic suction is used to make a variety of devices, from doorbells (in which an iron rod is sucked into a coil to strike a chime) to pinball machines (in which current goes through a coil, sucking in a rod attached to the flipper) to the starter switch on your car.

When the direction of current is reversed, the poles of the electromagnet reverse. Knowing this, you might think that when you bring the nail near the same end of the electromagnet as you did previously, the nail would now be repelled by the electromagnet, rather than attracted and sucked into it again. But when you try it, the nail does the same thing it did before. That's because the nail's iron atoms all reorient so that they line up with their opposite poles pointing toward whatever pole the electromagnet presents. Thus the nail will always be attracted to the electromagnet and will never be repelled.

You can find which end of the coil is the magnetic north pole with a magnetic compass, or by using the "right-hand rule." Wrap the fingers of your right hand around the coil in the direction the current is flowing (that is, away from the positive terminal of the battery and toward the negative terminal), and your thumb will point to the north end of the coil.

Imagine holding a current-carrying wire in your right hand.

Point your thumb in the direction of current flow (that is, from positive to negative) . . .

. . . and your fingers will point in the direction of the magnetic field.

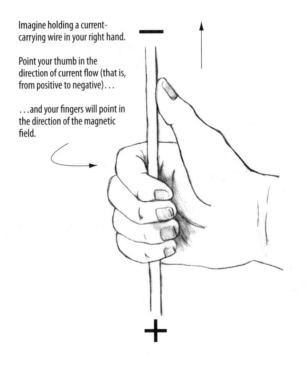

MOTOR EFFECT

A magnet exerts a force on current-carrying wire.

Materials

- Four to six small donut or disk magnets (available from RadioShack)
- A wooden board approximately 2 × 4 × 6 inches (5 × 10 × 15 cm)
- Masking tape
- A 1.5-volt alkaline D-cell battery
- Approximately 2 feet (60 cm) of flexible wire, such as solid or multi-strand hookup wire or magnet wire (available at RadioShack)
- A knife or sandpaper

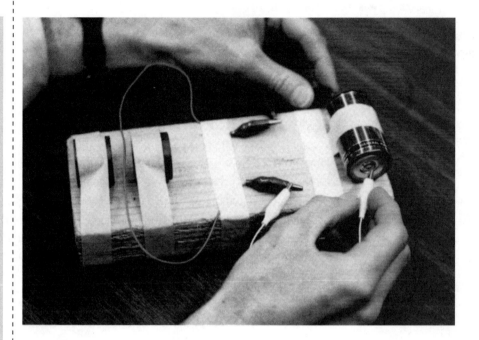

Introduction

This simple device shows that when an electrical current flows through a magnetic field, a force is exerted on the current. This force can be used to make an electric motor.

Assembly

(15 minutes or less)

1. Group the magnets into a single cylindrical pile.

2. Place the pile on the board so that it can be rolled along the board.

3. Split the pile in the middle, leaving a gap of about 1/2 inch (1.25 cm) between the faces of the two groups.

4. Arrange the groups so that a north pole faces a south pole across the gap, then tape the two groups to the board.

5. Tape the battery onto the board as shown in the photo.

6. Remove the insulation from the ends of the wire. (Use a knife for stranded wire, or use sandpaper to remove the nearly invisible insulating enamel from magnet wire.)

7. Loop the wire through the gap between the magnets, with the ends of the wire close enough to the battery to touch it. The wire should not be touching the board.

This experiment creates just a short pulse of motion. A motor requires continuous motion. This problem was solved originally in the early 1800s by the invention of commutators. A commutator is a sliding contact that not only makes electrical contact with a rotating loop of wire but also allows the current direction to reverse every half-cycle of rotation.

The first electric motors were constructed in 1821 by Michael Faraday in England and improved in 1831 by Joseph Henry in the United States.

To Do and Notice

(5 minutes or more)

Touch one end of the wire to the positive side of the battery and simultaneously touch the other end of the wire to the negative side. The wire loop will jump either up or down.

If you reverse the direction of current flow, the wire will jump in the opposite direction. To reverse the current, attach the lead that was connected to the positive end of the battery to the negative end and vice versa. (The result is the same as turning the battery around.)

What's Going On?

The magnetic field of the magnets exerts a force on the electric current flowing in the wire. The wire will move up or down, depending on the direction of the current and the direction of the magnetic field of the magnets.

To predict the direction of movement, you can use a mathematical tool called the "right-hand rule." Put your right hand near the section of wire that goes between the disk magnets. Make your hand flat, with your thumb sticking out to the side. (Your thumb should be at a right angle to your fingers.) Place your hand so your thumb points along the wire in the direction that the electric current is flowing (current flows from the positive terminal of the battery to the negative terminal) and so that your fingers point from the north pole of the magnets toward their south pole. (You can find the north pole of the magnets by using a compass; the south end of a compass will point toward the north pole of a magnet.) Your palm will then naturally "push" in the direction of the magnetic force on the wire.

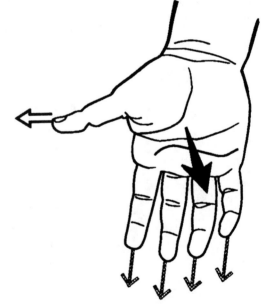

The deflecting force that a magnet exerts on a current-carrying wire is the mechanism behind the operation of most electric motors. Curiously (and happily for our sense of symmetry!), the reverse effect is also true: Move a loop of wire across the pole of a magnet, and a current will begin to flow in the wire. This, of course, is the principle of the electric generator. The electric current you generate by moving this single loop of wire through the weak magnetic field of the disk magnets is too weak to detect with all but the most sensitive of microammeters.

RADIOACTIVE DECAY MODEL
Substitute coins for radiation.

Introduction
Throwing one hundred coins, removing all those that come up tails, and placing them in piles, gives us a hands-on model for radioactive decay. The piles graphically show the meaning of the term "half-life."

Assembly
None necessary.

To Do and Notice
(30 minutes or more)

Toss the pennies onto a table surface. Remove all the pennies that land tail side up and put them flat on the left side of the table, arranged in a tall column.

Gather up the remaining pennies and toss them again. Remove the pennies that land tail side up, and arrange them in a second column, right beside the first column. Repeat this experiment until all of the pennies have been removed. If no pennies come up tails on a toss, leave an empty column.

You can do the same thing with wooden cubes, removing the cubes that land red side up.

Etcetera

Some radioactive nuclei, called mothers, decay into other radioactive nuclei, called daughters. To simulate this process, start with 100 nickels. Toss them and replace the nickels that land tail side up with pennies. Toss the pennies and the nickels together. Make a column with all the pennies that land tail side up, and replace all the nickels that land tail side up with more pennies. The nickels represent the mother nuclei; the pennies, the daughter nuclei. Notice that the columns of decayed pennies grow at first and then decay.

What's Going On?

The chance that any penny will come up tails on any toss is always the same, 50 percent. However, once a penny has come up tails, it is removed. Thus, about half the pennies are left after the first toss.

Even though half of the remaining pennies come up tails on the second toss, there are fewer pennies to start with. After the first toss, about 1/2 of the original pennies are left; after the second, about 1/4; then 1/8, 1/16, and so on. These numbers can be written in terms of powers, or exponents, of 1/2: $(1/2)^1$, $(1/2)^2$, $(1/2)^3$, and $(1/2)^4$. This type of pattern—in which a quantity repeatedly decreases by a fixed fraction (in this case, 1/2)—is known as exponential decay.

Each time you toss the remaining pennies, about half of them are removed. The time it takes for half of the remaining pennies to be removed is called the half-life. The half-life of the pennies in this model is about one toss.

If you're using painted wooden cubes, the probability that a cube will land red side up is 1/6. (Each cube has six sides, and only one of those sides is painted red.) It takes three tosses for about half the cubes to be removed, so the half-life of the cubes is about three tosses. After one toss, 5/6 remain; after two tosses, 5/6 of 5/6, or 25/36, remain; and after three tosses, $(5/6)^3$ = 125/216 of the cubes are left.

Tossing the coins or cubes is an unpredictable, random process. Rarely will exactly 1/2 of the coins or 1/6 of the cubes decay on the first toss. However, if you repeat the first toss many, many times, the average number of coins that decay will approach 1/2 (or cubes that decay will approach 1/6).

In this model, the removal of a penny or a cube corresponds to the decay of a radioactive nucleus. The chance that a particular radioactive nucleus in a sample of identical nuclei will decay in each second is the same for each second that passes, just as the chance that a penny would come up tails was the same for each toss (1/2) or the chance that a cube would come up red was the same for each toss (1/6).

The smaller the chance of decay, the longer the half-life (time for half of the sample to decay) of the particular radioactive isotope. The cubes, for instance, have a longer half-life than the pennies. For uranium 238, the chance of decay is small: Its half-life is 4.5 billion years. For radon 217, the chance of decay is large: Its half-life is one thousandth of a second.

SHORT CIRCUIT
What happens when you blow a fuse?

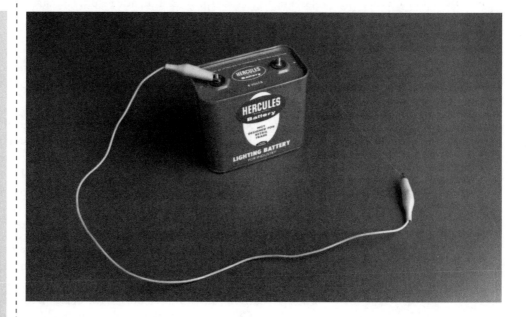

Materials

- A length of copper wire with alligator clips attached to each end (or a test lead) from any electronics supply store
- A fresh 6-volt or 12-volt lantern battery
- A 5- to 6-inch (13 to 15 cm) length of very fine steel wire, obtained by separating one strand from ordinary braided galvanized picture-hanging wire

NOTE

Braided copper wire and aluminum wire are available, but will not work here; iron wire can work, but is not commonly available. Whatever you use, be sure to stay away from plastic-coated wire, which can burn if it gets hot.

⚠ CAUTION

Electricity can really heat things up!
The wires in this Snack can get hot, so be careful.

Introduction

Current flowing through a wire heats the wire. The length of a wire affects its resistance, which determines how much current flows in the wire and how hot the wire gets.

Assembly

(5 minutes or less)

1. Attach one end of the clip lead to one of the battery terminals.

2. Attach one end of the fine iron wire to the other terminal.

3. Attach the other end of the clip lead to the other end of the iron wire, placing the clip as far from the terminal as possible.

One strand of unbraided picture-hanging wire

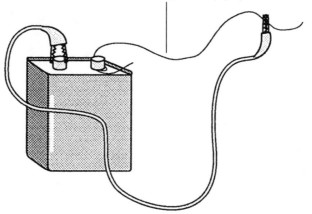

Etcetera

Try this Snack with pieces of aluminum foil 1/4-inch (6 mm) wide and 6 inches (15 cm) long. Observe the striking colors made by the aluminum-oxide layers formed when the aluminum gets hot.

To Do and Notice

(15 minutes or more)

Observe what happens to the steel wire after you connect the clip. Move the clip on the steel wire a little closer to the battery and watch what happens. Keep moving the lead closer until you see the final dramatic result. (Be careful! The wire gets very hot!)

What's Going On?

The thin steel wire is a good conductor of electricity, but not as good as the copper wire, which is deliberately chosen to have very low resistance. Thus most of the resistance of the circuit is in the steel wire.

When you connect the clip to the steel wire, the voltage of the battery pushes electrons through the circuit against the resistance of the steel wire, causing the steel wire to heat up. As you move the clip closer to the battery, the resistance of the steel wire decreases. Because the same voltage is applied across a lower resistance, more current flows, and the wire heats up more. Eventually, when you make the steel wire short enough, so much current flows that it melts the wire. Even the copper wire becomes warm.

In a normal electric circuit, an electric current powers an appliance, such as a refrigerator or TV. Every such appliance has a certain amount of resistance to the current flow, which keeps the current from reaching very large values. A short circuit occurs when the current finds a way to bypass the appliance on a path that has little or no resistance—for example, where frayed insulation bares a wire and allows it to touch the frame of the appliance, so the current can flow straight to the ground. In this situation, a very large current can occur, producing a lot of heat and a fire hazard.

Although houses today often have circuit breakers instead of fuses, fuses are still around. A fuse contains a thin strip of wire, somewhat like the thin steel wire in our experiment. The current that goes to appliances must also pass through this strip of wire. If a short circuit occurs—or even if too many appliances get hooked up to one wire so that too much current flows—the wire in the fuse heats up quickly and melts, breaking the circuit and preventing a fire from starting.

STRIPPED-DOWN MOTOR
Make a simple mini-motor.

Materials

- About 2 feet (60 cm) of solid (not stranded) enameled or insulated 20-gauge copper wire
- Wire strippers (if you're using insulated wire)
- Sandpaper (if you're using enameled wire)
- A black waterproof marking pen
- A paper, plastic foam, or plain plastic cup
- Five small disk or rectangular ceramic magnets (available at RadioShack)
- Two large paper clips
- Two electrical lead wires with alligator clips at both ends (available at RadioShack)
- Masking tape
- A battery or power supply
- A battery holder (see Assembly for instructions)

NOTE

We have successfully run motors on one 1.5-volt D battery; additional batteries seem to make it easier to get the motor to run. You may want to try 6-volt lantern batteries. We have also had excellent results using a power supply, or battery eliminator, set to about 4 volts. The advantage of the power supply is that it will supply a substantial current over a period of time. Unlike batteries, it doesn't have to be replaced. Experiment with what you have, and use whatever works!

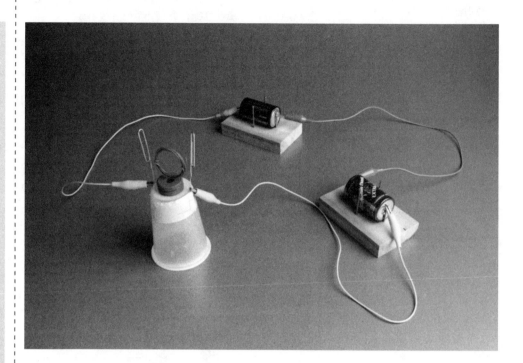

Introduction

A coil of wire becomes an electromagnet when current passes through it. The electromagnet interacts with a permanent magnet, causing the coil to spin. Voilà! You've created an electric motor.

Assembly

(30 minutes or more)

1. Wind the copper wire into a coil about 1 inch (2.5 cm) in diameter. Make four or five loops.

2. Wrap the ends of the wire around the coil a couple of times on opposite sides to hold the coil together. Leave 2 inches (5 cm) projecting from each side of the coil, and cut off any extra. (See diagram.)

3. If you are using insulated wire, strip the insulation off the ends of the wire projecting from the coil. If you are using enameled wire, use the sandpaper to remove the enamel.

4. Use the marking pen to color one side of one of the projecting ends black. (*Note:* It is very important that the orientation of the painted side corresponds to the orientation shown in the drawing. If the coil is held in a vertical plane, color the top half of one of the wires black.)

5. Turn the cup upside down and place two magnets on top in the center.

6. Attach three more magnets inside the cup, directly beneath the original two magnets. This will create a stronger magnetic field as well as hold the top magnets in place.

7. Unfold one end of each paper clip and tape them to opposite sides of the cup, with their unfolded ends down. (See diagram.)

8. Rest the ends of the coil in the cradles formed by the paper clips.

9. Adjust the height of the paper clips so that when the coil spins, it clears the magnets by about 1/16 inch (1.5 mm).

10. Adjust the coil and the clips until the coil stays balanced and centered while spinning freely on the clips. Good balance is important in getting the motor to operate well.

11. Once you've determined how long the projecting ends of the coil must be to rest in the paper-clip cradles, you may trim off any excess wire. (The length of the projecting ends depends on the separation of the paper-clip cradles, which in turn depends on the width of the base of the cup you are using. See diagram.)

12. If you're using a battery, place it in a battery holder. You can make your own from a block of wood and four nails, as shown in the diagram.

13. Use the clip leads to connect the battery or power supply to the paper clips, connecting one terminal of the battery to one paper clip and the other terminal to the other paper clip.

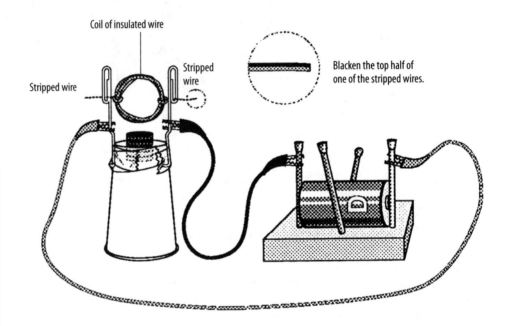

Coil of insulated wire

Stripped wire

Stripped wire

Stripped wire

Blacken the top half of one of the stripped wires.

To Do and Notice
(30 minutes or more)

Give the coil a spin to start it turning. If it doesn't keep spinning on its own, check to make sure that the coil assembly is well balanced when spinning, that the enamel has been thoroughly scraped off if enameled wire has been used, that the projecting end has been painted with black pen as noted, and that the coil and the magnet are close to each other but do not hit each other. You might also try adjusting the distance separating the cradles: This may affect the quality of the contact between the coil and the cradles.

Keep making adjustments until the motor works. Have patience! The success rate with this design has been quite good.

Etcetera

In this motor, the sliding electrical contact between the ends of the coil of wire and the paper clips turns off the current for half of each cycle. Such sliding contacts are known as commutators. Most direct-current electric motors use more complicated commutators that reverse the direction of current flow through the loop every half cycle. The more complicated motors are twice as powerful as the motor described here.

This motor can also be used to demonstrate how a generator works. Try hooking up the ends of the paper clips to a sensitive galvanometer instead of the battery. Spin the coil and see if any current registers on the meter.

What's Going On?

Current flows through the wire coil and creates an electromagnet. One face of the coil becomes a north pole; the other a south pole. The permanent magnet attracts its opposite pole on the coil and repels its like pole, causing the coil to spin.

Another way to describe the operation of the motor is to say that the permanent magnets exert forces on the electrical currents flowing through the loop of wire. When the loop of wire is in a vertical plane, the forces on the top and bottom wires of the loop will be in opposite directions. These oppositely directed forces produce a twisting force, or torque, on the loop of wire that will make it turn.

Why is it so important to paint half of one projecting wire black? Suppose that the permanent magnets are mounted with their north poles facing upward. The north pole of the permanent magnet will repel the north pole of the loop electromagnet and attract the south pole. But once the south pole of the loop electromagnet was next to the north pole of the permanent magnet, it would stay there. Any push on the loop would merely set it rocking about this equilibrium position.

By painting half of one end black, you prevent current from flowing for half of each spin. The magnetic field of the loop electromagnet is turned off for that half-spin. As the south pole of the loop electromagnet comes closest to the permanent magnet, the paint turns off the electric current. The inertia of the rotating coil carries it through half of a turn, past the insulating paint. When the electric current starts to flow again, the twisting force is in the same direction as it was before. The coil continues to rotate in the same direction.

PART THREE THE MAGIC WAND AND OTHER BRIGHT EXPLORATIONS OF LIGHT AND COLOR

Take a look out your window on a sunny day. What do you see?

Whatever the scenery outside your window, one answer is always true: You see light. It's really the only thing you can see, the only thing that your eyes can detect. You see trees or cars or clouds because sunlight is bouncing off these things and getting into your eyes.

All the colors you see come from light. The grass looks green because it reflects the green of sunlight and absorbs the other colors. A brilliant rainbow shines in the spray of a sunlit fountain because droplets of water spread white light out to reveal its hidden colors. A soap bubble shimmers with iridescence because white light reflected by the two sides of the thin soap film combines in a way that removes some colors and reveals others. Your eyes are designed to detect light and analyze the information it carries, making an image of the world so that you can see the view—or read this sentence.

The sunlight that reveals the world outside your window begins with the vibration of electrons, the negatively charged particles that orbit the nucleus of an atom. Vibrating electrons in the atmosphere of the sun send light out in all directions. When the sunlight gets in your eyes, light that has crossed 93 million miles makes electrons at the back of your eye wiggle, echoing the original vibration of electrons on the sun 8 minutes before. Wiggling electrons in your eye create the image of the world that you see.

That's one way to describe light—you can say where it begins and what it does. It's much more difficult to describe what light actually is. For centuries, scientists have been experimenting with light and trying to come up with a description that would explain the observations that they made. Along the way, they came up with two alternatives. You can think of light as a wave, like the waves in the ocean. That description will help explain some of the things that light does—such as the way a beam of light bends when it moves from air into water. Or you can think of light as a stream of particles (called photons), and that will help explain other aspects of light's behavior—like the way certain materials glow under ultraviolet light. But neither description alone can completely explain all the things light does.

However you describe it, light is fascinating stuff to experiment with. The instructions in this section will help you make your own observations about light and how it behaves. Though light is mysterious and tricky, these experiments require basic materials—mirrors and magnifying lenses and fish tanks and water—that should be easy to locate.

What can you do with such simple equipment? You can bend light, for one thing. That's called refraction, and lenses do it. You can bounce light around with mirrors and build an exhibit that lets you peer into infinity or one that puts you inside a kaleidoscope or one that creates an image that looks so real that you try to reach out and touch it.

You can investigate what happens when light waves meet and mix—in the thin film of a soap bubble or the gap between two plates of glass. Or you can sort light waves so that you have a set that are all wiggling in the same direction. That's called polarization. Polarized sunglasses eliminate glare and work by blocking all the light waves that wiggle in a particular direction.

Taken together, the experiments in this section let you get a handle on something that you can't even touch—that mysterious stuff we call light.

BLUE SKY

Now you can explain why the sky is [ ]
sunset is red.

Materials

→ A transparent plastic box, or a large beaker, jar, or aquarium

→ Tap water

→ A flashlight or other way to get a bright beam of light

→ Powdered milk

→ Blank white card to use as an image screen

→ Polarizing filter (such as a lens from an old pair of polarized sunglasses)

Introduction

When sunlight travels through the atmosphere, blue light scatters more than the other colors, leaving a dominant yellow-orange hue to the transmitted light. The scattered light makes the sky blue; the transmitted light ultimately makes the sunset reddish orange.

Assembly

(15 minutes or less)

1. Fill the container with water.

2. Place the light source so the beam shines through the container.

3. Add powdered milk a pinch at a time. Stir until you can clearly see the beam shining through the liquid.

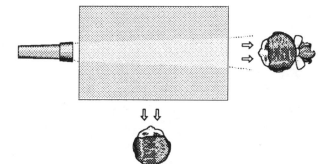

To Do and Notice

(15 minutes or less)

Look at the beam from the side of the tank and then from the end of the tank. You can also let the light project onto a white card held at the end of the tank. From the side, the beam looks bluish-white; from the end, it looks yellow-orange.

If you've added enough milk to the water, you'll be able to see the color of the beam change from blue-white to yellow-orange along the length of the beam.

The beam of light from a projector contains photons of light that are polarized in all directions—horizontally, vertically, and all angles in between. Consider only the vertically polarized light passing through the tank. This light can scatter to the side and remain vertically polarized, but it cannot scatter upward! To retain the characteristic of a transverse wave after scattering, only the vertically polarized light can be scattered sideways, and only the horizontally polarized light can be scattered upward. This is shown in the following drawing.

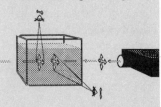

If you want to look at a narrower beam of light, use a computer projector to project the image of a white disk through your tank. You can use any image-creation software to make a white disk on a black background.

What's Going On?

The sun produces white light, which is made up of light of all colors: red, orange, yellow, green, blue, and violet.

Light is a wave, and each of these colors corresponds to a different frequency and therefore a different wavelength of light.

The colors in the rainbow spectrum are arranged according to their frequencies: Violet and blue light have higher frequencies than yellow, orange, and red light.

When the white light from the sun shines through the earth's atmosphere, it collides with gas molecules. These molecules scatter the light. The shorter the wavelength of the light, the more it is scattered by the atmosphere. Because its wavelength is so much shorter, blue light is scattered approximately ten times more than red light.

In addition, blue light's frequency is closer to the resonant frequency of the atoms and molecules that make up the air than red light's frequency is. That is, if the electrons bound to molecules in the air are pushed, they will oscillate with a natural frequency that is even higher than the frequency of blue light. Blue light pushes on the electrons with a frequency that is closer to their natural resonant frequency than that of red light. This causes the blue light to be reradiated out in all directions in a process called scattering. The red light that is not scattered continues on in its original direction. When you look up in the sky, the scattered blue light is the light that you see.

Why does the setting sun look reddish orange? When the sun is on the horizon, its light takes a longer path through the atmosphere to your eyes than when the sun is directly overhead. By the time the light of the setting sun reaches your eyes, most of the colors of light have been scattered out. The light you finally see is reddish orange.

Violet light has an even shorter wavelength than blue light: It scatters even more than blue light does. So why isn't the sky violet? Because there's just not enough of it. The sun puts out much more blue light than violet light, so most of the scattered light in the sky is blue.

Scattering can polarize light. Place a polarizing filter between the flashlight and the tank. Turn the filter while one person views the transmitted beam from the top and another views it from the side. Notice that when the person looking down from the top sees a bright beam, the person looking in from the side will see a dim beam, and vice versa.

You can also hold the polarizing filter between your eyes and the tank and rotate the filter to make the beam look bright or dim. The filter and the scattering polarize the light. When the two polarizations are aligned, the beam will be bright; when they are at right angles, the beam will be dim.

BONE STRESS
Polarized light reveals stress patterns in clear plastic.

Materials
- Overhead projector and screen
- Two polarizing filters (if polarizing material is not readily available, you can use two lenses from an old pair of polarizing sunglasses)
- A transparent plastic picnic fork, CD jewel case, or other thin (1/16- to 1/8-inch [1.5 to 3 mm]) piece of transparent plastic

Introduction
When certain plastics are placed between two pieces of polarizing material, their stress patterns become dramatically visible in a brightly colored display. A stressed plastic object can be used to illustrate stresses found in bones.

Assembly
(15 minutes or less)

1. Set up your overhead projector so that the light shines on the screen.

2. Place one of the filters on the stage of the overhead projector. If the second piece of polarizer is large enough to cover most of the lens on the arm of the projector, then tape it there. (See drawing.)

3. If you're using the lenses from a pair of sunglasses, then devise a stand to hold the other lens a few inches above the stage of the projector, right over the first filter.

4. If you're using thin plastic, such as the plastic from a clear CD jewel case, cut it into a shape that can be flexed, such as the shape of the letters C, J, S, or K.

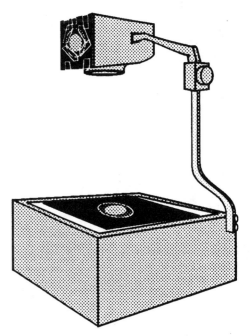

Etcetera

If you want to have a little fun with this, you can buy a clear polymer Nylabone dog chew toy at a pet store or supermarket. Flex it and see the stresses change dramatically.

To Do and Notice

(5 minutes or more)

Hold the fork or plastic shape above the first filter and below the second filter. Induce stress by squeezing the tines of the fork together or deforming the letter. Notice the colored stress pattern in the image of the plastic that is projected on the screen. Try rotating one of the polarizing filters. Some orientations will give more dramatic color effects than others.

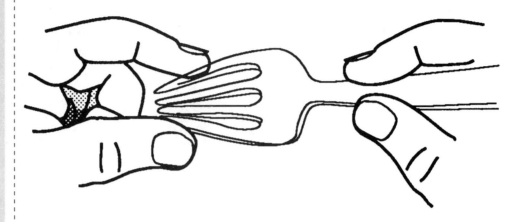

What's Going On?

The first polarizing filter limits the vibration of light waves to one plane—that is, it polarizes the light.

The white light from the overhead projector is made up of light of all colors. The plastic breaks the light waves that make up each color into two perpendicularly polarized waves. These two waves travel through the plastic at different speeds, which are determined by the light's color. When the two waves meet and recombine, they produce a polarization unique to that color.

The direction of polarization determines whether light of a certain color can pass through the second polarizing filter. If the new direction of polarization lines up with the second filter, light of that color passes through the filter and you see it. If the new direction of polarization does not line up with the second filter, light of that color is blocked. By rotating the filter, you can let different colors pass through, and the colors you observe will change.

Stressing the plastic alters its structure, which affects how rapidly light of different polarizations travels through the plastic. Where colored patterns change rapidly, stress is high. Where colored regions are spread out and change gradually, stress is low. Sharp corners, or areas that have been cut or stamped, are usually areas of stress concentration. Changing the stresses in the plastic will change the color patterns in the plastic.

Stress patterns and concentrations like the ones visible in the plastic are also present in your bones, as they flex under the daily loads imposed upon them.

BRIDGE LIGHT
A thin layer of air trapped between two pieces of Plexiglas produces rainbow-colored interference patterns.

Materials
- Two sheets of Plexiglas, about 1/8- or 1/4-inch (3 to 6 mm) thick and approximately 1-foot (30 cm) square (size is not critical)
- Sandpaper
- Alcohol and a soft cloth
- Electrical or duct tape
- A piece of dark construction paper
- A light source, such as a desk lamp
- One 3 × 5 inch (8 × 13 cm) piece of transparent red plastic

Introduction
When light hits two slightly separated transparent surfaces, part of the light will be reflected from each surface. If the distance between the surfaces is a multiple of half the wavelength of any one color of light, destructive and constructive interference will occur, producing an interference pattern.

Assembly
(15 minutes or less)

1. Peel the paper from the Plexiglas and smooth off all edges with sandpaper if necessary. Be careful not to scratch the surfaces.
2. Clean the top and bottom surfaces with alcohol and a soft cloth.
3. Press the Plexiglas plates tightly together and tape around the edges to hold them in place.
4. Tape a sheet of dark construction paper to one plate to make the interference patterns more visible.

To Do and Notice
(15 minutes or more)

Hold the plates, with the dark-paper side on the bottom, in any strong source of white light. Observe the rainbow-colored interference patterns. The patterns will change as you bend, twist, or press on the plates. Notice that the patterns strongly resemble the contour lines on a topographic map.

Place the red plastic between the light source and the plates. Notice that the patterns are now just red and black.

Etcetera

When you open a package of new, clean microscope slides, you can often see colored interference patterns created by the thin air space between the glass slides.

The beautiful rainbow colors you see in soap bubbles and on pieces of metal heated to high temperatures are produced in the same way: by light reflecting from the top and bottom of a thin transparent layer.

What's Going On?

Light waves reflect from the surfaces of two plastic sheets separated by a thin air gap. These light waves meet after reflecting from the two surfaces. When two waves meet, they can add together, cancel each other, or partially cancel each other. This adding and canceling of light waves—called constructive interference and destructive interference—creates the rainbow-colored patterns you see.

White light is made up of all different colors mixed together. When light waves of a particular color meet and cancel each other, that color is subtracted from white light. For example, if the blue light waves cancel, you see what is left of white light after the blue has been removed—it's yellow, the complementary color of blue.

When you place a red filter in front of the light source, only red and black fringes will appear. Where destructive interference takes place, there is no red light left to reach your eyes, so you see black. Where the waves constructively interfere, you see red.

The thickness of the gap between the plates determines which colors of light cancel out at any one point. For example, if the separation of the plates is roughly equal to one-half the wavelength of blue light (or some multiple of it), the crests of waves of blue light reflected from the top surface of the air gap will match up with the troughs of waves reflected from the bottom surface, causing the blue light to cancel out.

This is what happens: Imagine that the distance between the two plates is one-half the wavelength of blue light. When a wave hits the top of the air layer, part reflects and part continues on. Compared to the part that reflects from the top of the air layer, the part that continues on and reflects from the bottom travels an extra wavelength through the air layer (half a wavelength down and half a wavelength back). In addition, the wave that reflects from the bottom is inverted. The net effect is that the blue light waves reflected from the two surfaces recombine trough-to-peak and cancel each other out.

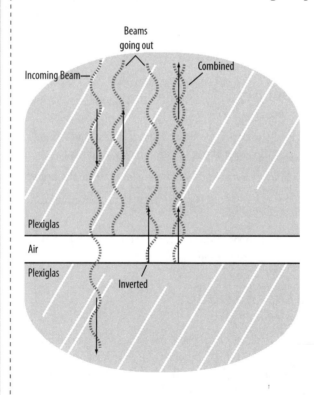

Because the interference pattern depends on the amount of separation between the plates, what you're actually seeing is a topographical map of the distance between plates.

COLOR TABLE
Color your perception.

Materials

- ➔ Several different colors of transparent plastic to use as colored filters, such as colored acetate report covers, colored acrylic plastic from a plastics store, or anything along those lines
- ➔ Assorted colored pictures from magazines, old wall calendars, or other sources
- ➔ Crayons, colored pencils, or colored pens
- ➔ White paper

Introduction

A brightly colored picture takes on a whole new look when you view it through a colored filter. A colored filter transmits some colors and absorbs others. Using a colored filter, you can decode secret messages written with colored pens or crayons.

Assembly

None needed.

To Do and Notice

(15 minutes or more)

Place one colored filter at a time over a colored picture and notice how the colors are affected. With a red filter, the picture appears entirely in shades of red plus black.

Print your name or a short message on a piece of white paper using a different color of crayon, pencil, or pen for each letter. Then look at the message through a red filter. You may notice that the red letters disappear, but you can still see blue or green letters. By figuring out which colors you still see and which you don't, you can write a secret message and then use the filter as the decoder.

What's Going On?

An ideal red filter transmits only red light and absorbs all other colors. In this ideal case, a picture containing red, green, and blue would appear red and black when viewed through a red filter.

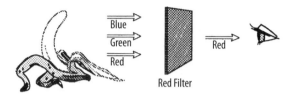

A red filter blocks green light and blue light: Only red light can get through to your eyes. The white banana and the yellow peel both reflect some red light, so the whole banana looks red.

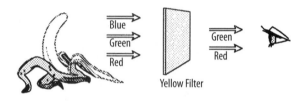

A yellow filter blocks blue light, so only red light and green light can get to your eyes. The white banana and the yellow peel both reflect some green light and some red light. The whole banana looks yellow because green light plus red light mix to make yellow light.

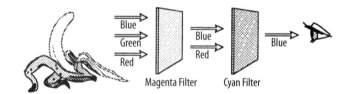

Here, a magenta filter blocks green light and a cyan filter blocks red light. Only blue light can pass through to your eyes. The banana looks blue because the white fruit reflects some blue light. But the yellow peel looks black. It reflects no blue light.

Likewise, a pure blue filter transmits only blue light, and a pure green filter transmits only green light. Any color from a picture that is not transmitted by the filter will be absorbed by the filter and will not be seen.

When you view multicolored writing through an ideal red filter, only red light reaches your eyes. Red light comes from both the red letters and the white paper (since white contains all colors). The red letters tend to disappear because they blend right in with the red light from the white paper. Letters that contain no red would appear black. Because most pigments are not perfectly pure, you may notice that more than just the red letters blend in with the background. That is, if a yellow letter reflects red (since yellow light can be made from a combination of red light and green light), the yellow letter would blend in with the background.

COLORED SHADOWS
Not all shadows are black.

Materials

- Red, green, and blue lightbulbs
- A way to plug in all three lightbulbs at the same time and simultaneously direct them onto the same white surface
- A white surface, such as a wall or piece of white poster board (white paper taped to stiff cardboard works well)
- Any solid object—a pencil, ruler, or similar

Introduction

When lights of different colors shine on the same spot on a white surface, the light reflecting from that spot to your eyes is called an additive mixture because it is the sum of all the light. We can learn about human color perception by using colored lights to make additive color mixtures.

Assembly
(15 minutes or less)

Set up the bulbs and screen in such a way that the light from all three bulbs falls on the same area of the screen and all bulbs are approximately the same distance from the screen. For best results, put the green bulb in between the red and the blue bulbs.

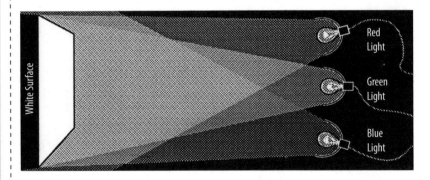

To Do and Notice
(30 minutes or more)

Make the room as dark as possible. Then turn on the three colored lights, aim them all at your white screen, and adjust the positions of the bulbs until you obtain the "whitest" light you can make on the screen.

Place a narrow opaque object, like a pencil, fairly close to the screen. Adjust the distance until you see three distinct colored shadows on the screen.

Remove the object, turn off one of the colored lights, and notice how the color on the screen changes. Put the object in front of the screen again and notice the colors of the shadows. Move the object close to the screen until the shadows overlap. Notice the color of the combined shadows.

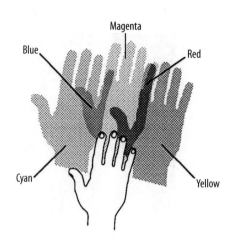

Repeat the preceding step with a different light turned off while the other two remain on, and then a third time until you've tried all combinations. Repeat again with only one color at a time on, and then with all three on. Vary the size of the object and the distance from the screen. Try using your hand as an object.

What's Going On?

The retina, which covers the back of your eye, contains light receptors called rods and cones. Rods are used for night vision, but only let you see in shades of gray. You have only one type of rod but three types of cones, which are used for seeing whenever it's not very dark, and let you see in color.

All three types of cones respond to a wide range of wavelengths, but one type is the most sensitive to long wavelengths (the red end of the spectrum), one to medium wavelengths, and one to short wavelengths (the blue end of the spectrum). With just these three types of cones we are able to perceive more than a million different shades of color.

When a red light, a blue light, and a green light are all shining on the screen, the screen looks white because these three colored lights stimulate all three types of cones in your eyes approximately equally, creating the sensation of white. Red, green, and blue are therefore called additive primaries of light.

With these three lights you can make shadows of seven different colors: blue, red, green, black, cyan (blue-green), magenta (a mixture of blue and red), and yellow (a mixture of red and green). If you block two of the three lights, you get a shadow of the third color: Block the red and green lights, for example, and you get a blue shadow. If you block all three lights, you get a black shadow. And if you block one of the three lights, you get a shadow whose color is a mixture of the two other colors. If the blue and green mix, they make cyan; red and blue make magenta; red and green make yellow.

If you turn off the red light, leaving on only the blue and green lights, the lights mix and the screen appears to be cyan, a blue-green color. When you hold the object in front of this cyan screen, you will see two shadows, one blue and one green. In one place the

---

Etcetera

If you let light from the three bulbs shine through a hole in a card that is held an appropriate distance from the screen, you will see three separate patches of colored light on the screen, one from each lamp. (Make the hole large enough to get a patch of color you can really see.) If you move the card closer to the screen, the patches of light will eventually overlap and you will see the mixtures of each pair of colors.

If you want to experiment further, you can find out what happens if you use different colors of paper for the screen. Try yellow, green, blue, red, or purple paper, and so on.

object blocks the light coming from the green bulb and therefore leaves a blue shadow; in another place it blocks the light from the blue bulb to make a green shadow. When you move the object close to the screen you get a very dark (black) shadow, where the object blocks both lights.

When you turn off the green light, leaving on the red and blue lights, the screen will appear to be magenta, a mixture of red and blue. The shadows will be red and blue.

When you turn off the blue light, leaving on the red and green lights, the screen will appear to be yellow. The shadows will be red and green.

It may seem strange that a red light and a green light mix to make yellow light on a white screen. A particular mixture of red and green light stimulates the cones in your eyes exactly as much as they're stimulated by yellow light—that is, by light from the yellow portion of the rainbow. Whenever the cones in your eye are stimulated in just these proportions, whether by a mixture of red and green light, or by yellow light alone, you'll see the color yellow.

CORNER REFLECTOR
See yourself as others see you.

Materials

- Three 6 × 6 inch (15 × 15 cm) mirrors (plastic mirrors are best, since there is less danger of breaking the mirror or cutting your fingers; they are available at plastics supply stores and can easily be cut to any size)

- Duct tape

- A piece of light cardboard or file folder

- Optional: A hacksaw, utility knife, or other way to cut mirror glass, if needed

ⓘ CAUTION

Be careful with mirrors! Keep yourself and your kids safe by always using plastic mirrors instead of glass. If you must use a glass mirror, tape the edges to minimize the possibility of cuts and glue one side to a suitable backing of cardboard or wood. Don't just spot-glue the mirror in a few places: The whole surface must be attached to the backing. That way, even if the mirror cracks or breaks, there will be no loose shards of glass.

Introduction

Two hinged mirrors create a kaleidoscope that shows multiple images of an object. The number of images depends on the angle between the mirrors. When you set the hinged mirrors on top of a third mirror, you create a reflector that always sends light back in the direction from which it came.

Assembly

(30 minutes or less)

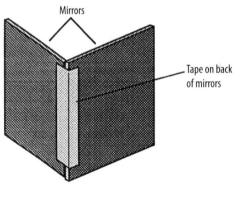

1. If you start with one large piece of mirror, cut three 6 × 6 inch (15 × 15 cm) pieces from the plastic or glass. You can cut the plastic with a fine saw, such as a hacksaw, or score it with a utility knife and then snap it off. It's not hard to cut glass; get someone who knows how to do it to show you—just be careful when you do it!

2. Once you have the three mirrors you need, use the duct tape to tape two of the mirrors together along one edge.

3. Put the tape on the back side of the mirror, making a hinge that opens and closes easily. Be sure the mirrors can move freely from 0 degrees to 180 degrees.

To Do and Notice

(15 minutes or more)

To make a kaleidoscope, set the hinged mirrors on the cardboard and place an object such as a pencil or some coins between them. Open the mirrors to different angles. Notice that the smaller the angle, the greater the number of images you see. Remove the

Etcetera

Throw a tennis ball at any wall or floor in the corner of a room. It should return to you after bouncing off the three surfaces.

Corner reflectors are used to make safety reflectors for cars, bicycles, and signs. They have also been used to bounce laser beams back to the earth from the surface of the moon.

objects and see what happens when you draw different designs in the space between the two mirrors.

Close your right eye and look at a single mirror straight on. Notice that the left eye of the image is closed. Now close your right eye and look at two mirrors that form a 90-degree angle. Notice that the right eye of this image is closed.

Now make a corner reflector by opening the two taped mirrors to 90 degrees and resting them on the third mirror, so that the three mirrors form a half cube (see diagram). Close one eye and stare right at the corner where the three mirrors join. Move your head and notice that the pupil of your open eye always falls right at the corner. Open both eyes and look at the corner. One eye may appear to be closer to the corner than the other. This is your dominant eye.

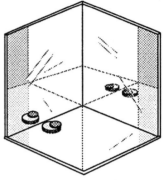

What's Going On?

In a corner reflector, multiple reflections reverse the image and invert it.

When you put an object between the two hinged mirrors, light from the object bounces back and forth between the mirrors before it reaches your eyes. An image is formed each time the light bounces off a mirror.

The number of images you see in the mirrors depends on the angle that the mirrors form. As you make the angle between the mirrors smaller, the light bounces back and forth more times, and you see more images.

The illustration below shows how an image is formed in the corner of two mirrors at 90 degrees. Light rays bounce off each mirror at the same angle that they hit the mirror: Physicists say that the angle of reflection is equal to the angle of incidence. Mirrors at other angles behave similarly, but the ray diagrams may get more complex.

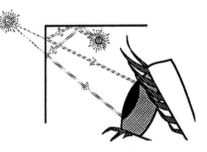

The inside corner of a corner reflector (where the three mirrors meet) sends light back parallel to its original path. If you pointed a thin beam of laser light right near the corner, the beam would bounce from mirror to mirror and then exit parallel to the entering beam. Light from the center of your eye bounces straight back to the center of your eye, so the image of your eye seems to be centered in the corner made by the mirrors.

For another way to use this Snack, tape five square mirrors together with the mirrored surfaces facing inward to form a box. Place a sixth mirror, turned at a 45-degree angle, over the open side so you can look into the box and also let some light in. Try other configurations of mirrors in three dimensions and see what you can discover.

To do a quantitative experiment, mark the following angles on a piece of cardboard: 180 degrees, 90 degrees, 60 degrees, 45 degrees, 36 degrees, 30 degrees, and 20 degrees. These angles are chosen so that when they are divided into 360 degrees they produce an even integer. Mount the hinged mirrors at each of these angles and place an object between them. Count the number of images you see. You should be able to verify the following rule: 360 divided by the angle between the mirrors, minus one, gives the number of images. At 60 degrees, for example, (360/60)−1 = 5, so you should see five images of the object.

CRITICAL ANGLE
Why your phone calls don't leak out of optical fibers.

Introduction

A transparent material such as glass or water can actually reflect light better than any mirror. All you have to do is look at it from the proper angle.

Assembly

(15 minutes or less)

1. Fill the aquarium with water.

2. Add the milk a drop at a time, stirring after each drop, until you can see the light beam pass through the water. If you use powdered milk, add a pinch at a time.

To Do and Notice

(15 minutes or more)

Direct the light beam upward through the water so that it hits the surface of the water from underneath. You can shine the beam into the water through the transparent bottom of the aquarium, or in through a side wall. (With the Mini Maglite, you can seal the light in a watertight plastic bag and place the light right in the water!) The beam will be more visible if you can dim the room lights.

Point the beam so that it hits the surface of the water at just about a right angle. In the aquarium, you may be able to see both the reflected beam, which bounces back into the water, and the refracted beam, which comes out of the water and into the air. (Dust in the air helps you see the refracted beam. You can add chalk dust to the air. You can also search for the beam and track it with a piece of paper.) Notice that most of the beam leaves the water and only a faint beam is reflected back down into the water.

Etcetera

Total internal reflection helps transmit telephone messages along optical fibers. Any light that is not aligned parallel to the axis of the fiber hits the wall of the fiber and is reflected (totally!) back inward, since the angle of incidence with which the light hits the wall is much larger than the critical angle.

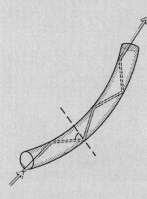

This helps prevent the signal from weakening too rapidly over long distances, or from leaking out when the fiber goes around a curve. This demonstration can also be done by replacing the aquarium and water with a small transparent plastic block, which can be bought at a local plastics supply store.

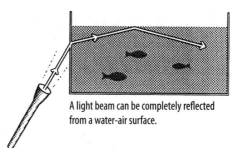

A light beam can be completely reflected from a water-air surface.

Slowly change the angle at which the beam of light hits the surface of the water. Notice that the beam reflected into the water grows brighter as the beam transmitted into the air becomes dimmer. Also notice that the transmitted beam is bent, or refracted.

Experiment until you find the angle at which the transmitted beam completely disappears. At this angle, called the critical angle, all the light is reflected back into the water.

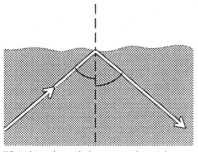

When the angles marked are greater than 49 degrees, light is totally reflected from a water-air surface.

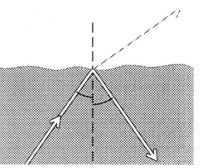

When the angles marked are less than 49 degrees, some light leaves the water.

What's Going On?

In general, when a beam of light (the incident beam) hits the interface between two transparent materials, such as air and water, part of the beam is reflected and part of it continues through the interface and on into the other material. The light beam is bent, or refracted, as it passes from one material into the next.

The farther the beam is from perpendicular when it hits the surface, the more strongly it is bent. If the light is moving from a material with a low speed of light into a material with a higher speed of light (for example, from water into air), the bending is toward the surface. At some angle, the bending will be so strong that the refracted beam will be directed right along the surface; that is, none of it will get out into the air.

Beyond that angle (the critical angle), all the light is reflected back into the water, so the reflected beam is as bright as the incident beam. This phenomenon is called total internal reflection, because very nearly 100 percent of the beam is reflected, which is better than the very best mirror surfaces.

The critical angle for water is measured between the beam and a line perpendicular to the surface, and is 49 degrees.

CYLINDRICAL MIRROR

This cylindrical mirror lets you see yourself as others see you.

Materials

- Construction paper or other stiff paper backing
- One 8½ × 11 inch (22 × 28 cm) sheet of aluminized Mylar
- One transparent page protector (available in stationery stores)

Introduction

A flat mirror will always reflect an image that is right side up and reversed right to left. A cylindrical mirror can produce images that are flipped upside down and images that are not reversed. The image you see in a cylindrical mirror depends on the orientation of the mirror and the distance between you and the mirror.

Assembly

(5 minutes or less)

1. Put the stiff paper backing behind the Mylar and slide them both into the transparent page protector.

2. Bend the Mylar to form a portion of a cylinder. When you bend the Mylar, be sure that the long side is parallel to the axis of the cylinder.

To Do and Notice

(15 minutes or more)

Hold the cylindrical mirror so that its long axis is horizontal. Curve the Mylar slightly and look into the mirror. Position yourself so that you can clearly see a reflection of your face. Notice how the image changes when you move closer to or farther from the mirror. When you move far enough away from the mirror, your image will flip upside down.

Wink your right eye. Which eye does the image wink? The image may wink its left eye or its right eye, depending on how far your face is from the mirror. When you are close to the mirror and your image is right side up, the image winks its left eye. When it's upside down, the image winks its right eye. (If you have trouble deciding which eye the image is winking, have someone stand beside the mirror and do what the image does—that is, wink the same eye as the image. Then ask your partner which eye it is. If the image is upside down, your partner's head will have to be upside down, too. The easiest way for your partner to get this effect is to turn around, bend over as far as possible, and look back at you from there.)

Now orient the cylindrical mirror so its long axis is vertical. Notice how the image changes when you move closer to and farther from the mirror. Wink your right eye and notice how the image in the mirror responds. When you are close, the image will wink its left eye. When you are far away, it will wink its right eye.

What's Going On?

You see the world because light gets into your eyes. You see these words, for example, because light reflecting from this page enters your eyes and makes an image on your retina.

When you make a visual picture of the world, you assume that the light entering your eyes has traveled in a straight line to reach you. But mirrors and other shiny objects change the path of the light, bouncing it back in an organized fashion. When you look into a mirror, you see your image because light reflecting from your face bounces off the mirror and back into your eyes. Your eyes and brain assume that the light has traveled in a straight line to reach your eyes, so you see an image of your face out there in front of or behind the mirror.

When you look into an ordinary flat mirror, the image of your face is right side up: Your hair is on top of your head and your chin is underneath. To reach your eyes, the light from your hair hits the mirror at a slight angle and then bounces into your eyes from above—which is why you see your hair on top and your image as right side up.

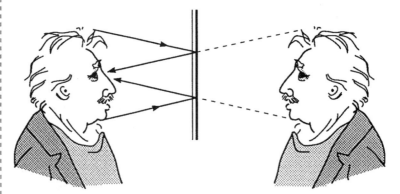

Light from your hair bounces off the mirror and enters your eyes from above; light from your chin enters your eyes from below.

When you look into a cylindrical mirror with the axis of the mirror horizontal and with your face a foot or more away from the mirror, your image is upside down. That's because the light from your hair bounces off the curved mirror and comes to your eyes from below.

Etcetera

Here's a classic tricky question: "If a flat mirror reverses right and left, why doesn't it reverse up and down?"

The answer is that a flat mirror actually reverses in and out. That is, light that travels "in" to the mirror is bounced back "out" of the mirror. This reversal does not change up into down, but it does change right into left. Consider the outline of the hand below. Is it a right hand or a left hand? You cannot tell which hand it is unless you know whether the palm of the hand is facing "in" to the page or "out" of the page. So right and left depend on in and out.

This can be either a right or left hand, depending on which way the palm is facing.

To make sense of the angle at which the light is entering your eyes, your eyes and brain must see the image of your face as upside down and a little bit in front of the mirror.

As everyone knows, a flat mirror reverses your right side and your left side. How does it do that? Suppose you are standing face to face with someone. If your right ear points toward the east, the other person's left ear will point toward the east. Now, instead of facing another person, suppose you are facing a flat mirror with your right ear pointing to the east. The light from your right ear will bounce off the flat mirror and enter your eyes from the east. Even though your east ear is the east ear of the image, your right ear has become the left ear of the image! (Yes, this is a little mind-boggling at first reading. But once you get it, it will seem simple.)

Now look into the cylindrical mirror with its axis vertical. Stand at least a foot away from the mirror. Once again, place your right ear so that it points to the east. Light from your right ear bounces off the curved mirror and enters your eyes from the west. Light from your right ear appears to come from the right ear of the image. In this cylindrical mirror, you see yourself as others see you. You see the image of your face just a little bit in front of the mirror.

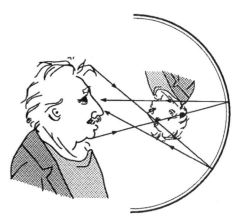
The light bouncing from a curved mirror makes an inverted image.

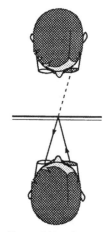
Light scattered by your right eye bounces off a flat mirror in the same way a ball would bounce off the mirror.

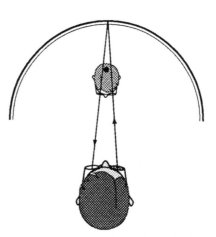
In a concave curved mirror, light from the right (east) bounces off the mirror and forms an image of the eye on the right (west) side of the face in the mirror.

DIFFRACTION
Light can bend around edges.

Materials

- Two clean new pencils with erasers
- A piece of transparent tape (any thin tape will do)
- A Mini Maglite flashlight (do not substitute other flashlights) or a candle with matches or a lighter (or, if you'd rather, you can make your own bright point source of light by using leads with alligator clips to attach a Mini Maglite flashlight-bulb to two AA batteries in a battery holder)
- Optional: Pieces of cloth, a feather, plastic diffraction grating, metal screen, a human hair

Introduction

Light bends when it passes around an edge or through a slit. This bending is called diffraction. You can easily demonstrate diffraction using a candle or a small bright flashlightbulb and a slit made with two pencils. The diffraction pattern—the pattern of dark and light created when light bends around an edge or edges—shows that light has wavelike properties.

Assembly
(5 minutes or less)

1. Light the candle or, if you are using a Mini Maglite, unscrew the top of the flashlight. The tiny lamp will come on and shine brightly.
2. Wrap one layer of tape around the top of one of the pencils, just below the eraser.

To Do and Notice
(15 minutes or more)

Place the light at least one arm's-length away from you.

Hold the two pencils vertically, side by side, with the erasers at the top. The tape wrapped around one pencil should keep the pencils slightly apart, forming a thin slit between them, just below the tape. Hold the pencils close to one eye (about 1 inch [2.5 cm] away) and look at the light source through the slit between the pencils. Squeeze the pencils together, making the slit smaller. Notice that there is a line of light

Etcetera

In a dimly lit room, look at a Mini Maglite bulb with one eye (a candle will not work). Notice the lines of light radiating out from the light source, like the seeds radiating out from the center of a dandelion.

How can you find the origin of these lines? Rotate the light source and notice that the lines of light do not rotate. Rotate your head and notice that the lines do rotate. Hold your hand or an index card in front of your eye so that it doesn't quite block your view of the light source.

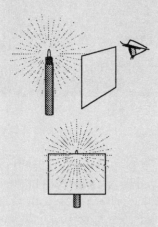

Notice that you still see a full circle of lines radiating out from the light source. The effect actually happens in your eye, as lines of light are spread out onto your retina by imperfections in the tissues of your cornea.

---

perpendicular to the slit. While looking through the slit, rotate the pencils until they are horizontal, and notice that the line of light becomes vertical.

If you look closely you may see that the line is composed of tiny blobs of light. As you squeeze the slit together, the blobs of light grow larger and spread apart, moving away from the central light source and becoming easier to see. Notice that the blobs have blue and red edges and that the blue edges are closer to the light source.

Stretch a hair tight and hold it about 1 inch (2.5 cm) from your eye. Move the hair until it is between your eye and the light source, and notice that the light is spread into a line of blobs by the hair, just as it was by the slit. Rotate the hair and watch the line of blobs rotate.

Look at the light through a piece of cloth, a feather, a diffraction grating, or a piece of metal screen. Rotate each object while you look through it.

What's Going On?

The black bands between the blobs of light show that a wave is associated with the light. The light waves that go through the slit spread out, overlap, and add together, producing the diffraction pattern you see. Where the crest of one wave overlaps with the crest of another wave, the two waves combine to make a bigger wave, and you see a bright blob of light. Where the trough of one wave overlaps with the crest of another wave, the waves cancel each other out, and you see a dark band.

The angle at which the light bends is proportional to the wavelength of the light. Red light, for instance, has a longer wavelength than blue light, so it bends more than blue light does. This different amount of bending gives the blobs their colored edges: blue on the inside, red on the outside.

The narrower the slit, the more the light spreads out. In fact, the angle between two adjacent dark bands in the diffraction pattern is inversely proportional to the width of the slit.

Thin objects, such as a strand of hair, also diffract light. Light that passes around the hair spreads out, overlaps, and produces a diffraction pattern. Cloth and feathers, which are both made up of many smaller, thinner parts, produce complicated diffraction patterns.

DISAPPEARING GLASS RODS
You can make glass objects disappear.

Materials

- A beaker
- Wesson oil (regular, not lite)
- One or more Pyrex stirring rods or other small, clear glass objects, such as marbles or lenses
- Optional: Glass eyedropper, glass magnifying lens

⚠ CAUTION

Be careful with glass!
Handling glass is always hazardous.

Introduction

Glass objects are visible because they reflect some of the light that shines on them and bend or refract the light that shines through them. If you eliminate reflection from and refraction by a glass object, you can make that object disappear.

Assembly

Pour some Wesson oil into the beaker.

To Do and Notice

(15 minutes or more)

Immerse a glass object in the oil. Notice that the object becomes more difficult to see. Only a ghostly image of the object remains. (*Note:* If you do this as a demonstration, keep your audience at a distance to make it harder for them to see the ghost object.)

Experiment with a variety of glass objects, such as clear marbles, lenses, and odd glassware. Some will disappear in the oil more completely than others.

You can make an eyedropper vanish before your eyes by immersing it and then sucking oil up into the dropper.

If you have a magnifying glass, immerse it in the oil. Notice that it does not magnify images when it is submerged.

Etcetera

times called optical density,
but optical density is not the
same as mass density. Two
materials can have different
mass densities even when
they have the same index
of refraction. Though Pyrex
glass and Wesson oil have
similar indices of refraction,
Pyrex sinks in Wesson oil
because it has a higher mass
density than the oil. Wesson oil has a higher index
of refraction than water
($n = 1.33$), but a lower mass
density, so it floats on water.
The index of refraction
depends not only on density
but also on the chemical
composition of a material.

You can make Pyrex glass
disappear by immersing
it in mineral oil. However,
mineral oil comes in dif-
ferent weights, and each
variety has a different index
of refraction. To match
the index of refraction of
Pyrex glass, you'll need a
mixture of mineral oils of
different weights. To create
the proper mixture, place
a Pyrex glass object into a
large glass beaker and pour
in enough heavy mineral
oil to submerge it partially.
Slowly add light mineral
oil and stir. Watch the glass
object as you pour. Most
Pyrex glass will disappear
when the mixture is two
parts heavy mineral oil to
one part light mineral oil.
Notice the swirling refraction patterns as you mix
the oils.

Karo syrup has an index of
refraction close to that of
glass. Karo can be diluted
with water to match some
types of glass. Other light-
colored corn syrups may
also work—you may want to
experiment and find out.

What's Going On?

You see a glass object because it both reflects and refracts light. When light traveling through air encounters a glass surface at an angle, some of the light reflects. The rest of the light keeps going, but it bends or refracts as it moves from the air to the glass.

When light passes from air into glass, it slows down. It's this change in speed that causes the light to reflect and refract as it moves from one clear material (air) to another (glass). Every material has an index of refraction that is linked to the speed of light in the material. The higher a material's index of refraction, the slower light travels in that material.

The smaller the difference in speed between two clear materials, the less reflection will occur at the boundary and the less refraction will occur for the transmitted light. If a transparent object is surrounded by another material that has the same index of refraction, then the speed of light will not change as it enters the object. No reflection and no refraction will take place, and the object will be invisible.

Wesson oil has nearly the same index of refraction (n) as Pyrex glass ($n = 1.474$). Differ-ent types of glass have different indices of refraction. In Wesson oil, Pyrex disappears, but other types of glass, such as crown glass or flint glass, remain visible. Fortunately for us, a great deal of laboratory glassware and home kitchen glassware is made from Pyrex glass.

For most Pyrex glass, the index-matching with Wesson oil is not perfect. That's because Pyrex glass has internal strains that make its index of refraction vary at different places in the object. Even if you can match the index of refraction for one part of a Pyrex stir-ring rod, for example, the match will not be perfect for other parts of the rod. That's why a ghostly image of the rod remains even with the best index matching.

The index of refraction of the oil (and of the glass, too) is a function of temperature. This demonstration will work better on some days than others.

DUCK-INTO KALEIDOSCOPE
Make multiple images of yourself.

Introduction

With this mirrored kaleidoscope, you can create hundreds of images of whatever you place inside. The basic structure is a triangle, but mirror tiles can be formed into other shapes and angles as well.

Assembly

(30 minutes or less)

1. Place the six mirror tiles in a row, as shown, and tape each tile to the tiles on either side with duct tape (shown as dark stripes on the drawing). Leave just enough room for the tape to flex and act as a hinge—and be sure to tape over any sharp edges.

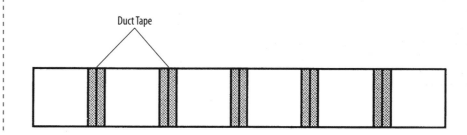

Duct Tape

Etcetera

If you have extra mirrors, experiment by making other closed geometrical shapes such as a square, a rectangle, or a hexagon. Put each shape over your head, or place an object in the center of the shape, and see the reflections.

2. Stand the pieces of cardboard on a table so that the long sides are horizontal.

3. Fold up the bottom 3 inches (7.5 cm) of each piece of cardboard to form a lip.

4. Tape the three cardboard pieces together to form a large equilateral triangle, 2 feet (60 cm) on each side, with the lip on the inside.

5. Insert the mirror tiles into the cardboard form so that the bottom edges of the mirrors rest inside the cardboard lip. Be sure that the mirrors are facing to the inside.

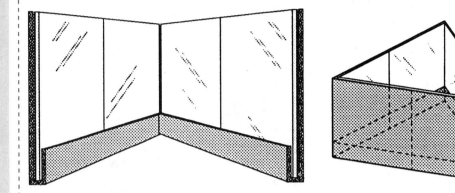

To Do and Notice

(5 minutes or more)

Put the kaleidoscope over your head and you'll see a million faces!

What's Going On?

In a kaleidoscope you see reflections of reflections.

GIANT LENS

A lens creates an image that hangs in midair.

Materials

- A large plastic page-magnifier Fresnel lens, 6 × 9 inches (15 × 22 cm) or larger (be sure you don't get a wide-angle viewer lens: if you look through the lens at a hand held an inch or so beyond the lens, the hand should appear larger, not smaller)
- Two or three large binder clips
- String
- Objects to look at and a lamp or computer screen
- Large sheet of white paper
- Two soda straws
- Common pins
- Corrugated cardboard or foamcore sheet, 9 × 9 inches (22 × 22 cm)
- A partner

⚠ CAUTION

Don't use the sun!
An image you make with the sun can become so hot that it can burn the paper and so bright that it can damage your eyes.

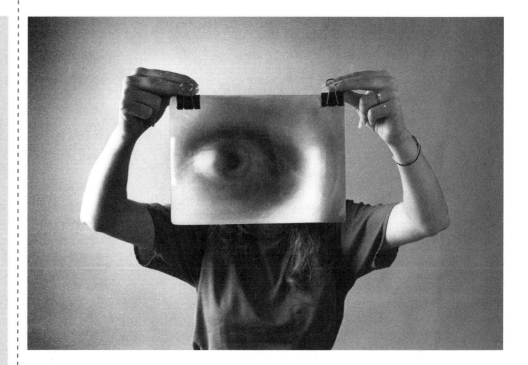

Introduction

A large hanging lens creates upside-down images of distant objects and right-side-up images of nearby objects. You can locate the upside-down images by using a piece of white paper as a screen. The right-side-up images are harder to find.

Assembly

(10 minutes or less)

Hang the lens from the ceiling at about head height using the clips and string, or use the clips to support the lens on a tabletop, as shown in the drawing.

To Do and Notice

(30 minutes or more)

Stand a few feet back from the lens and look through it at objects on the other side. Distant objects will appear upside down; nearby objects will appear right side up.

Stand close to the lens. Hold your hand close to the lens on the other side. You will notice that your hand is magnified and right side up.

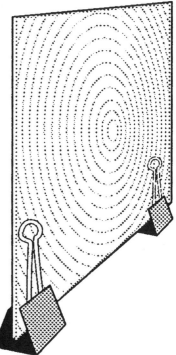

Stand an arm's length from one side of the lens; have a friend stand an arm's length from the other side. Look at your friend's face through the lens. Have your friend move closer to the lens as you back away, keeping the same two-arm's-length distance between the two of you. Then reverse this procedure: You step closer to the lens while your friend moves away. Notice how your friend's face appears, and ask how your face appears.

Find an object that is brightly illuminated (such as a lightbulb or computer screen), and dim the lights in the rest of the room. Hold the lens at least several feet from the object. Hold a large piece of white paper against the side of the lens that faces away from the object. Slowly move the paper until an image of the object comes into focus.

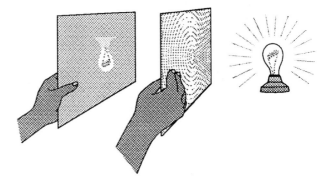

What's Going On?

Light from any point on an object spreads out in all directions. When the spreading light hits the page magnifier lens, it is bent toward the axis of the lens. (The page magnifier is called a positive, or converging, lens because it bends light rays together.)

Page magnifiers have a focal length of about 10 inches (25 cm). A focal length is the distance from the lens to an image the lens makes of a distant object. If an object is farther than one focal length (10 inches [25 cm]) from the lens, the lens can bend all the light that arrives from one point on the object until it comes back to a point on the other side of the lens. This point is a point on the image of the object. If you put white paper at the place where the light rays meet, an image will appear on the paper. An image that can be focused on a piece of paper is called a real image. (See Figure 1.)

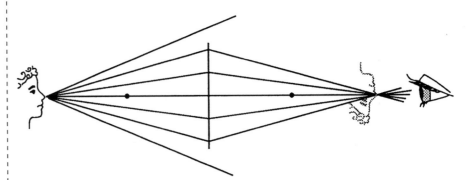

Figure 1. Your eye-brain system follows the light back to the point from which it spreads. This type of image is called a real image.

However, you don't need the white paper to see the image. Simply move about 1 foot (30 cm) farther away from the lens than the location of the image, and look at the lens. You will see the image hanging in space. Move your head slightly from side to side and watch the image move. (Actually, your eye-brain system may refuse to interpret the image as hanging in the air. It is so unusual to see something hanging in the air that

Etcetera

The Fresnel lenses used here are made out of wedges of plastic. The wedges must be thicker at the edge in order to bend light more, and thinner in the center. Run your finger over the ridges of the Fresnel lens and notice that the ridges are higher near the edge and lower and smoother near the center.

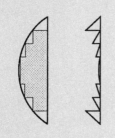

The Fresnel lens is named for August Fresnel, who figured out how to make these lenses for the French lighthouse commission in the late 1800s. Lighthouses needed large lenses to gather the light from a lamp and make it into a beam. If such a lens were ground out of glass, it would be thick, heavy, and expensive. Fresnel realized that the bending of light at the lens occurred at its curved surface, and that the thick glass had a minimal role in image formation. He figured out a way to maintain the curvature of the surface while getting rid of the useless glass. He made his lighthouse lenses out of prisms.

your brain may insist that the image is on the surface of the lens or even behind the lens—but the image actually is hanging in space.)

If an object is closer to the lens than the focal point, the lens cannot bend the light spreading from the object enough to return it to a point. To your eye-brain system, it looks as if there's an image on the same side of the lens as the object. This type of image is called a virtual image. A virtual image cannot be focused on a piece of paper. (See Figure 2.)

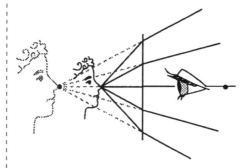

Figure 2. Your eye-brain system follows the light back to the point from which it appears to spread. This type of image is called a virtual image.

Building an Image Locator

You can find the location of a real or virtual image by building an image locator. Push a pin through one end of each soda straw. Use the pins to attach the straws to adjacent corners of the 9 × 9 inch (22 × 22 cm) corrugated cardboard sheet. Push another pin through the other end of one straw to mount it along one edge of the cardboard. The other straw will be free to rotate.

Mount the image locator firmly in place so you can look through the straw fixed to one edge and see one point on the image (see diagram). Then rotate the other straw until you can look through it and see the same point on the image. (You'll have to move your head to look through the second straw.) The image is located where two imaginary lines, one drawn through each straw, cross. If the image is a real image, you can place a piece of paper there and see it on the paper.

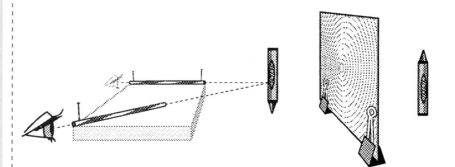

Finding the Focal Length of Your Lens

You can also find the focal length of your particular lens using a bright light source (but not the sun!) that is more than 30 feet (9 m) away. Hold a piece of paper against the lens on the side opposite the light. Move the paper away from the lens until a sharp image of the light appears on the paper. The distance from the lens to the image is the focal length.

INVERSE-SQUARE LAW

Why the world gets dark so fast outside the circle of the campfire.

Materials

- A Mini Maglite flashlight (no substitutes!) or make your own economical point source of light with a square of heavy cardboard, a Mini Maglite replacement bulb, two batteries in a battery holder—either AAA, AA, C, or D—and clip leads to connect them—see Assembly Note for details)
- Utility knife or scissors
- Cardboard or foamcore
- A file card
- Graph paper with 1/2-inch (12 mm) or 1/4-inch (6 mm) squares

NOTE

This Snack can be modified using a sheet of prepunched perfboard instead of graph paper.

ASSEMBLY NOTE

If you're making your own light source, use the clip leads to wire the bulb in series with the batteries, as shown in the diagram. Cut a small hole in the cardboard and push the bulb through the hole so it fits tightly and gives you something to hold onto.

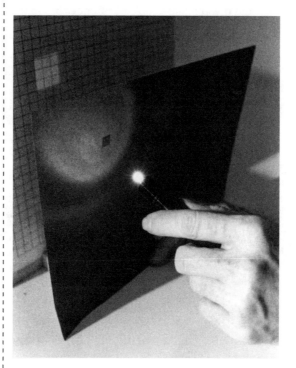

Introduction

We all know that the farther away we get, the dimmer a light will look. The question of how much dimmer it looks was answered a long time ago. Here's an easy way to repeat that discovery.

Assembly

(15 minutes or less if you use a Mini Maglite; 30 minutes or less if you make your own light source)

1. Unscrew the front reflector assembly of the Mini Maglite to expose the bulb. The bulb will come on and stay on when the reflector assembly is removed.

2. Now cut a $1/2 \times 1/2$ inch (1.25×1.25 cm) square hole in the file card.

3. Hold or mount the card 1 inch (2.5 cm) in front of the light source. The square of light made when the light shines through this hole will shine on the graph paper (see "To Do and Notice," later in this Snack).

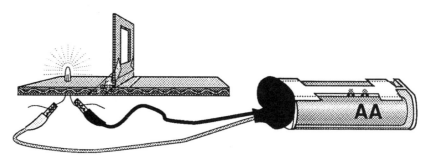

Etcetera

The inverse-square law applies not only to the intensity of light but also to gravitational and electrical forces. The pull of the earth's gravity drops off at $1/r^2$, where r is the distance from the center of the earth. The attraction or repulsion between two electric charges also decreases with the distance at $1/r^2$, where r is the distance between the two charges.

To Do and Notice

(15 minutes or more)

Keep the distance between the bulb and the card with the square hole constant at 1 inch (2.5 cm). Put the graph paper at different distances from the bulb, and count how many squares on the graph paper are lit at each distance. The results will be easier to understand if you make a table of "number of squares lit" versus "distance." Be sure to measure the distance from the bulb.

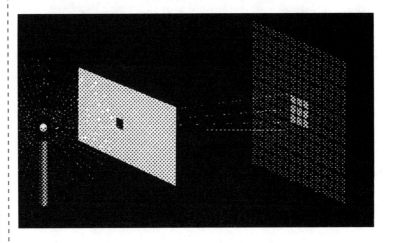

What's Going On?

What you see will be somewhat different depending on which version you make, but the principle is the same.

As you move the graph paper, light from the Mini Maglite spreads out equally in all directions. As the distance from the bulb to the graph paper increases, the same amount of light spreads over a larger and larger area, and the light reaching each square becomes correspondingly less intense. For example, adjust the distance from the bulb to the graph paper to 1 inch (2.5 cm). At this distance, the graph paper touches the card. A single 1/2-inch (1.25 cm) square area will be illuminated. When the graph paper is moved 2 inches (5 cm) from the card, four 1/2-inch (1.25 cm) squares will be illuminated on the graph paper. When the graph paper is moved 3 inches (8 cm) from the card, nine squares will be illuminated. At 4 inches (10 cm), sixteen squares will be illuminated, and so on. The area illuminated will increase as the square of the distance.

The intensity of light is the power per area. Since the energy that comes through the hole you cut is spread out over a larger area, the intensity of the light decreases. Since the area increases as the square of the distance, the intensity of the light must decrease as the inverse square of the distance. Thus, intensity follows the inverse-square law.

LOOK INTO INFINITY

Images of images of images can repeat forever.

Materials

- ➔ Two square pieces of plexi-mirror measuring 12 × 12 inches (30 × 30 cm), available from plastics stores (or substitute a 12 × 12 inch [30 × 30 cm] glass mirror tile or any two mirrors for the plexi-mirror; size is not crucial)
- ➔ Some kind of stand (see Assembly)
- ➔ Optional: Hole saw, router

⚠ CAUTION

Be careful with mirrors! Keep yourself and your kids safe by always using plastic mirrors instead of glass. If you must use a glass mirror, tape the edges to minimize the possibility of cuts and glue one side to a suitable backing of cardboard or wood. Don't just spot-glue the mirror in a few places: The whole surface must be attached to the backing. That way, even if the mirror cracks or breaks, there will be no loose shards of glass.

Introduction

If you have ever been between two mirrors that face each other, such as in a barbershop or a beauty salon, you will be familiar with the seemingly endless line of images fading into the distance. This Snack recreates the effect.

Assembly

(15 minutes or less)

1. Cut a hole about 1 inch (2.5 cm) in diameter near the center of one of the mirrors. You can use a hole saw, or you can have this done for you at the plastics store. You can get the effect without the hole, but the hole gives a more interesting perspective. If you don't care about the hole, you can use glass mirror tiles instead of a plexi-mirror. You can even create the hole on a glass mirror tile by scraping away the silver backing.

2. Stand the mirrors so that their reflecting surfaces face each other and are parallel to each other. The mirrors can be anywhere from a few inches to a foot apart. You can make a wooden stand for each mirror by cutting a slit along the length of the flat side of a piece of 1 × 4 inch (2.5 × 10 cm) pine. Then slip the mirror into the slit. You can also stand each mirror between two pieces of wood held together by rubber bands, or place two full soda cans (or any heavy objects) so that one is on each side of the mirror, supporting it.

An interesting handheld variation of this Snack involves gluing the two mirrors to a block of foam rubber, which acts as a spacer. Mirrors 6 × 6 inches (15 × 15 cm) work well for this portable version, but mirror size is not crucial. The foam should separate the mirrors by 2 or 3 inches (5 to 8 cm).

An even simpler handheld version uses pieces of sponge as spacers, with rubber bands holding the mirrors together. Use a soft sponge—the cheap ones used for washing cars work well. One or two holes can be drilled into the mirror.

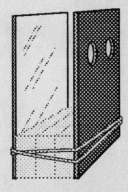

Squeeze the foam or sponge so the mirrors are not quite parallel to each other, and you'll see a pattern of images that curves off into infinity!

To Do and Notice

(5 minutes or more)

With the reflecting surfaces facing each other, look through the hole into the space between the mirrors. (If you didn't bother making a hole, just look over the top of one mirror.) You can also try placing either your finger or some other object between the mirrors.

If you place an object between the mirrors, notice the repetitious pattern in the orientation and spacing of the images. Objects with contrasting colors on the front and back (such as red and white) show this well. Successive images alternate from front view to back view. If the original object is closer to one mirror than the other, the distance between successive images will alternate from close together to far apart—making the images seem to be grouped in pairs, with a front side always facing a front side, or a back side always facing a back side.

What's Going On?

In this ray diagram, the solid lines show the actual path of the light rays; the dashed lines show the path of the light rays projected by your brain. You see images where the dashed lines come together.

This ray diagram shows the rays that come from the front of an object and those that come from the back. After the first reflection, you see one image in each mirror where the dashed lines come together (1). After the second reflection, you see a second image in each mirror (2), then a third (3), and so on.

As you look at the images formed in one of the mirrors on the diagram, notice that there is an alternation of front and back views, that the images appear to be grouped in pairs, and that a front side is always facing a front side and a back side is always facing a back side. This corresponds to what you actually observe in the mirrors.

MAGIC WAND
See pictures in thin air.

Materials

- → A moveable screen (a piece of white poster board will do)
- → A projectable image and a way to see it (a 35 mm slide and slide projector work best, if you can still get them, but a computer projector or an overhead projector will also work)
- → A pencil, wooden dowel, or meter- or yardstick "wand"
- → Optional: A piece of black cloth

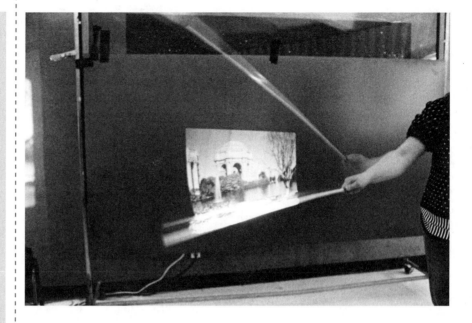

Introduction

When you view a slide show or a movie, where is the picture? Is it on the film, in the air, on the screen, or in the eye of the viewer? This Snack will help you investigate and understand how you see.

Assembly

(15 minutes or less)

1. Turn on the projector, and focus the image on the screen held about 6 feet (2 m) away.

2. Remove the screen.

3. If you can arrange it so the light from the projector travels out through a door or window after it passes the point where the screen was, or onto the surface of a black cloth, the out-of-focus image that will end up being projected onto a surface within the room will be less distracting to viewers.

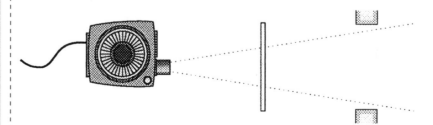

NOTE

Some computer projectors create color images by projecting a red image, then a green image, and then a blue image, one after the other, very rapidly. If you do this experiment with such a projector you'll see bands of color as you whip the wand through the image.

Etcetera

Persistence of vision is what allows you to see a television picture on a cathode-ray tube television, in which one bright dot of light—produced when an electron beam collides with phosphors on the inside front of the picture tube—sweeps across the television screen (plasma and LCD TVs work differently).

The dot moves across the screen one horizontal line at a time, sweeping out the entire 525 lines that fill the picture area every 1/30 of a second. Yet you do not see a flying dot; you see a complete picture.

You can do a fun 3-D version of this Snack if the slide you project is of a simple shape, such as a white circle. Hold a stiff piece of white cardboard or foamcore where the screen would be, and then sweep the board back and forth through the image, moving the flat side toward and away from the projector. The circle will become a white cylinder hanging in space.

To Do and Notice

(5 minutes or more)

Hold the wand horizontally in the place where the screen was located. Then wave the wand rapidly up and down by flicking your wrist. Notice that the picture appears as the wand moves.

Wave the wand at an angle, or rotate it to trace out a cylinder or a cone. Notice the deformed image that you produce.

What's Going On?

The image you're projecting here is focused in the air, but you can't see it unless something reflects the light to your eyes. The moving wand reflects the light just as the screen does, except that the wand reflects the image piece by piece.

When this reflected light enters your eyes, it makes an image on your retina. Your eyes retain each piece of the image for about 1/30 of a second—long enough to let you put the pieces together to make a composite picture.

Your eye's tendency to hang onto an image for a fraction of a second is called persistence of vision. Persistence of vision occurs because the light detectors in your eyes, the rods and the cones, continue to fire electrical signals to your brain even after a very short pulse of light has come and gone.

The deformed images produced when you move the wand in the shape of a cylinder or cone are examples of a map projection. The flat image of the slide is projected onto a curved surface. The resulting deformations are like those that occur when the spherical surface of the earth is mapped onto a flat map.

You might wonder if you could see the image by looking directly into the slide projector from the place where the screen used to be. The light in most projectors is too bright to try this experiment. However, the answer is no. Your eye can only make images of the light that actually enters the pupil. When you put your eyes where the screen was, light from only a small part of the image enters your eye, so you cannot see the entire image.

PARABOLAS
It's all done with mirrors.

Materials
➡ A commercially made Mirage Maker or Mind Boggling Optic Mirage, or the smaller, less expensive 3-D Mirascope, all available from various online vendors

NOTE
At about $40, the Mirage Maker and Mind Boggling Optic Mirage are relatively expensive, but these commercially available devices are a great investment if you can afford to buy one. Purchasing a unit is the only realistic way we could devise to replicate this exhibit. Large concave glass mirrors are available from scientific supply houses, but their cost approaches or exceeds that of the commercial devices. The 3-D Mirascope, at under $10, is a smaller, less expensive toy version, and will serve if you need to keep costs down. (Be careful— these mirrors are easily scratched!)

Introduction
What you perceive as an object in this Snack is really an image in space, created by two concave mirrors. This illusion would do credit to any magician.

Assembly
None required.

To Do and Notice
(5 minutes or more)

Put an object in the bottom of the apparatus. A coin works well, but a small, colorful object that looks like a push-button, resting on a "PUSH" sign, is an amusing alternative.

Notice that the object or button appears to be in the hole in the top of the device. Try to grab the object or push the button. There's nothing there!

What's Going On?
You are seeing an image formed by two concave mirrors facing one another. The object is placed at the center of the bottom mirror. The curvature of the mirrors is such that the object is at the focal point of the top mirror.

When light from a point on the object hits the top mirror, it reflects in parallel rays. These parallel rays hit the bottom mirror and reflect so that they reassemble to form a point located at one focal length from the bottom mirror. The mirrors are placed so

Etcetera

The image produced by this apparatus is known as a real image, because the light that forms it actually passes through the location of the image. However, if you place a piece of waxed paper or onionskin paper at the location of the real image, the image will not appear on the paper. The outside regions of the mirrors that do not reflect light to your eyes do reflect light to the paper. The edges of the mirrors have large aberrations and create an image so blurred that it cannot be seen. This image is also known as an aerial image because it appears in the air and not on a screen.

that the focal point of the bottom mirror is located at the hole in the top of the device. The end result is that light from every point on the object is assembled into an image in the hole.

The ray diagram may help explain this effect.

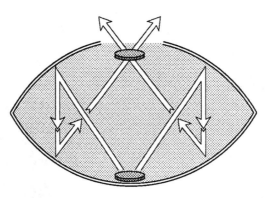

PINHOLE MAGNIFIER
Who needs expensive optical equipment?

Materials
- Utility knife
- A 3 × 5 inch (8 × 13 cm) file card
- Masking tape
- Aluminum foil
- A straight pin or needle
- A lamp with a dim (10 to 25 watt) lightbulb

Introduction

A pinhole in an index card can act like a magnifying glass, helping your eye focus on an object that is very close to you. However, by limiting the amount of light that reaches your eye from the object, the pinhole also makes the object appear dimmer.

Assembly
(5 minutes or less)

1. Cut a hole about 1-inch (2.5 cm) square in a file card.

2. Tape a piece of aluminum foil over the hole in the card and use the pin to punch a hole in the center of the foil. (You can make a good pinhole by placing the foil on a thick piece of cardboard and rotating a needle.)

To Do and Notice
(15 minutes or more)

Hold the card near your eye and look at the lightbulb from several feet away. Move closer to the bulb until you almost touch it, and notice the magnified writing on the bulb. Use the pinhole magnifier to examine other small brightly lit objects. You can, for example, examine a computer screen or a television screen up close using a pinhole magnifier.

Try using pins or needles with different diameters to make different-sized holes. Notice that the smaller the pinhole is, the dimmer your view. As the pinhole is made smaller, the image at first becomes sharper, but then is blurred by diffraction.

You can even form a pinhole by curling your index finger. Or try this as a magnifier:

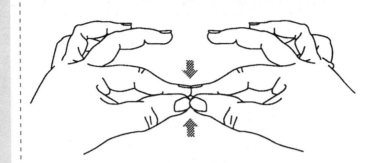

What's Going On?

The pinhole magnifier works on a very simple principle: The closer you get to an object, the bigger it looks to you. This is because the closer you are to the object, the larger the image the object forms on your retina (see Figure 1).

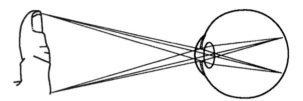

Figure 1. Focused Image

Unfortunately, however, there is a limit to this. If you get too close to the object, your eye is not able to bend some of the light rays enough to obtain a focused image. As a result, the image becomes blurry or fuzzy (see Figure 2).

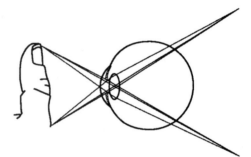

Figure 2. Blurry Image

The pinhole magnifier gets around this problem by limiting the rays that come to you from each part of the object (see Figure 3).

Sadly, there is a trade-off between the resolution, or sharpness, of an image and its brightness. A tiny pinhole produces a very sharp image, but, because it cuts down on the number of rays that enter your eye, the pinhole makes the object look much dimmer.

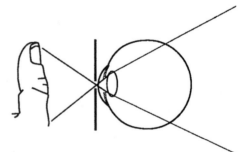

Figure 3. Pinhole Image

POLARIZED LIGHT MOSAIC
With polarized light, you can make a stained glass window without glass.

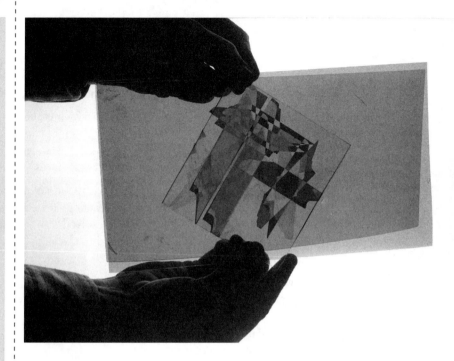

Materials

→ Transparent tape with a shiny, nonmatte surface (Scotch brand tape won't work, but some brands of inexpensive 2-inch-wide transparent packing tape will; you'll need to test the brand you choose—see the "Note" section)

→ A piece of glass or Plexiglas; plastic generally will not work (see "Note" section on following page)

→ Two sheets of polarizing material (you can use two lenses from an old pair of polarizing sunglasses, but since the lenses are small, the pattern or picture you'll be able to view will be limited in size; larger polarizing filters are available from Edmund Scientific)

→ Overhead projector

! CAUTION

Be careful with glass! Handling glass is always hazardous. Tape the edges to minimize the possibility of cuts.

Introduction

Using transparent tape and polarizing material, you can make and project beautifully colored patterns reminiscent of abstract or geometric stained-glass windows. Rotating the polarizer as you view the patterns makes the colors change. With a little creativity, you can also create colorful renditions of objects or scenes.

Assembly

(15 minutes or less)

1. Put strips of tape on the glass or Plexiglas in a crisscross or random pattern. Be sure that there are several areas where two or three strips of tape overlap and crisscross. You can use multiple layers of crisscrossed tape to create pictures, or you can cut the tape to form pictures, letters, or words.

2. Sandwich the glass between the polarizers and place the resulting package on the overhead projector.

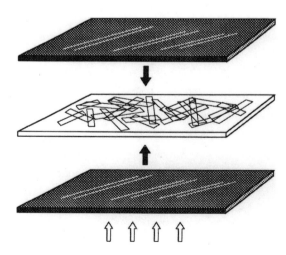

To Do and Notice

(15 minutes or less)

Rotate the top polarizer and observe the color changes.

What's Going On?

The colors you see here result from differences in the speed of polarized light as it travels through the transparent tape.

In transparent tape, long polymer molecules are stretched parallel to the length of the tape. Light polarized parallel to the stretch of the molecules travels through the tape more slowly than light polarized perpendicular to the stretch.

Every material has an index of refraction, which is the ratio of the speed of light in a vacuum to the speed of light in the material. Light travels through the tape you used in this demonstration at two different speeds. (Materials with this property are called birefringent, which is derived from the Greek words for "doubly refracting.")

When polarized light enters the tape, its direction of polarization will probably not line up with the length of tape. If the light is polarized in a direction that does not line up, its direction of polarization will be resolved into two perpendicular components. One of these components will be parallel to the length of the tape, and one will be perpendicular.

The waves that compose these two components are initially in step with each other. But as they travel at different speeds through the tape, they go out of step—that is, the crest of one wave no longer lines up with the crest of the other. When these out-of-step light waves emerge from the tape on the other side, they recombine, making light with a polarization different from the original light's.

The thicker the tape is, the more out of step the components will become, and the greater the change in the polarization will be. If, for example, the two waves recombine after one has been delayed by one-half a wavelength, the direction of polarization of the light will be rotated by 90 degrees.

The white light shining from the overhead projector is made up of light of all different colors, or wavelengths. Since the index of refraction of the tape is different for each color of light, each color has its own unique pair of speeds as it passes through the tape. The result is that the polarization of each color is changed by a different amount for a given thickness of tape.

Etcetera

If you can find a 35 mm slide projector, punch the film out of an old 35 mm slide and crisscross layers of tape over the opening. Place a piece of polarizing material inside the projector just in back of the slide and rotate a second piece in front of the lens. As the front polarizer is rotated, your creations will change colors. Colors are determined by the orientation of pieces and thickness of the layers. Rotate the polarizer to the rhythm of your favorite music, and you will have a do-it-yourself light show.

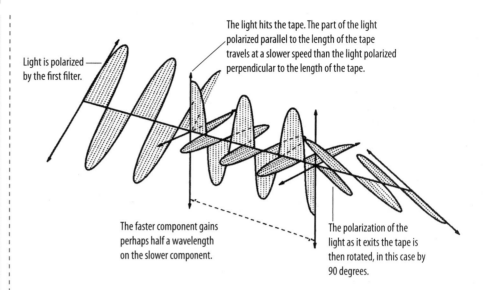

The light hits the tape. The part of the light polarized parallel to the length of the tape travels at a slower speed than the light polarized perpendicular to the length of the tape.

Light is polarized by the first filter.

The faster component gains perhaps half a wavelength on the slower component.

The polarization of the light as it exits the tape is then rotated, in this case by 90 degrees.

When a second piece of polarizer is placed over the tape and rotated, it transmits different colors at different angles. This accounts for the color combinations you see at a given angle, and for the changes in color as the polarizer is rotated.

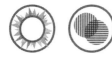

POLARIZED SUNGLASSES

If you rotate a pair of polarizing sunglasses, you'll find that they cut road glare much better in some positions than in others.

Materials
- One clear lightbulb with socket and cord
- One piece of shiny opaque plastic, such as a black plastic party plate
- One or two pieces of polarizing material (such as old lenses from polarizing sunglasses)

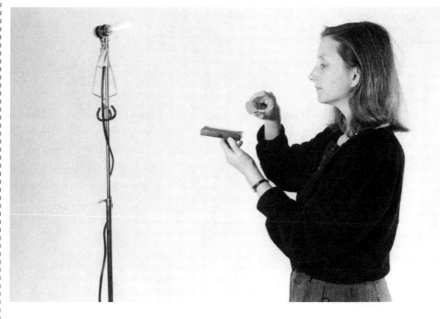

Introduction

When light reflects from water, asphalt, or other nonmetallic surfaces, it becomes polarized—that is, the reflected light is usually vibrating more in one direction than others. Polarizing sunglasses reduce this reflection, known as glare, but only when the polarizing lenses are oriented properly.

Assembly

None necessary.

To Do and Notice

(15 minutes or more)

Place the lit bulb with its filament parallel to the surface of the plastic. Orient the bulb so you can see the reflection of the bulb in the plastic.

Look at the reflection through a piece of polarizer. Rotate the polarizer and vary the angle at which you look at the plastic until you get the dimmest reflection. You'll probably get the best results when there's about a 35-degree angle between your eyes and the piece of plastic (see drawing). Rotate the polarizer 90 degrees as you watch the reflection. The reflection should become notably brighter.

Observe reflections elsewhere around you. Rotate the polarizer and vary the angle of viewing to vary the brightness. Try looking at a reflection from a metallic surface, such as an ordinary mirror. There should be no difference in the brightness of an image reflected in the mirror as you rotate the polarizer or vary the angle of viewing.

Etcetera

Light becomes completely polarized parallel to the surface at one particular angle of reflection, called Brewster's angle. Brewster's angle for water is 53 degrees; for glass it is 56 degrees; for plastic the angle varies but, in general, will be somewhere between these two numbers. Brewster's angle is traditionally measured from a line that is perpendicular to a surface. To find the angle measured directly from the surface you must subtract Brewster's angle from 90 degrees.

Look at the sky through the polarizing lens. Notice that the brightness of the sky changes as you rotate the polarizer. That's because the light in the sky is polarized.

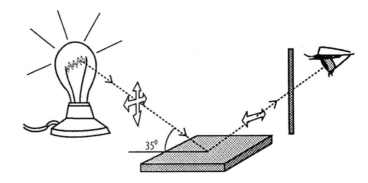

Look through a polarizer at the surface of a pond on a bright, sunny day. Rotate the polarizer and notice that at one orientation of the polarizer, the surface reflections are greatly reduced and you can see beneath the surface of the water. Rotate the polarizer 90 degrees from this orientation, and the surface reflections block your view of the underwater world. This is why people wear polarizing sunglasses when they go fishing.

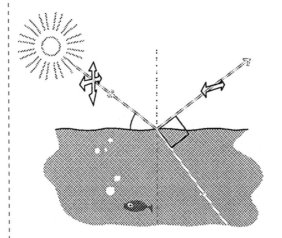

What's Going On?

The lightbulb produces unpolarized light—each photon is vibrating in its own different direction.

Nonmetallic surfaces, such as black plastic, tend to reflect light that is vibrating parallel to the surface and transmit or absorb light vibrating in all other directions. If the black plastic is horizontal, then it reflects light that is vibrating horizontally, creating horizontally polarized light. The horizontal black plastic reflects less light that is vibrating vertically.

The polarizer lets through light vibrating in one direction and absorbs light vibrating in all other directions. When the black surface is horizontal, the reflection looks dimmest when you hold the filter so it lets through just vertically vibrating light. The reflection looks brightest when you hold the filter so it lets through just horizontally vibrating light.

Horizontal surfaces in the environment, such as the asphalt of a street or the surface of a lake, reflect light that is vibrating horizontally. Polarizing sunglasses absorb this horizontally oriented glare. If you tilt your head sideways, this horizontally oriented glare passes through the glasses, making the surface look brighter.

ROTATING LIGHT

Polarized light passing through sugar water "rotates" to reveal beautiful colors.

Materials

- ➔ A clear plastic or glass (100 mL) graduated cylinder (or make your own using epoxy glue, plastic cement, or a silicone seal, a square of clear plastic or glass about 3 × 3 inches [8 × 8 cm], and a 6-inch [15 cm] length of clear, rigid plastic tubing that's about 2 inches [5 cm] in diameter: see Assembly for instructions)

- ➔ Karo syrup (other light-colored corn syrups may work)

- ➔ Two pieces of polarizing material, such as the lenses from an old pair of polarizing sunglasses

- ➔ A light source (brightly illuminated sheet of white paper, overhead projector, or flashlight)

- ➔ Optional: A clear plastic cylinder 1 inch (2.5 cm) in diameter (either solid or hollow, with one closed end), colored filters, other liquids that can take the place of the Karo syrup

Introduction

White light is made up of all the colors in the rainbow. When polarized white light passes through a sugar solution, each color's direction of polarization is changed by a different amount. It is possible to see the colors change as the depth of the solution changes or as the polarizing filter is rotated.

Assembly

(5 minutes or less if you use a graduated cylinder; 30 minutes or less if you make your own container)

1. If you want to make your own container, attach one end of the plastic tube to the square of clear acrylic using epoxy, plastic cement, or silicone seal (see the diagram).

2. Fill the tube with several inches of Karo syrup.

3. Put one piece of polarizing material under the bottom of the base and hold the other above the top of the tube.

4. Place a light source below the bottom polarizer.

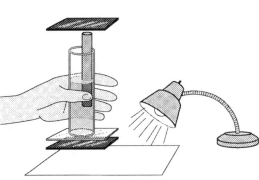

Etcetera

Materials that change the orientation of polarized light are called optically active materials. Some optically active solutions rotate the direction of polarization clockwise, to the right; others rotate it counterclockwise, to the left.

All organically produced glucose rotates the direction of polarization of light clockwise. This sugar is called d-glucose. Another sugar, called l-glucose, rotates the direction of polarization counterclockwise. It can only be made by inorganic chemical synthesis. Both d-glucose and l-glucose have the same chemical formula: $C_6H_{12}O_6$. However, the atoms in each of these isomers are arranged in a different pattern. The left-handed sugar (l-glucose) tastes just as sweet as the right-handed one (d-glucose), but your body can't use it as an energy source. That's how left-handed sugars can produce sweetness without calories.

All the proteins in your body and in all organisms on earth are made from amino acids that rotate the direction of polarization of light counterclockwise. On the other hand, laboratory-synthesized amino acids, and amino acids found on meteorites, are made up of equal numbers of amino acids that rotate light to the right and amino acids that rotate light to the left. No one knows why this is so.

To Do and Notice

(30 minutes or more)

Look down through the tube at the light source. Slowly rotate the polarizing filter and notice the color changes in the syrup.

Now hold the filter still and change the depth of the syrup. Pour more syrup into the tube. (If you have the optional tube or cylinder, you can push the cylinder or the closed end of the tube down into the solution.) Notice that the color changes with changes in the syrup's depth. If you rotate the filter and change the depth at just the right speeds, you should be able to keep the color constant.

You can perform a quantitative experiment by placing a colored filter under the tube. Suppose you use a blue filter. In order to see the blue as you add syrup, you must slowly rotate the upper polarizing filter. Determine the change in the depth of syrup required to rotate the direction of polarization of blue light by one full turn. Then try the same experiment with a red filter. With red light, a greater depth of syrup is needed.

Try a variety of transparent liquids and solutions such as honey and sugar syrup. Some are better than others at changing the direction of polarization.

What's Going On?

Light from most ordinary light sources wiggles up and down, left and right, and diagonally. Your polarizing filter lets through only the light that is vibrating in one particular direction. In this polarized light, the light waves all wiggle in the same direction.

To understand what this means, picture waves traveling along a rope. If the waves vibrate up and down, they are vertically polarized. Vertically polarized rope waves can pass through the slots between the vertical slats in a fence; waves vibrating in other directions are blocked by the slats. If you orient a polarizing filter properly, vertically polarized light waves can pass through the filter, while waves vibrating in other directions are blocked.

The light emerging from the light source at the bottom of the tube is unpolarized. That means it vibrates in all directions perpendicular to the light's direction of motion. The polarizing filter under the sugar solution polarizes this light so it vibrates in one direction only.

When polarized light passes through the Karo syrup, the direction of its polarization is changed. Light vibrating from to side to side, for example, might end up vibrating at a 45-degree angle. The amount of rotation depends on the depth of the syrup: The angle of rotation is proportional to the depth. It also depends on the concentration of the syrup: The more concentrated the syrup, the greater the rotation. Finally, the angle of rotation depends on the wavelength or color of the light. Blue light, with its shorter wavelength, rotates more than longer-wavelength red light.

When the white light emerges from the sugar solution, each color in the light has its own direction of polarization. When viewed without a polarizing filter, this light still appears white because our unaided eyes cannot detect the direction of polarization of light. However, when you look through a second polarizing filter, you see only the light that is vibrating in a direction that can pass through the filter. Only certain wavelengths or colors of light have the appropriate polarization. The intensity of the other colors in the light, which have different directions of vibration, is diminished. If a certain color of light has its polarization perpendicular to the axis of the polarizing filter, it is blocked out completely. (Think about the fence again. The rope waves won't get through if they are vibrating perpendicular to the slats.) As you rotate the filter, each orientation of the rotated filter produces a different dominant color, as does each different depth of sugar solution.

SOAP FILM PAINTING
A soap film becomes an ever-changing work of art.

Materials

Note: To cut the lengths called for here, you will need a total of 18 to 20 feet (5.5 to 6 m) of half-inch PVC pipe, Schedule 40.

➲ Two lengths of half-inch PVC pipe, each 30 inches (76 cm) long (for sides of frame)

➲ Two lengths of half-inch PVC pipe, each 26.5 inches (67 cm) long (for top and bottom of frame)

➲ One length of half-inch PVC pipe, 25 inches (63.5 cm) long (for soap-film bar)

➲ Four lengths of half-inch PVC pipe, 5 inches (13 cm) long (for leg verticals)

➲ Four lengths of half-inch PVC pipe, 7 inches (18 cm) long (for leg horizontals)

➲ Two lengths of half-inch PVC pipe, 3.5 inches (9 cm) long (for bottom of soap-film frame)

➲ One length of half-inch PVC pipe, a half inch (1.25 cm) long (or other small object you can attach to act as a pull handle and keep the string from slipping through the screw eyes on the top bar)

➲ Eight half-inch PVC 90-degree elbows

➲ Two half-inch PVC crosses

➲ A few extra pieces of PVC pipe (for activities)

➲ PVC cutter, hacksaw blade, or other way to cut PVC pipe

(continued)

Introduction

Under the influence of gravity, a thin soap film constantly changes thickness, creating an ever-shifting array of colors.

Assembly

(1.5 hours or less)

1. Assemble as shown in the illustrations.

- Eight screw eyes (size 112 works well)

- Wallpaper tray (PVC dimensions noted above and shown in the photo accommodate a wallpaper tray with dimensions 33 × 7.5 × 4.5 inches [83 × 19 × 11.5 cm]; adjust dimensions as necessary if a different-sized tray is used)

- Strong string, about 10 feet (3 m)—good-quality braided twine works well, as does braided fishing line

- Electric drill

- Drill bit—a 3/32-inch drill bit works for the size 112 screw eyes (note that the drill size for the string holes depends on the string used; the holes should be large enough to let the pipe travel freely on the string)

- A variety of objects to experiment with (sharpened pencils, knitting needles, paper cups, and so on)

- Bubble solution made from 2/3 cup (150 mL) Dawn dishwashing liquid and 1 tablespoon glycerin (available in drugstores) in 1 gallon (3.8 L) of water

- A partner

- Optional: Siphon or lab syringe, epoxy

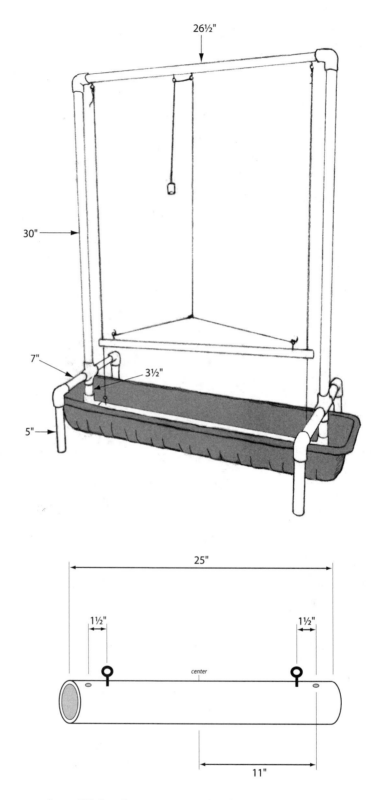

2. When you're done, fill the plastic tray with bubble solution until at least the entire lower half of the pipe is submerged.

- Make sure the measurements for locating the guide wire (string) holes are consistent on the top, middle, and bottom pieces.

- The two vertical strings that act as guide strings for the movable pipe should be tied as taut as possible to allow the movable pipe to travel freely up and down.

- Try using a siphon or lab syringe to empty the tray. You may find this easier and less messy than trying to pour from it!

- You can make a permanent version of this Snack by using epoxy to glue the joints. If the joints are not glued, however, the parts can be disassembled for storage. (In an unglued version, note that soap solution may leak into the bottom pipes and unsealed screw holes. If this happens, no harm done, but beware when taking it apart!)

- If you have trouble making a lasting soap film, try using distilled water instead of tap water. Aging the solution for at least a day before use significantly increases the lifetime of the film.

To Do and Notice

(15 minutes or more)

It's easiest to do these activities with two people: one to pull the string to make the soap film and the other to explore its behavior.

Using the solution in the tray, thoroughly wet the strings and any other surfaces that will come into contact with the soap film (so the film doesn't immediately pop).

Pull the string to raise the bar out of the soapy water and make a soap film. Notice the changing colors reflected by the film. Note that the colored patterns are most easily seen if you stand with your back to a white surface and view the soap film against a black background.

Shake the frame back and forth and notice the pattern of waves on the film.

Stand a few feet away and blow gently onto the soap film. Notice that it stretches out into a bulge when you blow and returns to its original flat shape when you stop.

Put a dry finger through the film and the film will pop. Coat your finger with the bubble solution and try again. This time, you should be able to push your finger into the soap film without the film popping. Try coating other objects in bubble solution: Does the tip of a sharpened pencil work? A knitting needle? The bottom of a paper cup? Can you pass an object through the film to a friend on the other side?

Now try coating a small piece of PVC pipe entirely in bubble solution. Can you push one end through the film and pop the bubble inside (if one forms) to make a "hole" in the soap film?

What's Going On?

A soap film is a soapy water sandwich, with two outside layers of soap molecules forming boundaries around a layer of soapy water. The thickness of the soap film changes as the water drains down the inside of the film.

When light strikes the front surface of the soap film, some of the light is reflected (about 4 percent). The remainder of the wave is transmitted through to the rear surface. At the rear surface of the soap film, more of the light is reflected back to your eyes. The light reflecting from the front of the film meets up with the light reflecting from the back of the film, and the waves combine.

The beautiful colors you see on the soap film are due to interference patterns, created when light reflects off the two surfaces of the thin soap film. Interference patterns are created when two reflected waves line up in phase or out of phase. If two waves line up in phase, with crests together and troughs together, we say that the waves are interfering constructively. When two waves line up out of phase, crest to trough, we say that the waves are interfering destructively.

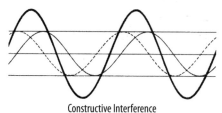
Constructive Interference

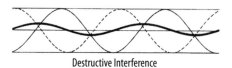
Destructive Interference

White light can be considered a mixture of three additive primary colors: red, green, and blue. If the thickness of the soap film is just

Etcetera

Exploring the properties of soap films can often help explain the properties of plasma membranes and the mechanics of transport across membranes. Cells need to import some materials, such as oxygen and nutrients, and export others, such as waste. At the boundary of every cell is a plasma membrane that regulates what goes into and out of the cell.

Plasma membranes are similar to soap films in several ways. Both are flexible, bilayered structures formed by molecules with hydrophilic (water-attracting) and hydrophobic (water-repelling) ends. While plasma membranes don't "pop" when confronted by unlike substances, both plasma membranes and soap films are selectively permeable, allowing certain substances to move through them. In some cases, proteins even provide channels or tunnels for the passage of molecules or ions, just as you could pass an object through the short length of soap-coated PVC pipe. And moving the PVC pipe around in the soap film can model the way proteins move around within plasma membranes.

right to cause the destructive interference of one of the additive primaries, you will perceive a mixture of the two remaining colors:

$$\text{white} - \text{red} = \text{blue} + \text{green} = \text{cyan (bluish green)}$$

$$\text{white} - \text{green} = \text{red} + \text{blue} = \text{magenta (reddish blue)}$$

$$\text{white} - \text{blue} = \text{red} + \text{green} = \text{yellow}$$

Therefore, everywhere you see yellow, the film is just the right thickness to destructively interfere with the blue light waves, removing them. Where you see cyan, the red light has been removed. And where you see magenta, the green light has been removed.

The surface tension that allows a soap film to form is caused by the tendency of water to minimize its surface area. When a finger, pencil, or piece of PVC pipe is coated with bubble solution and inserted into the soap film, the film stays in contact with a like solution and remains continuous. A dry finger, however, interrupts that continuity, making it impossible to maintain surface tension, and the bubble bursts.

SPECTRA
Fingerprints for light sources.

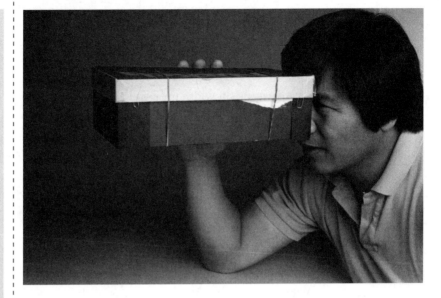

Introduction

Using a diffraction grating, you can observe that what seems to be a single color of light may really be a combination of colors, called a spectrum. You can also compare the spectra produced by different light sources.

Assembly
(30 minutes or less)

1. At one end of the shoebox or mailing tube, cut a rectangular hole measuring about 3/4-inch (2 cm) wide by 1¹/₂-inches (3.5 cm) high.

2. Cover the hole with pieces of index card to create a vertical slit about 3/16-inch (5 mm) wide.

3. Tape these pieces lightly in place for now, because you may want to adjust the width of the slit before permanently securing them.

4. At the opposite end from the slit, cut an opening measuring about 2 × 2 inches (5 × 5 cm). If you're using a mailing tube, simply remove the cap at the far end.

5. Cover this opening with a slide-mounted grating or a piece of grating material cut from a sheet. It's important that the scratches on the grating are parallel to the slit in the other end of the tube or box, but you may not be able to judge this until you try out your device.

6. Tape the grating lightly in place for now, and move it if necessary as directed in Step 10.

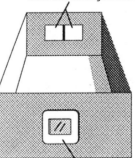

Index cards covering the hole to make a slit

Hole covered by diffraction grating

Etcetera

In addition to examining commonly available light sources, you might want to examine the spectra produced by specific gases. Power supplies and a variety of gas tubes are sold by scientific supply companies. Try to find a neon sign-making shop that gives tours, and see how the different gases that fill the glass tubes glow in different spectra.

7. If you are using a shoebox, put the top on the box.

8. Hold the shoebox or the tube so the slit is facing a light source. (Light from an ordinary lamp is a good starter.) Be sure the slit is oriented vertically.

9. Look through the diffraction grating into the box or the tube. You should see colors. The spectrum of the light source should extend to the left and right of the slit.

10. If you don't see the spectrum extending to both sides, the scratches on the grating are not parallel to the slit. Turn the grating one-quarter turn and look again. Adjust as necessary until the spectrum extends to the left and right of the vertical slit, and then tape the grating securely in place.

11. Adjust the slit width until you obtain a spectrum that is both reasonably bright and reasonably well defined.

The result is a simple spectroscope, a device used to form and examine the unique combination of colors that make up any light. These colors are called a spectrum (plural: spectra).

To Do and Notice

(30 minutes or more)

Compare the spectra of various sources: Different kinds of light will give you different spectra.

When you view different light sources, look for specific colors and notice the spacing between colored lines. The heated tungsten filament of an incandescent lightbulb produces a continuous spectrum, and one color shades into another. The electrically excited mercury vapor in a fluorescent bulb produces distinct colored lines; the phosphors that coat the inside of the bulb produce a continuous spectrum.

Some other suggested light sources are a candle flame, the flame from a Bunsen burner, a flashlight, a camping lantern, yellow streetlights (sodium produces the color), blue streetlights (mercury vapor produces the color), and neon signs.

Different light sources produce different spectra. You can see the solar spectrum by looking at sunlight reflecting off a piece of white paper. (Never look directly at the sun.)

When atoms of different materials are excited by electric current or another source of energy, they glow with a unique spectrum. Atoms of different elements have different colors in their spectra. These characteristic color patterns represent specific atoms just as fingerprints serve to identify specific people.

A diffraction grating acts like a prism, spreading light into its component colors. The light you see from a light source is the sum of all these colors. Each color corresponds to a different frequency of light. While prisms sort light by frequency, diffraction gratings sort light by wavelength, with violet light (the shortest wavelength of visible light) at one end of the spectrum and red light (the longest wavelength of visible light) at the other.

When atoms in a dilute gas (like the mercury vapor in a mercury street light) radiate light, the light can be seen through a diffraction grating as a line spectrum, made up of bright lines of color. Each line in the spectrum of such a gas corresponds to one frequency of light emission, and is produced by an electron changing energy levels in the atom.

In solids, liquids, and densely packed gases, the situation is not so simple. As atoms emit light, they collide with other atoms. This changes the frequency of the light each atom emits. That's why solids, liquids, and dense gases have broad bands of light in their spectra.

SPHERICAL REFLECTIONS
Discover art and science in a myriad of spherical reflections.

Materials

- ➜ Utility or X-Acto knife
- ➜ A sheet of Styrofoam (cooked oatmeal can be used as a more ecological substitute)
- ➜ A box with sides higher than the diameter of the balls
- ➜ Black construction paper or flat black latex paint (oil-based paint will dissolve the Styrofoam)
- ➜ Christmas-tree balls with mirror-reflective surfaces (any color will work; hooks and collars removed)

⚠ CAUTION

Be careful with glass!
Handling glass is always hazardous.

Introduction

Christmas-tree balls packed together in a box create an array of spherical reflectors. Each sphere reflects a unique image of the world. Study the properties of spherical mirrors while you create a colorful mosaic of reflections.

Assembly

(30 minutes or less)

1. Cut the Styrofoam to fit the bottom of the box. (If you prefer not to use Styrofoam, pour in freshly cooked oatmeal thick enough to embed the neck of each bulb—about 1/2 inch [1.25 cm] thick—and let cool.)

2. Cover the Styrofoam or oatmeal with a piece of black construction paper cut to size, or paint the Styrofoam or congealed oatmeal flat black.

3. Lay the Christmas-tree balls in the box in a single layer, packed as closely as possible.

4. Gently but firmly push the stem end of each ball into the Styrofoam or oatmeal so that it's held securely. If you're using construction paper instead of paint, push the stem end of each ball into the construction paper so that it makes a mark, then cut the paper at the marked points to make insertion into the foam easier, reducing the chance that a ball will shatter in your hand when you place it.

Etcetera

Convex mirrors are often used as security mirrors in stores, since they reveal a broad field of view. Convex rearview car mirrors have a written warning cautioning that objects are actually closer than they appear. Your brain assumes that when an object that is known to be large—a car, for instance—has a small image in a mirror, then the object is far away. In a convex mirror, however, an image that appears quite small can actually be very close.

Where the balls come together, light can reflect from one ball to another many times. This results in images of images of images, each becoming smaller and smaller. Looking into the spaces between Christmas-tree balls in an array is a good way to see a fractal pattern.

To Do and Notice

(5 minutes or more)

Look at the spherical mirrors from various angles. Notice that the image in each mirror is a little different from the image in the neighboring mirrors. That's because each mirror "sees" the world from a slightly different vantage point. Notice that if you point your finger at one sphere, the image of your finger in all the other mirrors will point at the chosen mirror.

Also notice that your image is very small in the mirrors, and that it appears quite far away.

What's Going On?

Each Christmas-tree ball is a convex mirror—a mirror that curves out toward the source of light. Convex mirrors reflect images that are smaller than life-sized.

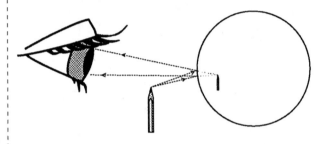

In the ray diagram shown here, notice the reflection of two rays of light from a particular point at the tip of the pencil. Your eye and brain follow these reflected rays backward along a straight line to their apparent intersection behind the mirror. All other reflected rays from the point also seem to originate at this intersection. The reflected rays from all other points on the pencil also appear to intersect at specific points behind the mirror. All these intersection points put together create what's called a virtual image.

TOUCH THE SPRING
You can see it, but you can't touch it!

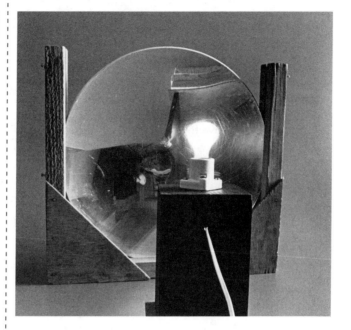

Introduction

You can place an object in front of a concave mirror so that it is not visible to the viewer, but the viewer can see the mirror image of the object formed in space. Try to touch the image and your hand moves right through what seems to be a solid object. This is a magician's illusion at its finest.

Assembly
(1 hour or less)

1. Make a small wooden box with one open side as shown in the drawing. The height of the box should be slightly less than half the height of the mirror, and it should be wide enough and deep enough to hold the lightbulb.

2. Paint all surfaces of the box black.

3. Mount the socket that has no electrical cord or plug so that it is centered on top of the box.

4. Mount the other socket (the one with the cord and plug) upside down inside the box, directly beneath the empty socket, as shown in the drawing.

5. Build the mirror support as shown in the drawing, and place the mirror in it. (Be careful! These mirrors are easily scratched.)

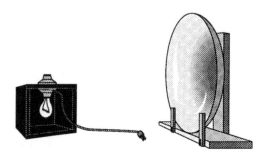

Materials

- Wood to build a support stand for the mirror and a small box for the lightbulb (see photo and drawings)
- Two light sockets, one with an electrical cord and plug
- One 3 × 5 inch (8 × 13 cm) file card
- A 16-inch (40 cm) diameter concave mirror, or you can use the bottom mirror from a commercially made Mirage Maker or Mind Boggling Optic Mirage, or the smaller, less-expensive 3-D Mirascope (all available from scientific supply houses and various vendors online)
- A lightbulb, 40 to 75 watts (if you are using the toy-sized 3-D Mirascope, however, be sure to use a flashlight bulb instead of a full-sized bulb)

Etcetera

Though we use a lightbulb here, you can also make a real image of a nonglowing object. (In the original Exploratorium exhibit, we used a spring as the object—hence the name of the Snack.)

A small plastic animal, like a toy cow or pig, can be fun to use. You can add an additional flourish by shining a flashlight onto the image of the toy animal. A spot of light will appear on the image! The mirror collects the light from the flashlight and then images it onto the real toy animal.

A closely related Exploratorium exhibit that you can create with the same concave mirror is called Shake Hands with Yourself. In this exhibit, your hand is placed two focal lengths from a concave mirror, resulting in a real, inverted image the same size as your hand. This image is also located two focal lengths from the mirror. Thus, your actual hand can touch the image of your hand, and you can "shake hands with yourself."

To Do and Notice

(30 minutes or more)

Plug in the lightbulb and place the box with its open side facing the mirror. To find the focal length of the mirror, place the mirror far from the lightbulb—at least 20 feet (6 m) away—so that its concave (hollow) side is facing the lightbulb. The mirror will then make a real image of the lightbulb close to the focal point of the mirror. Find the distance from the center of the mirror to the image of the lightbulb, and you will find the focal length of the mirror.

To find the location of the image, take the file card and hold it near the center of—and touching—the surface of the mirror. Move the card slowly away from the mirror. When the image of the bulb is in sharp focus, the card is near the mirror's focal point.

Place the mirror two focal lengths from the lightbulb. The concave mirror will reflect an image of the glowing bulb. This image will appear in space in front of the mirror. By carefully adjusting the vertical and horizontal position of the box, you can position the image so that it appears to be in the empty socket on top of the box. (You may have to place magazines or books under the box to adjust its height.)

The illusion works best in a darkened room. Have people stand back about 15 feet (5 m) so they see a bulb in the upper socket. Then have them move slowly toward the bulb. They may have to bend or straighten slightly or move right or left slightly to maintain an undistorted image. When they are about 6 feet (2 m) from the image of the bulb, pass your hand through it. The illusion of your hand passing right through a lightbulb is impressive, even when everything is out in the open.

In the Exploratorium exhibit, everything is inside a large cabinet. To touch the image, you must reach through a small opening. The cabinet hides all the clues and enhances the illusion but is a more elaborate construction project with associated storage problems.

What's Going On?

The image you see is formed by the concave spherical mirror. Light rays spreading out from one point on the lightbulb are reflected by the concave mirror so that they come back together at a point in space, creating a real image of that point.

The rays continue on through this convergence point and strike your eye. The lens of your eye brings the rays together once again to create an image on your retina. Your eye and brain can't tell the difference between a retinal image of the reflected bulb and a retinal image of the actual bulb.

In some respects, however, the reflected image of the lightbulb differs from the actual bulb. Placing an object behind the reflected image will obscure the lightbulb. Many people feel queasy when they see this seemingly unnatural occurrence.

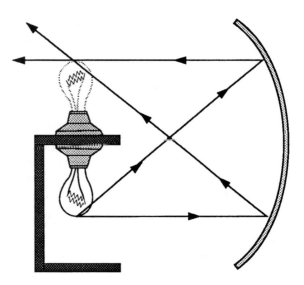

WATER SPHERE LENS
Make a lens and a magnifying glass by filling a bowl with water.

Materials

- A Florence (round-bottomed) flask or transparent spherical bowl, such as a fishbowl
- Water
- A candle or a clear light-bulb with socket
- A white card to use as a viewing screen
- A sheet of newspaper

Introduction

A round bowl of water can act as both a magnifier and a lens!

Assembly

Fill the flask or fishbowl with water to make a water-sphere lens.

To Do and Notice
(15 minutes or more)

Place the light source (lightbulb or candle) more than 1 foot (30 cm) from the water-sphere lens. Hold the white card against the side of the lens opposite the light source. Move the card away from the sphere until you see an image of the filament (or flame) on the card. Notice that the image is inverted.

Move the light source up and notice that its image moves down.

Move the light very close to the water sphere, and notice that you cannot find an image on the card at any distance.

Look through the water-sphere lens at a newspaper held close to the other side of the sphere. Notice that the sphere acts as a magnifying glass. Vary the light-to-lens distance and notice how the image-to-lens distance changes. Also notice how the image changes size.

⚠ CAUTION

Respect the sun!
If you use the sun as your light source, the focused sunlight may be hot enough to burn the paper card. Be careful!

What's Going On?

Light rays from the bulb or candle bend when they enter the water-filled sphere and bend again when they leave the sphere, as shown in the following diagram. The only light rays that don't bend are the ones that enter the sphere at a straight-on, 90-degree angle—that is, the ones that pass through the center of the bowl.

The sphere acts just like a lens, focusing the light that passes through into an image on the other side. The image must lie on a straight line from the object through the center of the lens.

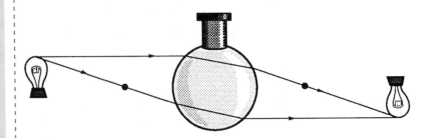

The image is upside down and reversed right to left. The motion of the image is also reversed: When the object moves up, the image moves down; when the object moves closer to the sphere, the image moves farther away. It might help to picture a seesaw: When one side moves up, the other side moves down.

Every lens has a focal point, which is a spot where light rays from far away converge after passing through the lens. The distance from the center of the lens to the focal point is called the focal length. Measure the focal length of your lens by finding a bright light source that's more than 30 feet (9 m) away. Using the white card, find the distance from the lens to the image. This is the focal length.

If an object is closer than one focal length to the center of the water-sphere lens, the lens can't bend the light rays from the object enough to bring them back together to form an image. However, when you look through the water-sphere lens at a nearby object, the lens of your eye can complete the bending, forming an image on your retina. The image on your retina made with the help of the water-sphere lens is larger than the largest image you could make with your eye alone. The water-sphere lens is thus a magnifying glass.

The image you see may be fuzzy and distorted, but should be recognizable. It also may show color distortion. The fuzziness is due to spherical aberration—a sphere is not the perfect shape for a lens; the colors are due to chromatic aberration—each different color of light bends by a different amount as it enters or leaves the lens.

PART FOUR   THE SPINNING BLACKBOARD AND OTHER DYNAMIC EXPLORATIONS OF FORCE AND MOTION

Chances are you know more about the principles of physics than you suspect. Just to get by in the world, you need to understand something about forces and how they affect motion.

Suppose, for example, you had a choice: You could stand in the path of a charging rhino, or you could stand in the path of a charging mouse. You surely know that it would be harder to stop the rhino than it would be to stop the mouse. That means you have an intuitive understanding of Newton's Second Law of Motion, which says that the force you need to make something slow down (or speed up) depends on how massive that something is. Because the rhino is considerably more massive than the mouse, it takes more force to stop it.

You rely on your knowledge of physics in many situations. Imagine that you had to balance on a narrow board and walk like a tightrope walker over a deep abyss. To help yourself balance, you'd probably stretch your arms out to the sides. You know that extending your arms makes balancing easier, even if you don't know why.

Or suppose the rear wheels of your car are stuck in an icy ditch. If you gun the engine, the wheels spin. Some friends come to help you push the car out, but even when you work together, you can't push the car out all at once. So you start rocking it. You push it forward, let it roll back, then push it forward again, matching the timing of your pushes to the rhythm of the car's movement. With each forward push, the car moves farther—until it finally rolls up out of the ditch. When you rock the car, you are applying a small force repeatedly at just the right time in order to cause a very large motion—a process physicists call resonance.

The experiments in this section are designed to help you examine some of the physical principles that you apply in your everyday life. With the Momentum Machine, for example, you can go for a spin and learn more about how changing your weight distribution can change your motion. You'll also find out why ice skaters and ballet dancers twirl faster when they pull their arms in.

Three experiments involving resonance—Resonant Pendulum, Resonant Rings, and Resonator—will help you understand how rocking a car helps you get it out of a ditch. Along the way, you'll also learn about one reason an earthquake may knock down some buildings and leave others standing. And with Bicycle Wheel Gyro, you can make a giant gyroscope from a bicycle wheel and experience firsthand the forces that a gyroscope exerts.

Taken together, the experiments in this section will help you understand some basic physical principles and link them to your existing knowledge of the world around you.

BALANCING BALL
Suspend a ball in a stream of air.

Materials

Small Version

- A hair dryer (blower)
- A spherical balloon or table tennis ball
- Tissue paper
- Optional: A stand for the blower, a partner

Large Version

- A vacuum cleaner such as a Shop-Vac, which has a reversible hose so it can be used as blower
- A lightweight vinyl beach ball
- Tissue paper
- Optional: A stand for the vacuum cleaner hose, a partner

Introduction

A ball stably levitated on an invisible stream of air is a dramatic sight. When you try to pull the ball out of the air stream, you can feel a force pulling it back in. You can also feel that the air stream is being deflected by the ball. This Snack shows the force that gives airplanes lift.

Assembly

None required. Note, though, that depending on the blower you choose, some experimentation may be necessary to find a satisfactory ball. You might want a partner to help you, or you can devise some sort of stand for the blower. That way, your hands will be free to experiment with the ball in the air stream.

To Do and Notice
(5 minutes or more)

Blow a stream of air straight up. Carefully balance the ball above the air stream. Pull it slowly out of the flow. Notice that when only half the ball is out of the air stream, you can feel it being sucked back in. Let go of the ball and notice that it oscillates back and forth and then settles down near the center of the air stream.

With one hand, pull the ball partially out of the air stream. With the other hand, dangle a piece of tissue paper and search for the air stream above the ball. Notice that the ball deflects the air stream outward. In the large version of this Snack, you can actually feel the deflected air stream hit your hand.

Tilt the air stream to one side and notice that the ball can still be suspended.

Balance the ball in the air stream and then move the blower and the ball toward a wall (try the corner of a room). Notice the great increase in the height of the suspended ball.

What's Going On?

When the ball is suspended in the air stream, the air flowing upward hits the bottom of the ball and slows down, generating a region of higher pressure. The high-pressure region of air under the ball holds the ball up against the pull of gravity.

When you pull the ball partially out of the air stream, the air flows around the curve of the ball that is nearest the center of the air stream. Air rushes in an arc around the top of the ball and then continues outward above the ball.

This outward-flowing air exerts an inward force on the ball, just like the downward flow of air beneath a helicopter exerts an upward force on the blades of the helicopter. This explanation is based on Newton's law of action and reaction.

Another way of looking at this is that as the air arcs around the ball, the air pressure on the ball decreases, allowing the normal atmospheric pressure of the calm air on the other side of the ball to push the ball back into the air stream.

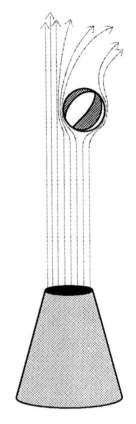

People immediately raise several questions when they hear the second explanation: Why does air flowing over a surface in an arc exert less pressure on that surface? To answer this question, consider a rider on a rollercoaster car going over the top of a hill at high speed. The force the rider exerts on the seat decreases as the car goes over the top of the hill. In the same way, the air that arcs around the side of the ball exerts less force on the ball.

Why does air follow the surface of the sphere? Consider what would happen if the air did not curve around the ball. An "air shadow" would be formed above the ball. This air shadow would be a region of low pressure. The air would then flow into the low-pressure air shadow. So the air flows around the ball.

An alternative explanation is provided by the Bernoulli principle. If you pull the ball far enough out of the air stream, then the air flows over only one side of the ball. In fact, the air stream speeds up as it flows around the ball. This is because the middle of the ball sticks farther into the air stream than the top or bottom. Since the same amount of air must flow past all parts of the ball each second, it must flow faster where it is pinched together at the middle. The Bernoulli principle states that where air speeds up, its pressure drops. The difference in pressure between the still air and the moving air pushes the ball back into the center of the air stream.

When you approach a wall with the balanced ball, the high-pressure region under the ball becomes a region of even higher pressure. The air that hits the bottom of the ball can no longer expand outward in the direction of the wall, so it drives the ball to a greater height.

BALANCING STICK
Does it matter which end is up?

Materials

➔ A lump of clay

➔ One 1/2-inch (1.25 cm) wooden dowel, approximately 3 feet (1 m) long

Introduction

The distribution of the mass of an object determines the position of its center of gravity, its angular momentum, and your ability to balance it!

Assembly
(5 minutes or less)

Place a lump of clay about the size of your fist 8 inches (20 cm) from the end of the dowel.

To Do and Notice
(5 minutes or more)

Balance the stick on the tip of your finger, putting your finger under the end that's near the clay. Now turn the stick over and balance it with the clay on the top. Notice that the stick is easier to balance when the clay is near the top.

What's Going On?

The dowel rotates more slowly when the mass is at the top, allowing you more time to adjust and maintain balance. When the mass is at the bottom, the stick has less rotational inertia and tips more quickly. The farther away the mass is located from the axis of rotation (such as in your hand), the greater the rotational inertia and the more

Etcetera

Instead of demonstrating the Snack in advance, give a group of people the clay and dowel separately, tell them to put the ball of clay on the dowel so the dowel sticks out at both ends, and challenge them to see who can balance the dowel the longest. Let them discover the role of the clay.

slowly the stick turns. An object with a large mass is said to have a great deal of inertia. Just as it is hard to change the motion of an object that has a large inertia, it is hard to change the rotational motion of an object with a large rotational inertia.

You can feel the change in inertia when you do the following experiment. Grab the end of the dowel that's near the clay. Hold the dowel vertically, and rapidly move the dowel back and forth with the same motion you would use to cast a fishing line. Next, turn the dowel upside down, and hold it at the end that is farthest from the clay. Repeat the casting motion. Notice that it is much harder to move the dowel rapidly when the clay is near the top. The mass of the stick has not changed, but the distribution of the mass of the stick with respect to your hand has changed. The rotational inertia depends on the distribution of the mass of the stick.

BERNOULLI LEVITATOR
Suspend an object in the air by blowing down on it.

Materials

Small Version

- Scissors
- Index card
- Pushpin or thumbtack
- Large wood or plastic thread spool
- Optional: Drinking straws, scissors

Large Version

- Scissors
- A cardboard box with one side somewhat larger than the plate
- A stiff paper or plastic plate
- Hair dryer or vacuum-cleaner blower
- Pushpin or thumbtack

NOTE

If more than one person is going to use this, construct the following sanitary version:

1. Cut a 2-inch (5 cm) long piece of straw for each person.

2. At each person's turn, have the participant push one end of the straw into the hole in the spool of thread.

3. If any straw does not fit, cut a 1/2-inch (1.25 cm) slit near the end of the straw (so the pieces can pinch together) and push the straw into the spool.

Introduction

The Bernoulli principle explains how atomizers work and why windows are sometimes sucked out of their frames as two trains rush past each other. You can choose from two versions of this Snack—a small personal-sized version or a large demonstration-sized version.

Assembly

Small Version
(5 minutes or less)

1. Trim an index card to a 3 × 3 inch (7.5 × 7.5 cm) square.

2. Push the pushpin into the card's center.

Large Version
(15 minutes or less)

1. Cut the flaps off the top of the box, and turn the box so that the opening faces to the side.

2. Put the side of the box that is larger than the plate on top, and cut a hole in the center slightly smaller than the outlet of the hair dryer or vacuum hose.

3. Stick a pushpin through the center of the plate and set this assembly inside the box.

To Do and Notice

Small Version

(5 minutes or more)

Hold the card against the bottom of the spool with the pushpin or thumbtack sticking into the spool's hole. The pushpin keeps the card from drifting off to the side.

Blow strongly through the hole in the top of the spool and let go of the card. If the card falls at first, experiment with different-sized cards or spools until you can make the card hang suspended beneath the spool.

Large Version

Turn on the blower and direct it down through the hole. If you use a vacuum cleaner, be sure to use it as a blower. If you use a hair dryer, turn the heat off if you can. (If you can't, the hair dryer may overheat and automatically turn off. It will work again as soon as it cools down.)

Bring the plate up toward the hole from below. Contrary to what you might expect, as the plate approaches the hole it will be sucked up and held in place by the air blowing down. The pushpin should keep the plate from drifting off to the side.

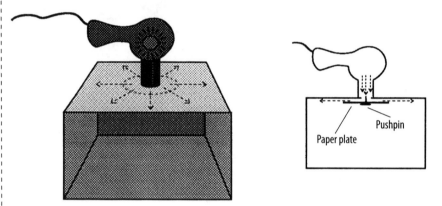

Paper plate

Pushpin

What's Going On?

When you blow into the spool or through the box, the air goes through the opening, hits the card or plate, and accelerates outward. The energy needed to accelerate the air comes from the energy stored as compression of the gas, so the gas expands and its pressure drops.

As air (or any other fluid) accelerates, its pressure drops. This is known as the Bernoulli principle. In the small version of this Snack, the air rushing between the spool and the card exerts less pressure above the card than the still air underneath the card. The still air pushes the card toward the spool and holds the card up against gravity. In the larger version, the same principle is at work, holding the plate up against the hole in the box.

BICYCLE WHEEL GYRO
A bicycle wheel acts like a giant gyroscope.

Materials
- Two handles (plastic handles from a hardware store work perfectly and are cheap; get the kind of handle that's designed to screw onto a file)
- A bicycle wheel (cheap or free from a thrift shop, bike store, or friend)
- A low-friction rotating stool or platform (typing or computer chairs often work well)
- A partner
- Optional: Eyebolt, drill, spoke guards, chain or rope suspended from a large stand or a ceiling

Introduction

A spinning bicycle wheel resists efforts to tilt it and point the axle in a new direction. Any rapidly spinning wheel exhibits this gyroscopic property. In this Snack, you can use this tendency to take yourself for a spin.

Assembly

(15 minutes or less)

1. Screw the handles onto each side of the wheel's axle. You may have to remove the outer nuts to clear enough axle for the handles. You may want to put plastic spoke guards on the hubs first to protect your fingers from the spinning wheel.

2. If you have the eyebolt, drill a hole in the end of one handle for it.

3. Mount the screw eye in the hole.

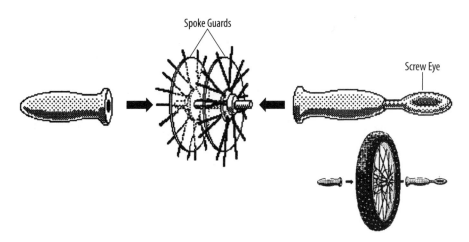

Spoke Guards

Screw Eye

Etcetera

Astronauts have experimented with toy gyroscopes in the weightless environment of the space shuttle. Even when an astronaut gave the spinning gyro a shove, the toy's axle stubbornly resisted changing direction.

Spacecraft use small gyroscopes to sense their orientation in space. When the spacecraft turns, a freely floating gyroscope will not turn with it. Larger gyroscopes are also used to change the orientation of the spacecraft. The spacecraft can exert a torque on a rapidly spinning, massive gyroscope, which will in turn exert an equal and opposite torque on the spacecraft, causing it to turn.

To Do and Notice

(15 minutes or more)

Hold the wheel by the handles while another person gets it spinning as fast as possible. Sit on the stool with your feet off the floor, and tilt the wheel. If the stool has sufficiently low friction, it should start to turn. Tilt the wheel in the other direction and see what happens.

Get the wheel spinning, and then use the eyebolt in the end of the handle to hang the wheel from a hook mounted to the free end of a chain or rope. Hold the wheel so that the axle is horizontal, then release it. The axle will remain more or less horizontal while it moves slowly in a circle.

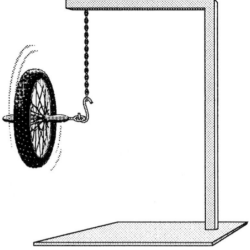

If you don't have a chain or rope, rest the eyebolt on your fingertips. Be sure to practice this before you try a demonstration. You will have to move with the wheel as it slowly turns in a circle.

What's Going On?

A rotating bicycle wheel has angular momentum, which is a property involving the speed of rotation, the mass of the wheel, and how the mass is distributed. For example, most of a bicycle wheel's mass is concentrated along the wheel's rim, rather than at the center, and this causes a larger angular momentum at a given speed. Angular momentum is characterized by both size and direction.

The bicycle wheel, you, and the chair form a system that obeys the principle of conservation of angular momentum. This means that any change in angular momentum within the system must be accompanied by an equal and opposite change, so the net effect is zero.

Suppose you are now sitting on the stool with the bicycle wheel spinning. One way to change the angular momentum of the bicycle wheel is to change its direction. To do this, you must exert a twisting force, called a torque, on the wheel. The bicycle wheel will then exert an equal and opposite torque on you. (That's because for every action there is an equal and opposite reaction.) Thus, when you twist the bicycle wheel in space, the bicycle wheel will twist you the opposite way. If you are sitting on a low-friction pivot, the twisting force of the bicycle wheel will cause you to turn. The change in angular momentum of the wheel is compensated for by your own change in angular momentum. The system as a whole ends up obeying the principle of conservation of angular momentum.

Unfortunately, the gyroscopic precession of the wheel hanging from the rope is not explainable in as straightforward a manner as the rotating stool effect. However, the effect itself is well worth experiencing, even though its explanation is too difficult to undertake here. For more information, consult any college physics text on the subject of precession.

BUBBLE SUSPENSION
Soap bubbles float on a cushion of carbon dioxide gas.

Materials
- Dry ice
- A small aquarium
- Leather gloves (thicker is better to protect from the dry ice)
- Bubble solution—you can use a commercial solution such as Wonder Bubbles, or make your own using the Exploratorium's recipe: Gently mix 2/3 cup (160 mL) Dawn dishwashing liquid and 1 tablespoon (15 mL) glycerin (available at most drugstores) with 1 gallon (3.8 L) of water
- Bubble wand

NOTE
If you have trouble making good bubbles, try using distilled water instead of tap water. Aging the solution for at least a day before use significantly increases the lifetime of the bubbles.

⚠ CAUTION
Use protective gloves when handling dry ice! Never touch it with your bare skin.

Introduction
This beautiful investigation illustrates the principles of buoyancy and semipermeability.

Assembly
(5 minutes or more)

Put on protective gloves, and then place a slab of dry ice flat in the bottom of the aquarium. Allow a few minutes for a layer of carbon dioxide gas to accumulate.

To Do and Notice
(15 minutes or more)

Blow bubbles so they float down into the aquarium. The bubbles will descend and then hover on the denser layer of carbon dioxide gas accumulating above the dry ice. After a few minutes, notice that the bubbles begin to expand and sink. Notice how some of the bubbles freeze on the dry ice.

What's Going On?
As dry ice turns from a solid to a vapor, or sublimes, it produces carbon dioxide gas. Carbon dioxide is denser than air. (Carbon dioxide molecules have an atomic mass of

Etcetera

You can do many experiments to show some of the interesting features of bubbles. Here are two:

What happens when bubbles of different sizes collide? Sometimes they make a single larger bubble, other times they join as two bubbles with a flat or bulging wall between them. If the two bubbles are the same size, the wall is flat between them, because the pressure is equal on both sides. If the two bubbles are of different sizes, the wall will bulge away from the smaller of the two bubbles because the smaller bubble will have a higher pressure inside.

How does a bubble respond to a comb that has been charged by rubbing it with a wool cloth? The near side of the bubble is given an opposite charge by the comb as ions in the bubble with the same charge as the comb are driven to the far side. The bubble is then said to be electrically polarized. The electrically polarized bubble is then attracted to the comb.

44 amu [atomic mass units]. Air is made up mostly of nitrogen, 28 amu, and oxygen, 32 amu.) The denser carbon dioxide gas forms a layer on the bottom of the aquarium.

A bubble is full of air. It floats on the carbon dioxide layer, just like a helium balloon floating in the air. You might expect that the air in the bubble would cool and contract near the dry ice, but the bubble actually expands slightly. The soapy wall of the bubble allows carbon dioxide to pass through but keeps air molecules inside. Initially, the concentration of carbon dioxide gas is low inside the bubble and high outside the bubble.

The gas gradually diffuses into the bubble, a process called osmosis. The bubble film is a semipermeable membrane—a surface that allows some substances to pass through while preventing others from doing so at all. The cells in your body have the same property. Water, oxygen, and carbon dioxide easily enter some cells, whereas other molecules do not. The added carbon dioxide makes the bubble denser, causing it to gradually sink. The carbon dioxide at the bottom of the tank is cold enough to freeze the bubble.

BUBBLE TRAY
Create giant bubbles!

Materials

- Bubble solution—you can use a commercial solution such as Wonder Bubbles, or make your own using the Exploratorium's recipe: Gently mix 2/3 cup (160 mL) Dawn dishwashing liquid and 1 tablespoon (15 mL) glycerin (available at most drugstores) with 1 gallon (3.8 L) of water
- Wire coat hanger
- Shallow tub or tray about 18 inches (45 cm) in diameter, such as a potted-plant drain dish, pizza pan, or cafeteria tray
- Optional: Yarn

NOTE

If you have trouble making good bubbles, try using distilled water instead of tap water. Aging the solution for at least a day before use significantly increases the lifetime of the bubbles.

Introduction

Bubbles are fascinating. What gives them their shape? What makes them break or last? What causes the colors and patterns in the soap film, and why do they change?

Assembly

(5 minutes or less; 30 minutes or less using yarn)

Bend the coat hanger into a flat hoop with the hook sticking up at an angle to serve as a handle. Bubbles will form more consistently when the hoop is as circular as possible. If you wrap yarn tightly around the wire of the hoop, the yarn will absorb the bubble solution, which will make the hoop easier to use.

To Do and Notice

(15 minutes or more)

Fill the shallow tray with bubble solution and submerge the hoop in it. Tilt the hoop toward you until it's almost vertical, and then gently lift it from the tray. You should have a bubble film extending across the hoop. Swing the hoop through the air to make a giant bubble. When you have a big bubble, twist the hoop to seal it off at the end.

What shapes do the bubbles take once they are free of the hoop? What roles do convection and air currents play in a bubble's movement? Look for patterns and colors in the bubbles. Dip the hoop in the solution and hold the film up to the light without forming a bubble. What patterns (and changes in patterns) do you observe?

Etcetera

You can make a variety of devices to create large bubbles. One of the easiest is a length of string (or, still better, fuzzy yarn) threaded through two drinking straws, with the ends tied to make a loop any size you want. Not only will this device make large bubbles, but you can twist the straws to make film surfaces with different shapes.

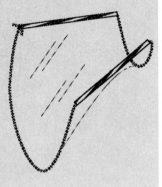

What's Going On?

The strong mutual attraction of water molecules for each other is known as surface tension. Normally, surface tension makes it impossible to stretch the water out to make a thin film. Soap reduces surface tension and allows a film to form. Because of surface tension, a soap film always pulls in as tightly as it can, just like a stretched balloon.

A soap film makes the smallest possible surface area for the volume it contains. If the bubble is floating in the air and makes no contact with other objects, it will form a sphere, because a sphere is the shape that has the smallest surface area compared to its volume. (Wind or vibration may distort the sphere.)

The patterns of different colors in a soap bubble are caused by interference. Light waves reflected from the inner and outer surfaces of the soap film interfere with each other constructively or destructively, depending on the thickness of the bubble and the wavelength (that is, the color) of the light. For example, if the soap film is thick enough to cause waves of red light to interfere destructively with each other, the red light is eliminated, leaving only blue and green to reach your eyes.

CENTER OF GRAVITY
How to balance a checkbook using the physics method.

Etcetera

Often, an object's center of gravity is also the center of its length. The next time you need to carry something uniformly long and thin—like a wooden pole or a length of pipe or metal (or, if you're a tightrope walker, that really long balancing stick)—finding the center of gravity by sliding your hands together near the middle of the object can also help you find its center. If you need to carry shorter lengths in your car, you can find the approximate center of the material this way, have it cut, and be confident that you've got two roughly equal-sized pieces

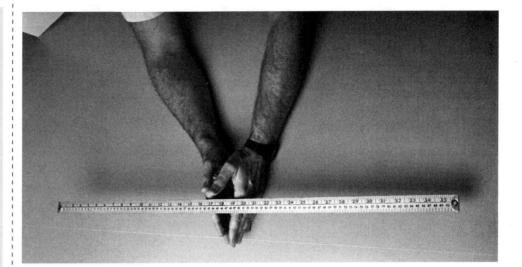

Introduction

Here's an easy way to find the center of gravity of a long, thin object, even if the object's weight is unevenly distributed.

Assembly

(None needed)

To Do and Notice

(5 minutes or more)

Support the stick by resting each of its ends on a finger. Slowly slide your fingers together until they meet. Your fingers will meet under the stick's center of gravity.

Attach the weight or a piece of clay to some point on the stick. Again support the stick on two fingers, and then slide your fingers together to locate the new center of gravity. Move the weight or piece of clay to some new place on the stick. Repeat the experiment. Your fingers will always meet right under the center of gravity.

The stick's center of gravity is the place where you could balance the stick on just one finger. When you first support the stick with two fingers, in general one finger (the one that is closer to the center of gravity) will be holding a little more of the weight than the other. When you try to move your fingers closer together, the one that is carrying less weight will slide more easily. This finger will continue to slide more easily until it gets closer to the center of gravity than the other finger, at which point the situation will reverse and the other finger will begin to slide faster. Your left and right fingers simply alternate moving until they meet at the center of gravity, where both fingers support equal weight.

COUPLED RESONANT PENDULUMS
These pendulums trade swings back and forth.

Materials

- A piece of string about 3 feet (1 m) long
- Two ring stands or other vertical supports for the string
- Two plastic 35 mm film cans, empty pill bottles, or similar containers
- Something to punch a hole with, such as a nail
- Two pieces of metal coat-hanger wire, each about 8 inches (20 cm) long
- Clay, coins, or washers for mass

Introduction

Two pendulums suspended from a common support will swing back and forth in intriguing patterns if the support allows the motion of one pendulum to influence the motion of the other.

Assembly

(30 minutes or less)

1. Stretch and secure the string between two ring stands placed about 20 to 30 inches (50 to 75 cm) apart.

2. In the center of each film can lid, punch a hole just large enough to insert one end of a coat-hanger wire.

3. Bend the end of the inserted wire so the lid won't slide off, but you can still put the lid on the can.

4. Bend the other end of the wire so it will hang freely from the string. The two hangers should be close to the same length.

5. Add equal amounts of clay, coins, or washers to each can and attach the lids.

6. Hang the pendulums so they are about equally spaced from each other and from the ring stands.

⚠ CAUTION

Be careful with metal!
The sharp ends of a wire can give you a very nasty cut.

Etcetera

It's easy to predict how often the two swinging cans will trade energy. Count the total number of swings per minute when you start both pendulums together and they swing back and forth, side by side. Compare that to the number of swings per minute when you start them opposite one another—that is, with one pulled forward and one pulled backward an equal distance from the string, and then released at the same time. The difference between those two numbers exactly equals the number of times per minute that the pendulums pass the energy back and forth if you start just one pendulum while the other hangs at rest. Physicists call these two particular motions normal modes of the two-pendulum system, and they call the difference between the frequencies of the normal modes a beat frequency.

To Do and Notice

(15 minutes or more)

Gently pull one pendulum back a short distance and let it go. As it swings back and forth, notice that the other pendulum also begins to move, picking up speed and amplitude with each swing. Notice that the pendulum you originally moved slows down with each swing and eventually stops, leaving the second pendulum briefly swinging by itself. But then the process begins to reverse, and soon the first pendulum is swinging again while the second one is stopped. The pendulums repeatedly transfer the motion back and forth between them this way as long as they continue to swing.

Experiment with different wire lengths and with different string tensions to produce more strongly or weakly interdependent coupled pendulums.

What's Going On?

Every pendulum has a natural or resonant frequency, which is the number of times it swings back and forth per second. The resonant frequency depends on the pendulum's length. Longer pendulums have lower frequencies.

Every time the first pendulum swings, it pulls on the connecting string and gives the second pendulum a small tug. Since the two pendulums have the same length, the pulls of the first pendulum on the second occur exactly at the natural frequency of the second pendulum, so it (the second pendulum) begins to swing too. However, the second pendulum will swing slightly out of phase with the first one. When the first pendulum is at the height of its swing, the second pendulum is still somewhere in the middle of its swing.

As soon as the second pendulum starts to swing, it starts pulling back on the first pendulum. These pulls are timed so that the first pendulum slows down. To picture this, it may help you to think of a playground swing. When you push on the swing at just the right moments, it goes higher and higher. When you push the swing at just the wrong moments, it slows down and stops. The second pendulum pulls on the first pendulum at just the "wrong" moments.

Eventually, the first pendulum is brought to rest; it has transferred all of its energy to the second pendulum. But now the original situation is exactly reversed, and the first pendulum is in a position to begin stealing energy back from the second. And so it goes, the energy repeatedly switching back and forth until friction and air resistance finally steal all of it away from both pendulums.

If the two pendulums are not the same length, then the tugs from the first pendulum's swings will not occur at the natural frequency of the second one. The two pendulums swing, but with an uneven, jerky motion.

DESCARTES DIVER

To paraphrase French philosopher René Descartes:
"I sink, therefore I am."

Materials

- Cup
- Water
- Several squeeze-condiment packets (soy sauce, ketchup, mustard, and so on)
- Clear plastic bottle with screw-on cap

BONUS!

Another simple diver can be made with a transparent plastic drinking straw (so you can see the water level inside—otherwise, any plastic straw will do), a tall cup of water, a water-filled plastic bottle, and a handful of paperclips. First cut the straw in half. Take one of the pieces, bend it in half, and insert enough paper clips (about 5 or 6, depending on the clips you're using) so the ends of the straw are held together and the assembly barely floats, paper-clip-end down, when dropped in a tall cup of water (adjust as necessary). Then drop the assembly into the water-filled plastic bottle. Make sure the bottle is absolutely full, tighten the cap, and squeeze to make the diver sink; release to make it rise again. The closer the straw is to being almost completely submerged at the start, the less you have to squeeze the bottle to get the diver to sink.

Introduction

Changes in fluid pressure affect the buoyancy of a Cartesian diver—made from a condiment packet! The diver floats, sinks, or hovers in response to pressure changes.

Assembly

(15 minutes or less)

1. Fill a cup with water and drop in your packets, one by one, to see how they'll work. The best packets to use in this Snack are the ones that just barely float.

2. After you've found the proper packet, fill an empty, clear plastic bottle to the very top with water. Shove your unopened condiment packet into the plastic bottle. Replace the cap and you're done!

To Do and Notice

(10 minutes or more)

Squeeze the plastic bottle to make the diver sink, and release it to make it rise.

Etcetera

If you want a challenge, try to make a diver that stays at the bottom when you stop squeezing the bottle. As the diver sinks, the pressure outside the packet increases slightly with the water's depth. This increase is in addition to the increase in the pressure you cause by squeezing the bottle. When the diver reaches the bottom and you stop squeezing, the pressure resulting from the increase in depth remains and continues to compress the air bubble a little. If the diver has been carefully balanced initially, so that it just barely floats, this small compression of the bubble will be enough to keep the diver submerged.

Change the shape of the diving bottle, and you can get an additional effect. If you use a thin, flat plastic bottle (like from shampoo or mouthwash), squeezing the different-shaped sides changes what happens inside the bottle. Choose a diver that just barely floats, put it in a bottle filled completely with water, and put the cap on. Squeeze on the wide sides of the bottle and you make the volume inside smaller: the pressure inside the bottle goes up, compressing the air bubble in the diver, and the diver sinks and remains on the bottom (as it does in the preceding activity). Squeeze on the narrow sides of the bottle and you make the volume inside larger: The pressure inside the bottle goes down, allowing the air bubble in the diver to expand, and the diver rises. With a round bottle, you won't be able to get the diver to rise again once it's on the bottom.

What's Going On?

The key to making this work is to choose a condiment-packet diver that barely floats. This works because, while many sauces are denser than water, it's actually the air bubble sealed inside the packet that determines whether it will sink or swim. Squeezing the bottle increases pressure on the condiment package, compressing the air bubble inside. When the higher pressure compresses the air in the packet, the packet displaces less water, thus decreasing its buoyancy and causing it to sink. When you release the sides of the bottle, the pressure decreases, and the air inside the packet expands once again. The packet's buoyancy increases, and the diver rises.

The Greek philosopher Archimedes was the first person to notice that the upward force that water exerts on an object, whether floating or submerged, is equal to the weight of the volume of water that the object displaces. That is, the buoyant force is equal to the weight of the displaced water.

DOWNHILL RACE

Two cylinders that look the same may roll down a hill at different rates.

Materials

- Two identical round metal cookie tins (such as those from butter cookies)
- Ten large metal washers about 1/4 pound (112 g) each (you might be able to use ten heavy-duty refrigerator magnets that will stick to the cookie tins)
- Double-sided foam stick-on tape or adhesive-backed Velcro
- A ramp

Introduction

Two objects with the same shape and the same mass may behave differently when they roll down a hill. How quickly an object accelerates depends partly on how its mass is distributed. A cylinder with a heavy hub accelerates more quickly than a cylinder with a heavy rim.

Assembly

(15 minutes or less)

1. Arrange five of the washers evenly around the bottom of one tin (see photo), pushed up against the outside rim.
2. Stack five washers in the middle of the bottom of the second tin (see photo).
3. Secure the washers with tape or Velcro. (If you're using magnets, they may stay in place without additional adjustment.)
4. Put the tops back on the tins.

To Do and Notice

(15 minutes or more)

Place both tins at the top of the ramp. Be sure the tops are on. Ask your friends to predict which tin will reach the bottom of the ramp first. Release the tins and let them roll down the ramp. The tin with the mass closer to the center will always reach the bottom first.

Etcetera

The use of lightweight "mag" wheels on cars is related to translational and rotational kinetic energy. Imagine that you had two cars of equal overall mass, but one had lightweight mag wheels and a heavy chassis, and the other had heavy steel wheels and a light chassis. Given the same energy input, the mag-wheel car would accelerate more rapidly, because less of the energy supplied would be needed to get the wheels rotating, and more would therefore appear as straight-line motion of the car as a whole.

It's also interesting to experiment with rolling cans of soup down an inclined plane. Solid soups roll down the incline at a slower rate than liquid soups. The liquid does not have to rotate with the can, so the potential energy of the liquid soup can go into linear motion, not into rotation of the soup.

What's Going On?

At the top of the ramp, both tins have identical potential energy, since both have the same mass and are at the same height. At the bottom of the ramp, each tin will have part of its original potential energy appearing as linear (or translational) kinetic energy and the rest appearing as rotational kinetic energy.

Though both tins have the same total mass, each has this mass distributed differently. It's harder to get the tin with its mass distributed along the rim rotating than it is to get the tin with its mass concentrated at the center rotating. The tin with its mass at the rim will use more of its original potential energy just to get rolling than will the tin with its mass concentrated at the center. Therefore the tin with its mass at the rim has less energy available to appear as translational kinetic energy, resulting in a lower linear speed. The tin with its mass concentrated around the rim will lose the race to the bottom of the ramp, and the tin with its mass concentrated at the center will win.

DRAWING BOARD

A pendulum moving in two directions creates beautiful designs.

Introduction

The Drawing Board consists of a marking pen that remains stationary and a platform that swings beneath the pen, acting as a pendulum. As the platform swings, the pen marks a sheet of paper that is fastened to the platform, generating beautiful, repetitive patterns, which grow smaller with each repetition. These colorful designs contain hidden lessons in physics.

Assembly

Rather than attempting to give detailed instructions for assembling this device, we have chosen instead to supply some close-up photos and helpful hints. The rest is left to the dedicated experimenter.

The penholder must be counterbalanced so that the pen exerts minimum pressure on the moving board while maintaining constant contact with the writing surface. The size and orientation of the pieces at the back end of the pen assembly can be adjusted to achieve a suitable balance.

To make the pen assembly shown in the photos, the pivot hole was drilled about 10 inches (25 cm) from the pen end. If the hole is drilled at a different location, the size and location of the mass at the far end of the arm should be adjusted accordingly.

The platform must have sufficient mass so that its motion does not die down too quickly. The platform shown in the photos is a 10 inch × 10 inch (25 cm × 25 cm) piece of half-inch particleboard, which has a significant mass. If a lighter platform is used, a

- Eight half-inch PVC 90-degree elbows (to connect parts of the frame and the swing-arm; see photo)
- Three half-inch PVC Ts (one to hold the marking pen; two to connect the vertical frame to the horizontal base)
- One wooden dowel (3/16 inch), cut to about 6 inches (15 cm) long (for drawing-arm pivot)
- Two half-inch PVC crosses (supports for the hanging platform)
- Five large binder clips (four to anchor strings; one to hold paper to platform)
- Two mini or micro binder clips (to anchor dowel in drawing arm)
- Four screw eyes (to connect string to hanging platform)
- Ruler
- Electric drill
- Drill bit, 13/64 inch
- PVC cutter, hacksaw blade, or other way to cut PVC pipe
- Paper (anything will work, including clean sides of used copy paper)
- Marking pens (Sharpie fine-point markers or similar), assorted colors
- Four pieces of string, each approximately 2 feet (60 cm) long; cut off extra after assembly if necessary
- A 10 × 10 inch (25 × 25 cm) platform board of some sort—particle board, plywood, or similar (see Assembly)
- Optional: Masking tape to wrap around pen if needed for fit.

mass can be affixed to the platform. If the location of the mass is adjustable, you may find that its placement will affect the pattern obtained.

The Drawing Board should produce a pattern that repeats the same basic shape over and over again, with each cycle getting smaller. If the pattern is not consistent from one cycle to the next, try adjusting the counterbalance weight on the penholder. Experiment to see what works best.

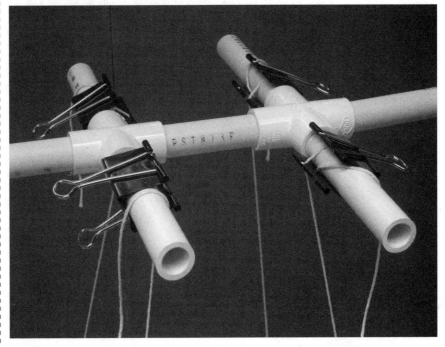

Using binder clips allows you to adjust the four pieces of string so that the drawing platform hangs level.

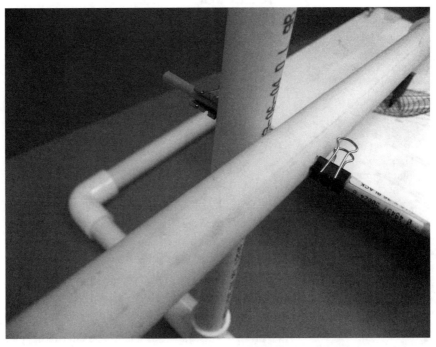

The wooden dowel for the drawing arm pivot is held in place with two mini or micro binder clips.

Etcetera

Some of the shapes you will produce with the Drawing Board are known as harmonograms, or Lissajous figures. An oscilloscope can easily produce these figures because the pattern on the scope face is generated by a single electron beam simultaneously moving vertically and horizontally on the screen. An oscilloscope can be thought of as an electronic Etch-a-Sketch.

One of our teachers had this Snack set up and running during an aftershock of California's 1989 Loma Prieta earthquake. The pen traced the pattern of motion generated by the aftershock. The operating principle behind the Drawing Board—a pen directly attached to the earth with a paper only loosely attached to the earth—is the operating principle behind the seismograph.

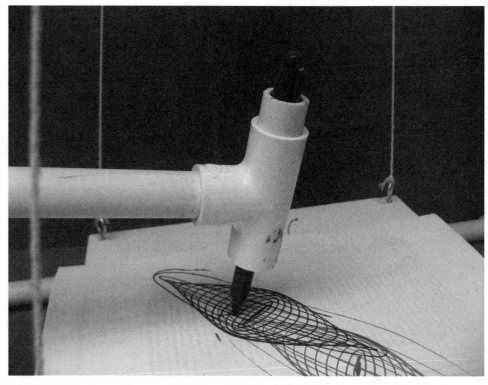

A standard Sharpie marking pen will fit into the half-inch PVC T pipe, but you can modify the holder to suit any size felt-tip marker. You can also fit the pen by wrapping it with masking tape.

To Do and Notice

(15 minutes or more)

Once the Drawing Board is adjusted, you can create wonderfully intricate designs. Push the board to start rotational as well as translational motion; lower the pen to start drawing and raise it to stop. Try drawing one to four patterns on the same paper using pens of different colors, changing the direction and force of the push with each new color.

What's Going On?

When you push on the platform, displacing it from its resting position, the four suspending strings exert forces on it to bring it back. You can think of these forces as acting in two directions perpendicular to each other: north-south and east-west, for example. The combination of these two simultaneous motions can produce a variety of curved forms, in the same way that careful use of the two knobs on an Etch-a-Sketch toy allows you to draw curves.

The diminishing size of each successive repetition of the pattern is a graphic demonstration of how friction steadily dissipates the energy of a moving object.

MOMENTUM MACHINE

How ice skaters, divers, and gymnasts get themselves spinning and twisting faster.

Materials

- → A rotating stool or chair
- → Two heavy masses (two bricks will do, but steel is even better); use the heaviest weights you can support at arm's length
- → A partner

⚠ CAUTION

What goes around may not come around!

A rapid spin may cause the chair to tip over! Be sure to grip the masses securely during the spin and after. Also, you may be dizzy when you get up, so be careful. Remember that you're holding heavy weights.

Introduction

You've probably seen an ice skater spinning on the tip of one skate suddenly start to spin dramatically faster. A diver or gymnast may also suddenly flip or twist much faster. This speeded-up rotation results from a sudden redistribution of mass. You can make yourself suddenly spin faster while sitting in a rotating chair.

Assembly

None required.

To Do and Notice

(5 minutes or more)

1. Sit in a chair with one of the masses in each hand and arms outstretched.

2. Have your partner start rotating you slowly, then have that person let go and move away.

3. Quickly pull the masses inward and notice that you rotate faster.

What's Going On?

Newton found that an object in motion tended to remain in motion, in a straight line and at a constant speed, unless it was acted upon by a net force. Today, we call this observation the law of conservation of momentum. The momentum of an object is the product of its mass and its velocity.

Etcetera

One method dancers and skaters use to avoid getting dizzy when they spin is called "spotting." As they begin spinning, they pick an object a fair distance away, look directly at it for as long as they can, and turn their head only when they have to, finding that same object again as they come back around. If you watch someone doing this, you can see that the person's body turns, and then the head follows, whipping around to find the object being spotted once again.

Your body senses balance and motion through the vestibular system, which is part of your inner ear. There, hair-like sensors react to the sloshing of surrounding fluid, which gives your brain information about your orientation with respect to gravity. The technique of spotting minimizes continuous motion of the head and gives that sloshing fluid a moment to settle down before it's set moving again. Try a gentle spin with and without spotting (preferably somewhere near a handy chair) and see how well it works for you.

There is an equivalent law for rotating objects. A rotating object tends to remain rotating with a constant angular momentum unless it is acted upon by an outside twisting force. The definition of angular momentum is more complex than that of linear momentum. Angular momentum is the product of two quantities known as angular velocity and moment of inertia. Angular velocity is merely velocity measured in degrees, or radians-per-second, rather than meters-per-second.

Moment of inertia depends on both the mass of an object and on how that mass is distributed. The farther from the axis of rotation the mass is located, the larger the moment of inertia. So your moment of inertia is smaller when your arms are held at your sides and larger when your arms are extended straight out.

If the motion of a rotating system is not affected by an outside twisting force, then angular momentum is conserved for this system, which means that the angular momentum stays the same.

A person sitting on a rotating chair or stool approximates a system in which angular momentum is conserved. The friction of the bearings on the chair stem serves as an outside twisting force, but this force is usually fairly low for such chairs. Because angular momentum is conserved, the product of angular velocity and moment of inertia must remain constant. This means that if one of these factors is increased, the other must decrease, and vice versa. If you're initially rotating with your arms outstretched, then when you draw your arms inward, your moment of inertia decreases. This means that your angular velocity must increase, and you spin faster.

The conservation of angular momentum explains why ice skaters start to spin faster when they suddenly draw their arms inward, or why divers or gymnasts who decrease their moment of inertia by going into the "tuck" position start to flip or twist at a faster rate.

NON-ROUND ROLLERS

A flat panel rolls smoothly on non-circular rollers, providing a decidedly counterintuitive experience.

Materials

- → Access to a photocopier
- → Glue, tape, or stapler
- → File folders, poster board, or similar stiff material
- → Scissors
- → Metric ruler
- → Drawing compass
- → A piece of poster board or Masonite, about 6 × 18 inches (15 × 45 cm)

Introduction

The most common closed and curved plane figure that has a constant width as it rotates is the circle. Surprisingly, however, there are other figures that have this property. They have a variety of shapes that you can construct with a compass and straightedge. The rollers you can build with this Snack behave in seemingly paradoxical ways.

Assembly

In this Snack, we offer several options. You can use a predrawn template to build a simple non-round roller (Version 1), perform the geometric constructions for the rollers yourself (Version 2), or construct simple non-round rollers of your own design (Version 3).

Version 1: Predrawn Template for a Simple Non-Round Roller

(30 minutes or less to make a set of two or three rollers)

1. Photocopy the patterns in Figure 1.

2. Glue the entire photocopied sheet to stiffer material (file folder or poster board).

3. Cut out the patterns. The large pattern is the axle, and the two smaller ones are the ends.

4. Fold the axle on the horizontal lines to make a triangular prism.

5. Fold Tab A over area A, and glue or tape them together.

6. Fold the axle flanges x and y outward.

7. Staple or glue the axle flanges to the corresponding lettered areas on the ends.

8. Make two or three of these rollers.

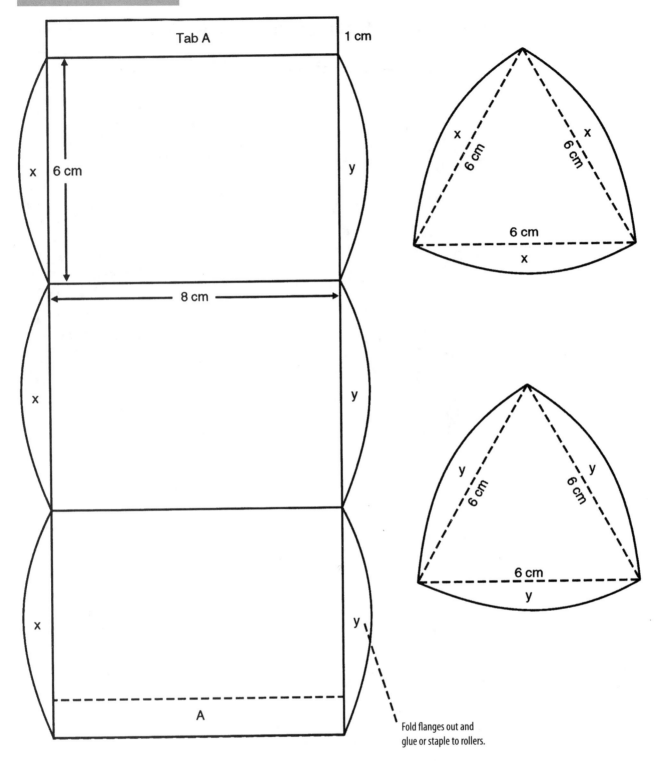

Tab A

1 cm

x   6 cm

8 cm

x   y

x   y

A

y

x   6 cm   6 cm   x

6 cm
x

y   6 cm   6 cm   y

6 cm
y

Fold flanges out and
glue or staple to rollers.

Figure 1. Pattern for simple non-round roller

Version 2: Geometric Constructions for a Simple Non-Round Roller
(1 hour or less)

1. Follow Steps 1–4 in Figure 2 to construct an equilateral triangle with circular arcs connecting its vertices. We suggest you start with a triangle about 2 inches (5 cm) on a side. After you are familiar with the process, you can make larger versions. This particular constant-width, non-round roller is called a Reuleaux triangle.

2. On a piece of file folder, draw four identical Reuleaux triangles and cut them out. These will serve as the wheels for a set of two rollers.

3. To make an axle, draw a rectangle measuring 3 inches × 6 inches (8 cm × 15 cm) on another piece of file folder. Divide this into three smaller rectangles, each measuring 3 inches × 2 inches (8 cm × 5 cm). On one end, add a 1/2 × 3 inch (1 cm × 8 cm) tab.

4. Finally, use the compass to make three arcs of radius 2 inches (5 cm) along each side of the three rectangles. Your drawing should be identical to the drawing in Figure 1.

5. Draw and cut out two or three rollers. Assemble as noted in Version 1.

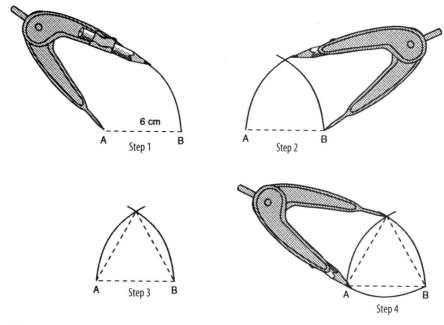

Figure 2

Version 3: Geometric Construction of a General Case of Non-Round Rollers
(1 hour or less)

Non-round, constant-width rollers of many different shapes can be made as noted in the following set of steps and shown in Figure 3. You'll need to build two or three of these rollers.

1. Draw a triangle of any size on a piece of cardboard. It does not have to be any particular type of triangle—any variety will do. Extend each side of the triangle beyond the triangle's vertices.

2. Find the longest side of the triangle and open the compass so that its gap is a little longer than that side. (In the picture shown, the longest side is BC.) Set the compass at point B and make arc EF between BA and BC.

3. Set the compass at point A, matching the pencil to point E. Make arc DE.

4. Set the compass at point C, matching the pencil to point F. Make arc FG.

5. Continue this process until the closed curve is complete. (*Note:* If, after the first arc is made, one of the subsequent arcs ends up going into the triangle, then you will not be able to continue around the outside. If this happens, you should consider how the triangle might be redrawn to avoid this, and try again. The drawing after Step 5 in Figure 3 shows all the circles that contribute to the roller.)

6. Construct the axle by drawing a diagram similar to the one shown (Figure 3, Step 6) onto a piece of cardboard.

7. Attach the axle to the roller ends. It is important that the roller ends be aligned with each other. The easiest way to accomplish this is to match the side of the axle with the corresponding sides of the triangle.

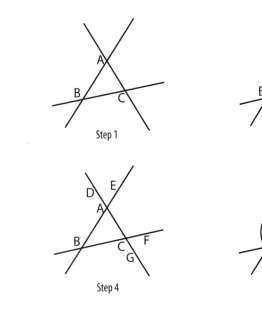

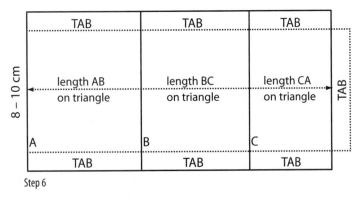

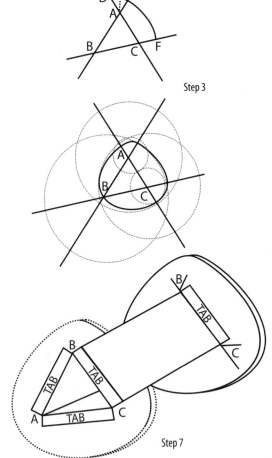

Figure 3

To Do and Notice

(5 minutes or more)

Build at least two identical rollers. Put them on a flat surface. Place the piece of Masonite or poster board on top of the rollers and roll it gently from side to side. The rollers should roll smoothly and the board should stay level. (See the photo at the beginning of this Snack.)

There is no standard definition of the center of a non-round roller. Define your own center, and see if it stays a constant height above the surface on which the rollers are rotating. Notice that there is no point on the roller that stays a constant height as the roller rolls. Any point you choose will bob up and down.

What's Going On?

In Versions 1 and 2, the roller always pivots on a vertex, even at the top and bottom, and the distance to the opposite contact point is always the same.

In Version 3, the width of the non-round roller at any point is defined by a straight line that runs through one of the vertices of the triangle and through the triangle itself. Each such straight line is the sum of two radii—the radius of one large arc and the radius of one small arc. For example, the straight line PO in Figure 4 is the sum of the radii of arc HG (a large arc) and arc DE (a small arc).

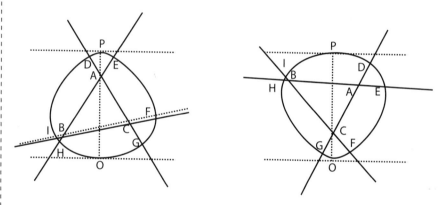

Figure 4

Suppose you have a roller like the one shown in Figure 4. Let's say the roller is resting on point O. As the roller rolls on arc HG, with its resting point approaching H, the board on top of the roller will be rolling on arc DE. The board will remain level because the roller's width (which is the sum of the radius of arc DE and the radius of arc HG) will be constant.

Suppose the roller rolls until it rests on point H. Its width is still the sum of two radii—the radius of arc HI and the radius of arc EF. Because arc HI and arc HG have point H in common, and because arc DE and arc EF have point E in common, the width of the roller must still be constant. As the roller continues rolling and reaches point I, the same argument applies, and the width of the roller is always the same.

Etcetera

A drill bit made in the shape of a Reuleaux triangle can be used to drill a square hole!

Figure 5 shows the roller in motion.

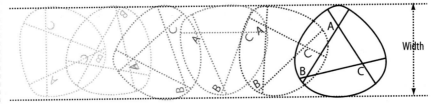

Figure 5

When you tried to choose a center for your non-round roller, you might logically have chosen the triangle's centroid. Another logical choice would be the point halfway between the top and bottom of the roller for a particular orientation. Neither of these points, however, stays at a constant height as the roller rolls. Instead, they describe an up-and-down motion. As you observed, no point on the roller stays a constant height as the roller rolls. For this reason, the rollers would make lousy car wheels. (Where would you put the axle?)

RESONANT PENDULUM
Big swings from little pulls grow.

Materials

- → An empty 1 gallon (3.8 L) metal paint can with lid (a steel bucket will work, but it may spill); an unopened can of paint will work as well
- → Sand to fill the paint can or bucket
- → A length of chain or rope (shorter than room height)
- → A large hook or eye bolt to attach the chain or rope securely to the ceiling
- → A ceramic magnet on a few feet of string
- → Optional: A second magnet on a string, a partner

Introduction

By exerting very small forces at just the right times, you can make a massive pendulum swing back and forth in very large swings.

Assembly
(30 minutes or less)

Fill the paint can with sand, close the lid to prevent spills, and suspend it from the ceiling with the chain or rope. The can should hang somewhere between waist height and ground level. The closer to the ground it hangs, the less traumatic the results if it should somehow fall.

To Do and Notice
(15 minutes or more)

Stand a few feet away and throw the magnet at the can. Your goal is to get the magnet to stick to the can. Once you have done this, pull gently on the string to set the can in motion. If you pull too hard and the magnet pulls off, try again. By pulling very gently on the string, but only pulling when the pendulum is moving toward you, you can gradually make the pendulum swing in very large swings.

If you have a second magnet on a string, a second person standing 90 degrees to the side of you can make the pendulum move along a diagonal line between the two of you by pulling gently at the same time that you do. If the two of you pull out of phase with each other, you can make the pendulum move in a circle.

Etcetera

This device can double as a dramatic potential-to-kinetic-to-potential energy demonstration. Pull the can to one side until it just reaches your nose. (Adjust the length of the rope as necessary to allow this.) Let go of the can (without pushing!) and stand very still. (Don't move your head forward!) The pendulum will return repeatedly without striking your face. A bowling ball with a large eyebolt screwed into a predrilled hole can be substituted for the paint can in this demonstration. The paint can or bowling ball will not hit you in the nose because of the law of conservation of energy. To swing farther, the pendulum must rise higher; to rise higher, it needs more energy. If no energy is added during the swing, the pendulum cannot hit you in the nose.

What's Going On?

A very small force, when applied repeatedly at just the right time, can induce a very large motion. This phenomenon is known as resonance. Perhaps the most familiar example of resonance in everyday life is swinging on a playground swing. The first push or pump sets the swing in motion. Each subsequent push or pump is delivered at just the right time to increase the amplitude of swing. If you continue pushing or pumping over a period of time, the swing will gradually go higher and higher.

Every pendulum, from a playground swing to your hanging paint can, has a frequency at which it tends to swing. This is the pendulum's natural frequency. To find the natural frequency of a pendulum, just pull it to the side and release it. The pendulum will swing back and forth at its natural frequency. If the frequency of pushes on a pendulum is close to the pendulum's natural frequency, the motion and the pushes will remain in step. Each successive push will increase the amplitude of the motion of the object.

You can measure your pendulum's natural frequency using a stopwatch or a timer. Time how long it takes the pendulum to swing back and forth ten times. Then divide this time by ten. You now have the period of one swing of the pendulum. The frequency is the inverse of the period. To get the frequency, just divide one by the period. For example, if ten swings take twenty seconds, then the period is two seconds. That means the frequency is 1 divided by 2, or one-half of a cycle per second (one-half hertz, or 0.5 Hz).

RESONANT RINGS
One reason not all buildings are equal in an earthquake.

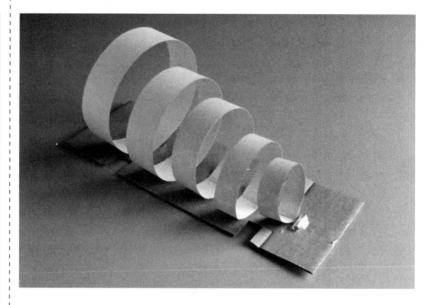

Introduction

This device graphically demonstrates that objects of different sizes and stiffness tend to vibrate at different frequencies.

Assembly

(15 minutes or less)

1. Cut four or five 1-inch (2.5 cm) wide strips from the construction paper. The longest strip should be about 20 inches (50 cm) long, and each successive strip should be about 3 inches (8 cm) shorter than the preceding one.

2. Form the strips into rings by taping the two ends of each strip together.

3. Tape the rings to the cardboard sheet as shown in the picture.

To Do and Notice

(5 minutes or more)

Shake the cardboard sheet back and forth. Start at very low frequencies and slowly increase the frequency of your shaking.

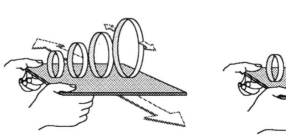
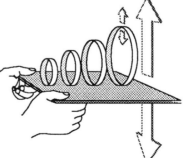

Etcetera

You can make the vibration frequency audible and more obvious by cutting a 1-inch (2.5 cm) section of a plastic drinking straw, inserting a BB into it, taping paper over the ends of the straw, and taping the straw to the cardboard sheet parallel to the end. As you shake the sheet, the BB will tap against the ends of the straw at the same frequency as your vibration.

Notice that different rings vibrate strongly, or resonate, at different frequencies. The largest ring will begin to vibrate strongly first, followed by the second largest, and so on. The smallest ring starts to vibrate at the highest frequencies.

Keep shaking the cardboard faster and faster, and notice that the largest ring will begin to vibrate strongly again. Each ring will vibrate at more than one frequency, but the shape of each ring will be different for each resonant frequency.

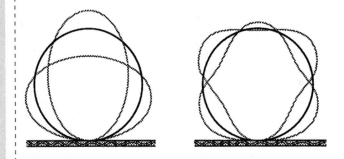

The rings will also have different resonant frequencies if you shake the board up and down instead of sideways.

What's Going On?

The frequencies at which each ring vibrates most easily—its resonant frequencies—are determined by several factors, including the ring's inertia (mass) and stiffness. Stiffer objects have higher resonant frequencies, whereas more massive ones have lower resonant frequencies.

The biggest ring has the largest mass and the least stiffness, so it has the lowest resonant frequency. Put another way, the largest ring takes more time than the smaller rings to respond to an accelerating force.

During earthquakes, two buildings of different sizes may respond very differently to the earth's vibrations, depending on how well each building's resonant frequencies match the "forcing" frequencies of the earthquake. Of course, a building's stiffness—determined by the manner of construction and materials used—is just as important as a building's size.

RESONATOR

If you vibrate something at just the right frequency, you can get a big reaction.

Materials

- ➔ A drill
- ➔ One 2 × 4 board measuring approximately 2 feet (60 cm) long
- ➔ Three 1/4-inch (6 mm) wooden dowels measuring 1½ feet (45 cm) long, 2 feet (60 cm) long, and 2½ feet (75 cm) long
- ➔ One 3/8-inch (9.5 mm) dowel measuring 2 feet (60 cm) long
- ➔ Hammer
- ➔ Four solid rubber balls at least 1 inch (2.5 cm) in diameter
- ➔ Optional: Carpenter's glue

ⓘ CAUTION

Take it easy with the shaking!
If you get the dowels vibrating too violently, watch out—they may break!

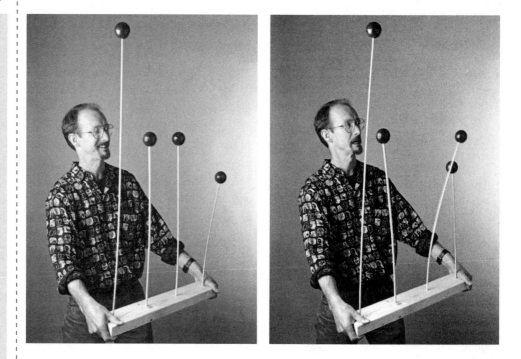

Introduction

In this Snack, wooden dowels of varying lengths, each loaded with the same mass, are vibrated at identical frequencies. When the vibration matches the resonant frequency of one of the dowels, that dowel vibrates with a large amplitude.

Assembly

(30 minutes or less)

1. Drill four holes approximately 4 inches (10 cm) apart along the center line of the wide face of the 2 × 4 (5 cm × 10 cm) board. The first three holes should be slightly smaller than 1/4 inch (6 mm), and the fourth hole should be slightly smaller than 3/8 inch (9.5 mm).

2. Gently hammer the dowels into the holes so they're held firmly in place. (If you prefer, you can drill holes that are the same size as the dowels and glue the dowels into the holes with carpenter's glue.)

3. Drill a 1/4-inch (6 mm) hole halfway through three of the rubber balls and a 3/8-inch (9.5 mm) hole halfway through the fourth ball. The best way to do this is to place the balls in a good vise and drill slowly.

4. Place a rubber ball on the end of each dowel. This adds a relatively large mass to each dowel. (Note that this will work even if you don't put rubber balls on the dowels, but the balls lower the resonant frequencies and make the motion easier to see. You can substitute lumps of clay or tennis balls, though tennis balls are hollow, so they tend to flop around on the ends of the dowels.)

Etcetera

Just as each dowel has its natural frequencies of vibration where resonance occurs, so most objects tend to vibrate at certain frequencies. You may have noticed that parts of your car rattle at a certain speed or that certain objects vibrate and buzz in response to a particular note from your stereo. These are everyday examples of resonance.

Resonance has also been responsible for some spectacular destruction. In earthquakes, buildings are often damaged when the frequency at which the ground is shaking comes very close to or matches one of the resonant frequencies of the buildings. In 1940, the Tacoma Narrows Bridge near Tacoma, Washington, vibrated itself to pieces when a strong wind pushed it at just the right frequency. In the 1960s, the wing of the Lockheed Electra jet failed repeatedly until engineers discovered that its resonant frequency was responsible for its destruction. In 1981, a suspended walkway at a Kansas City hotel collapsed when people dancing on the structure caused resonant vibration.

In the army, troops always march across a bridge out of step; army vehicles drive across spaced at irregular intervals. These practices avoid setting up vibrations at the bridge's resonant frequency.

To Do and Notice

(15 minutes or more)

Grip the 2×4 inch board at each end and slide it back and forth across a tabletop, moving it lengthwise. As you vary the rate of shaking, different dowels will swing back and forth with greater or lesser amplitude. When you are shaking at just the right frequency to cause one dowel to vibrate violently, another dowel may hardly be vibrating at all.

Notice which dowels vibrate violently at lower frequencies and which vibrate violently at higher frequencies.

What's Going On?

When you push someone on a swing, a series of small pushes makes the swing move through a large amplitude. To accomplish this, you time your pushes to match the swing's natural frequency, the rate at which the swing tends to move back and forth.

The same principle is at work in this Snack. When you shake the 2×4 assembly at just the right frequency, a series of small shakes adds up to a large vibration of a particular dowel. The shaking board sets the dowel vibrating. If the next shake is timed just right to reinforce the next vibration of the dowel, the vibration in the dowel builds up. This process of using a series of small inputs to create a large motion is known as resonance.

The longer the dowel, the more slowly it tends to vibrate, and the lower its natural frequency. Thus, the long dowel will resonate at lower frequencies than the short dowel.

Stiffer dowels have higher resonant frequencies. The 3/8-inch (9.5 mm) dowel is much stiffer than the 1/4-inch (6 mm) dowels, and so it tends to resonate at higher frequencies than the thinner dowels. Note also that each dowel may have more than one resonant frequency.

Not all objects resonate. Any object that dissipates energy faster than the energy is added will not resonate. Try, for example, shaking the dowels under water. The friction of the dowel moving through water will dissipate the energy faster than you add it. Because the motion of the dowel will not build up at any frequency, there is no resonance.

SOAP BUBBLES
Create geometric art with soap films.

Materials

- Plastic drinking or bar straws (bar straws, which have a smaller diameter than regular drinking straws, hold the pipe cleaners more tightly but are more expensive and sometimes harder to get; if you can't find them at grocery or liquor stores, try restaurant or party supply stores)

- Pipe cleaners (sometimes called chenille stems), available at school supply, hobby, or party stores

- A small bucket or container for the bubble solution—large enough so that bubble frames are entirely covered when they are dipped

- Bubble solution—you can use a commercial solution such as Wonder Bubbles, or make your own using the Exploratorium's recipe: Gently mix 2/3 cup (160 mL) Dawn dishwashing liquid and 1 tablespoon (15 mL) glycerin (available at most drugstores) with 1 gallon (3.8 L) of water

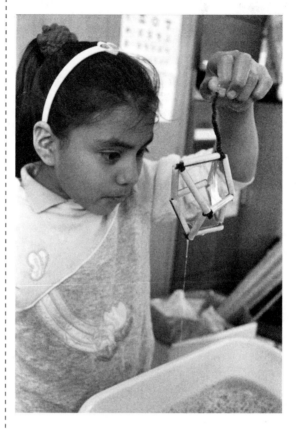

Introduction

Using pipe cleaners and drinking straws, you can make three-dimensional geometric frames: cubes, tetrahedrons, or shapes of your own design. When you dip these frames in a soap solution, the soap films that form on the frames are fascinating and colorful.

Assembly
(30 minutes or less)

1. Mix the soap solution in the bucket. Make sure you have enough to fully cover the frames when they are dipped. Note that bubble solution works best if it's aged at least a day before use. If you have any trouble making good bubbles, try using distilled water instead of tap water.

2. Form frames using the drinking straws for the straight pieces. Try constructing cubes or tetrahedrons, or just let your imagination run wild.

3. Connect two straws at a corner by inserting a doubled pipe cleaner into the end of each straw.

4. In places where three straws meet, fold the pipe cleaners as shown in the diagram.

5. Attach a pipe-cleaner handle to your frame.

Etcetera
If you look around for objects you can safely dip into the bubble mixture—from toys to kitchen implements—you might be surprised at the soap-film shapes you can create.

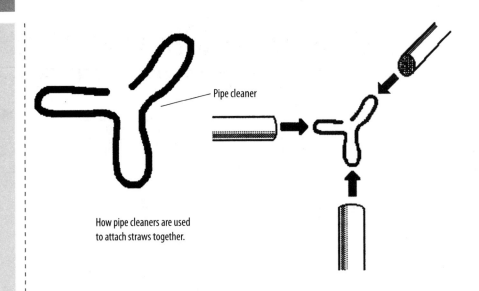

Pipe cleaner

How pipe cleaners are used to attach straws together.

To Do and Notice

(15 minutes or more)

Dip the frames into the soap solution, and observe the fascinating geometrical shapes that form. Also notice the shimmering colors in the soap film.

What's Going On?

As you lift your frame out of the solution, the soap film flows into a state of minimum energy. The soap film is in a state of minimum energy when it's covering the least possible amount of surface area. The intricate shapes you see inside the frame represent the minimum area the soap film can cover. You may notice that a soap film will sometimes take on different shapes when you dip the frame into the solution again and again. That's because there may be more than one way for the soap film to form a minimum surface area.

When light waves hit the soap film, they reflect and interfere with each other. This interference causes the shimmering colors you see.

White light is made of many different colors. When white light shines on the soap film, some light waves reflect from the front surface of the film and some reflect from the back surface of the film. When these two sets of reflected waves meet, they can add together, cancel each other out, or partially cancel, depending on the thickness of the film and the initial color of the light. When light waves of a particular color meet and cancel each other, that color is subtracted from white light. For example, if the red light waves cancel, then you see white light minus red light, which you perceive as blue-green light.

SPINNING BLACKBOARD
Create graceful loops and spirals by drawing on a spinning disk.

Materials
➡ Paper and marking pens or butcher paper and sand

➡ An old record player turntable if you can find one (a lazy Susan with a square or circular board placed on it will also work, but it will have to be rotated by hand)

➡ Optional: A disk cut out of cardboard

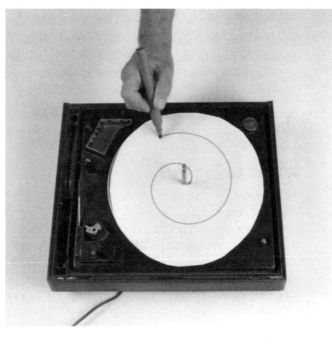

Introduction
When you draw on a spinning disk, you make unexpected patterns. You may draw a straight line, for instance, but what appears on the disk is a spiral. The patterns you make result from adding the motion of your hand to the spinning motion of the disk.

Assembly
(15 minutes or less)

Marking-Pen Version
Simply mount a piece of paper on the turntable. (If the turntable has grooves in it, cover it first with a sheet of cardboard.)

Sand Version
1. Fit a large piece of butcher paper between the turntable and the body of the record player to protect the mechanism from the sand. (Even though it's junk, you'll want it to survive long enough to repeat the Snack another time!)

2. Cover the turntable with a cardboard disk.

3. Spread a thin layer of sand evenly on the cardboard disk.

Etcetera

Like a speck of sand or an ant on the turntable, a person on the surface of the earth is in a rotating frame of reference. You can picture the earth as a giant turntable. If you are in the Southern Hemisphere looking north toward the equator, the earth is rotating clockwise. If a jetliner or a wind or an ocean current were traveling in a straight line from the South Pole toward the equator, you'd see them curve to the left.

From the Northern Hemisphere, the earth appears to rotate counterclockwise. Objects moving from the North Pole toward the equator appear to curve to the right of their direction of motion. In fact, objects moving in any direction appear to curve to the right. This explains why air flowing into the low-pressure center of a hurricane in the Northern Hemisphere bends to the right, and so flows around the hurricane in a counterclockwise direction.

To Do and Notice

(15 minutes or more)

Start the turntable rotating. Move a marking pen at a constant speed in a straight line from the center of the turntable to the edge. (On the sand-covered turntable, trace the straight line with your finger.) Notice the spiraling curve that appears on the turntable. This curve is called a spiral of Archimedes. Move your pen or finger out from the center at different speeds and notice how the spiral changes.

Try drawing other straight lines: For example, start at the edge of the turntable and draw a line toward the center, or start at the edge and draw a line making a 45-degree angle with the edge. Draw straight lines with different constant speeds to make new curves.

Draw many straight lines radiating out from a point halfway between the center and the edge of the turntable. Try to draw a triangle or a square on the rotating turntable.

What's Going On?

When you draw a straight line from the center of the spinning turntable toward the center of your body, the turntable rotates beneath your finger as you draw the line. Your finger traces a curve on the turntable. Because record players rotate clockwise, the line appears to curve to the left, when viewed from its starting point, which was at the center. The spiral made by your finger also appears to curve to the left. The pattern on the turntable shows the motion of your finger from the perspective, or frame of reference, of a speck of sand on the spinning turntable. (Physicists would say that the speck of sand is in a rotating frame of reference.)

Objects move in a straight line at a constant speed when there are no net forces on them. The person drawing the straight line can see no net forces on the pen or fingertip, but an ant rotating with the turntable sees the pen or fingertip curve in an arc and so believes that there must be a force pushing it into this curved path. In the rotating frame of reference, observers make up forces named centrifugal and Coriolis to explain the curvature of the line.

STRANGE ATTRACTOR

The attraction and repulsion of magnets produces entrancing, unpredictable motion.

Materials

- Four to six donut magnets (available at RadioShack)
- Paint, masking tape, or correction fluid
- Fishing line or string
- Ring stand and clamp

Introduction

Patterns of order can be found in apparently disordered systems. This pendulum—a magnet swinging over a small number of fixed magnets—is a very simple system that shows chaotic motion for some starting positions of the pendulum. The search for order in the chaos can be engrossing.

Assembly

(15 minutes or less)

Put all the magnets together in a stack so they stick together magnetically. By doing this, you are orienting the magnets so that all of the north poles point in one direction and all of the south poles point in the other direction. Take the stack apart and mark the top of each magnet with paint, tape, or correction fluid, thus identifying all the matching poles.

Use the string or fishing line to hang one magnet from the ring stand so that it is a free-swinging pendulum. You can hang the magnet in any orientation.

Arrange the other magnets on the ring stand base in an equilateral triangle measuring a couple of inches on a side. Position the magnets so that they all have the same pole up.

Adjust the length of the pendulum so that the free-swinging magnet will come as close as possible to the magnets on the ring-stand base without hitting them or the base itself. You can accomplish this either by changing the length of the string or by adjusting the position of the clamp.

To Do and Notice

(15 minutes or more)

Give the pendulum magnet a push, and watch!

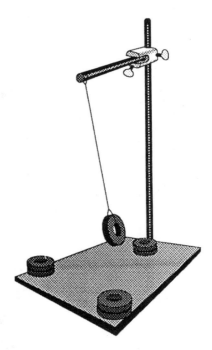

Vary the location and poles of the magnets to develop other patterns. You can arrange the magnets so they all have the same pole up, or you can mix them. Notice that a tiny change in the location of one of the fixed magnets or in the starting position of the pendulum magnet may cause the pendulum to develop a whole new pattern of swinging.

The force of gravity and the simple pushes and pulls of the magnets act together to influence the swinging pendulum in complex ways. It can be very difficult to predict where the pendulum is going to go next, even though you know which magnets are attracting it and which are repelling it.

This sort of unpredictable motion is often called chaotic motion. Strangely enough, there can be a subtle and complex kind of order to chaos. Scientists try to describe this order with models called strange attractors.

TAKE IT FROM THE TOP
How does this stack up?

Materials

→ Approximately fifteen to twenty uniform flat, rectangular blocks (the particular size is not crucial, as long as all blocks are the same—we've found that 1 × 4 × 9 inch [2.5 × 10 × 22.5 cm] finished pine works well)

Introduction

Simple wooden blocks can be stacked so that the top block extends completely past the end of the bottom block, seemingly in a dramatic defiance of gravity. To make this work, you must start moving the top block first and then proceed on down the stack, rather than starting from the bottom up. A mathematical pattern can be noted in the stacking.

Assembly

See "To Do and Notice."

To Do and Notice

(15 minutes or more)

Stack the blocks evenly on top of one another to make a vertical column.

Position the stack so that you are facing the long side of the blocks. Start at the top of the stack. Move the top block to the right so it overhangs the second block as far as possible without falling. Now move the top two blocks to the right as a unit so they overhang the third block as far as possible without falling. Move the top three blocks, and continue on down the stack. How many blocks must you move before the top block is completely beyond the balance point?

Notice that you can never move a given block over as far as you moved the previous one. The larger the stack of blocks you are moving, the smaller the distance you can move them before they become unbalanced and topple over.

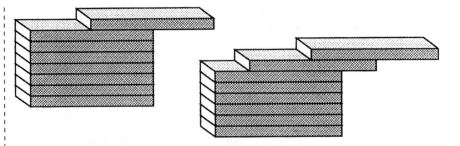

Etcetera

A stack of textbooks can provide an instantly available set of uniform "blocks." Teachers might try stacking the books as we have described when passing them out to students.

Other readily available stackable objects include flat rulers, index cards, or playing cards. You can also cut pieces of mat board or Masonite to any desired size, a method that's particularly handy if you want to make lots of smaller sets for individual use.

If you want to have some fun, glue together a duplicate set of the blocks that you stacked earlier. You can do this quickly with hot glue. Place the glued stack on top of a loose block that has a strong string attached to a screw eye in one end. You now have a great inertia demonstration. If you jerk the bottom block out swiftly, you won't upset the stack. Practice this a few times first, though! Also, be careful that the block you jerk doesn't hit someone! You will likely have more success if you position the bottom block with the screw eye facing away from the overhanging portion, rather than below it. You might also consider fudging a little by not quite moving each block to its extreme balance point before gluing it. If you manage to jerk the bottom block out before your audience discovers that the stack is glued, they will think that this is an amazing feat. (A little creative showmanship and acting can set the stage for this!) You can also find the center of gravity of the glued stack and show that the pivot point of the whole glued stack is directly under the center of gravity.

What's Going On?

When you move the top block over so that it just balances, its center of gravity, or balance point, rests over the edge of the block below. Each time you move a block, you are finding the center of gravity of a new stack of blocks—the block you move plus the blocks above it. The edge of each block acts as a fulcrum supporting all the blocks above it.

By considering the positions of the centers of gravity of the blocks as the stack is built, it can be shown that the first block will be moved 1/2 of a block length along the second block, the top two blocks will be moved 1/4 of a block length along the third block, the top three blocks will be moved 1/6 of a block length along the fourth block, the top four blocks will be moved 1/8 of a block length along the fifth block, and so on. Do you see the pattern?

How far will the nth block be moved along the block below it? The answer is: $1/2n$ of a block length along the $n + 1$ block. Unavoidable experimental error due to factors such as nonuniformity of blocks and inexact location of balance points will lead to actual values that are not quite in agreement with theory but that are still probably close enough to make the point.

VORTEX

Whirling water creates a tornado in a bottle.

Materials

- A Tornado Tube plastic connector (available from science museums, science stores, novelty stores, and some scientific supply companies), or you can make your own using a washer with a 3/8-inch (9.5 mm) hole and electrical tape
- Two 2-liter soda bottles
- Tap water
- Optional: A small dropper bottle of food coloring; bits of paper or glitter

Introduction

Water forms a spiraling, funnel-shaped vortex as it drains from a 2-liter soda bottle. A simple connector device allows the water to drain into a second bottle. The whole assembly can then be inverted and the process repeated.

Assembly

(5 minutes or less with the Tornado Tube; 15 minutes or less with the washer and electrical tape)

1. Fill one of the soda bottles about two-thirds full of water. For effect, you can add a little food coloring or some bits of paper or glitter to the water.

2. Screw the bottles onto both ends of the plastic connector. (Do not screw the connector on too tightly!) Or tape the bottles together with the washer between them.

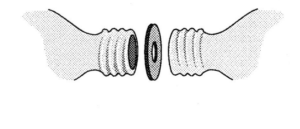

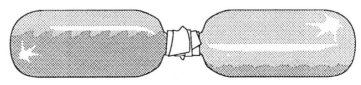

To Do and Notice

(15 minutes or more)

Place the connected bottles on a table with the filled bottle on top. Watch the water slowly drip down into the lower bottle as air simultaneously bubbles up into the top bottle. The flow of water may come to a complete stop.

With the filled bottle on top, rapidly rotate the bottles in a circle a few times. Place the assembly on a table. Observe the formation of a funnel-shaped vortex as the bottle drains.

Notice the shape of the vortex. Also, notice the flow of the water as it empties into the lower bottle.

You can make the vortex with a single bottle by twirling the bottle and holding it over a water basin or the ground to drain, but you lose the water and have to refill the bottle each time you use it.

What's Going On?

When the water is not rotating, surface tension creates a skin-like layer of water across the small hole in the center of the connector.

If the top bottle is full, the water can push out a bulge in this surface to form a bulbous drop, which then drips into the lower bottle. As water drops into the lower bottle, the pressure in the lower bottle builds until air bubbles are forced into the upper bottle. The pressure that the water exerts on the surface in the connector decreases as the water level in the upper bottle drops. When the water level and pressure drop low enough, the water surface can hold back the water and stop the flow completely.

If you spin the bottles around a few times, the water in the upper bottle starts rotating. As the water drains into the lower bottle, a vortex forms. The water is pulled down and forced toward the drain hole in the center by gravity. If we ignore the small friction forces, the angular momentum of the water stays the same as it moves inward. This means that the speed of the water around the center increases as it approaches the center of the bottle. (This is the same reason that the speed of rotating ice skaters increases when they pull in their arms.)

To make water move in a circle, forces called centripetal forces must act on the water. These "center-pulling" forces are created by a combination of air pressure, water pressure, and gravity.

You can tell where the centripetal forces are greater by looking at the slope of the water. Where the water is steeper, such as at the bottom of the vortex, the centripetal force on the water is greater. Water moving with higher speeds and in curves of smaller radius requires larger forces. The water at the bottom of the vortex is doing just this, and so the wall of the vortex is steepest at the bottom. (Think about race cars: Racetracks have steeper banks on high-speed, sharp corners to hold the cars in their circular paths around the track.)

The hole in the vortex allows air from the lower bottle to flow easily into the upper bottle. This enables the upper bottle to drain smoothly and completely.

WATER SPINNER
Rotating water has a curved surface.

Materials

- A clear, thin rectangular plastic box, about 12 × 12 × 1 inches (30 × 30 × 2.5 cm)—you can buy one ready-made, or you can easily glue one together from pieces of plastic available at a plastics store
- Silicone seal adhesive to make the box waterproof
- Strong glue
- Two wood or plastic blocks, each about 2 × 6 × 1/2 inches (5 × 15 × 1.25 cm), to fasten the box to the lazy Susan
- A lazy Susan or other appropriate turntable
- Tap water

Introduction

When you spin a tank of water on a lazy Susan, the surface of the water forms a curve called a parabola.

Assembly

(15 minutes or less with a ready-made box; one hour or less if you make your own box)

1. The seams of the box need to be watertight, so use the silicone seal adhesive to plug any leaks.

2. Cut a hole in the top of the box, or leave the top of the box open.

3. Glue the blocks to the lazy Susan alongside the box, to hold the box firmly in place.

Etcetera

Make a raft small enough to float inside your rotating box—a small, flat piece of wood with a toothpick mast works well. Place the raft on the water surface near the edge of the box, and then spin the box. The raft will stay in place even when it is on the slope of a hill of water. Its mast will always be perpendicular to the water.

To Do and Notice

(5 minutes or more)

Half-fill the box with water and rotate the lazy Susan. Notice the shape of the surface of the water.

What's Going On?

When the waves settle down, the surface of the water forms a curve called a parabola.

As the box spins, the water tends to continue moving in a straight line tangent to the circle. However, the box restrains the water and forces it to keep moving in a circle. The water near the edge of the box goes around in one large circle in the same time that the water near the center goes around in a small circle. That means the water near the edge travels faster than the water near the center. The faster an object moves in a circle, the larger the force necessary to hold it in the circle. This force is called the centripetal force.

The surface of a body of water in equilibrium is always perpendicular to the net forces on the water. The diagram below shows the forces on the water in relation to the tilt or slope of the water surface.

The diagram shows that the tilt or slope of the water surface indicates the size of the force holding the water in its circular path. The flat bottom of the parabola shows that little force is needed to hold the water there in its circular path, while the steep outer regions show that a large force is required in those areas.

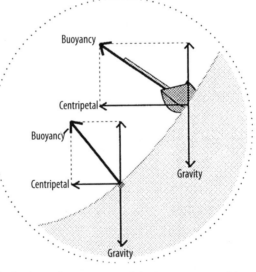

The horizontal component of the buoyancy provides the centripetal force.

You can prove to yourself that the water forms a parabola. A parabola has the equation $y = x^2$. Draw a parabola on a piece of graph paper and tape the paper to one side of your rectangular box so that you can look through the box and see the paper. Then rotate the box until you find the speed at which the bottom of the parabola you drew matches up with the lowest part of the water surface. (Note that the X and Y axes of this graph must have the same scale.) The water surface should exactly match the curve of the parabola drawing at every other point.

PART FIVE THE WIRE-HANGER CONCERTO AND OTHER EAR-SPLITTING EXPLORATIONS OF HOW WE HEAR THE WORLD

You may not think of your ear as a thing of beauty, but it is elegantly designed for the job it does. Your pinna, or outer ear, collects vibrating waves of air and funnels them down the ear canal to the eardrum. From there, like some crazy Rube Goldberg device, your ear pushes on this, which rattles that, which pulls on this, which pushes on that—all to transform those captured vibrations into the sounds you hear.

How and what we hear is the subject of the Snacks in this section. Some focus on the nature of sound, others on the process of hearing, and still others on some unusual ways to make sounds with homemade musical instruments.

Most of us spend our days surrounded by noises of every imaginable origin, from the trill of a bird to the thump of a neighbor's stereo to the blast of a train's whistle. Normally, the sounds around you blend into a complex wash of high and low pitches, but with the Pipes of Pan Snack, you can use a few cardboard mailing tubes, a length of wood, and some glue to pick those sounds apart: the longer the tube, the lower the pitches you can hear.

Turns out there's a lot of information in moving sounds, as well. Stop and listen to a row of cars whipping past you. If there's a radio blaring or a horn wailing, even better. The changing pitches of the sound you hear as cars approach and then pass by you is the subject of the Doppler Effect Snack—a phenomenon you can demonstrate with a simple soundmaker inside a rubber ball. In Falling Rhythm, dropping two weighted ropes can help you hear the way objects accelerate under gravity, and in Organ Pipe, changing the length of a tube changes how long it takes for a sound to travel up and down its length—a change you can hear with a tuning fork.

In Bee Hummer, Make Your Own Rainstick, and Coffee-Can Cuica, homemade versions of traditional instruments show some unexpected ways to make music, from the stick-and-slip sounds of a rag being tugged along the length of a stick to the vibrations of a flapping rubber band. Radiohead and Wire-Hanger Concerto, on the other hand, show ways you can hear music that's not carried through the air. Both these activities show you how to channel sound straight into your body—one through your teeth and into your skull; the other from vibrating metal, through a string, and then straight into your ear canal.

Taken together, the experiments in this section will help you find some of the hidden information in the sounds you hear and better understand how your sense of sound helps you navigate the world around you.

ANTI-SOUND SPRING

Send waves down a spring to watch them travel and interact.

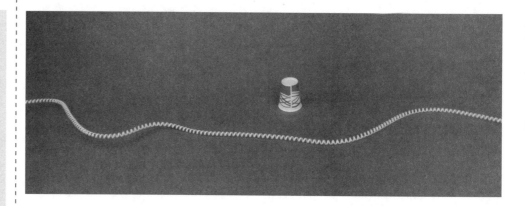

Materials

- A 25-foot (7.5 m) coiled phone cord
- Lightweight paper or plastic foam cup
- Masking tape 1/2-inch (1.25 cm) wide
- One or two friends (you may want to have a third person available to help set up the cup)

Introduction

In this simple exploration, a coiled phone cord slows the motion of a wave so you can see how a single pulse travels and what happens when two traveling wave pulses meet in the middle.

Assembly

None needed.

To Do and Notice

(30 minutes or more)

First, make a single pulse: Have your partner hold one end of the phone cord, or attach it firmly in place at about waist height. Stretch the cord so it's about 12 feet (4 meters) from you to your partner, and then jerk the hand holding the cord to the right about one hand-span and immediately back again to set a traveling pulse in motion. Notice that a rightward pulse travels down the cord, but a leftward pulse returns after bouncing off the far end of the cord.

If you have trouble seeing that the pulse is reversed when it is reflected, set the cord on the ground and stretch it to about 12 feet (4 meters). Mark a straight line on the ground under the cord using masking tape. The direction of motion of the pulses will be much more visible when compared to the reference tape.

If it isn't there already, set the cord on the ground and stretch it to 12 feet (4 meters). Place an empty paper or plastic foam cup next to the center of the cord. Once again, send a single pulse down the cord, making sure you move your hand to the side the cup is on when you make the pulse. It should hit the cup and knock it over.

Now make two pulses and add them together: This time, both you and your partner will set pulses in motion.

Keep the cord on the ground as it was before, stretched between you and your partner. Then set up the cup again at the center of the stretched cord. First, you and your partner should both send waves down the cord. Both pulses should be toward the side the cup

Etcetera

In a 1957 short story, science fiction author and futurist Sir Arthur C. Clarke (1917–2008; inventor of the communications satellite and author of *2001: A Space Odyssey*) envisioned a machine that could create silence in an opera-crazy society by adding mirrored sound waves to the unwanted din, thus canceling out the noise. In the late 1980s, the Bose Corporation developed just such a sound-cancellation system, making special headphones for the pilots of the noisy *Voyager* aircraft, the first aircraft to fly around the world without refueling. Today, sound-cancellation technology is used in personal electronics, as well as in commercial and military applications.

is on. Notice that when the pulses meet in the middle, you end up with an even bigger wave that knocks down the cup. Carefully time your pulses so that they both arrive at the center of the cord at the same time.

Set up the cup again.

This time, you and your partner should send waves through the cord in opposite directions: While you send a pulse on the same side as the cup, have your partner send an identical pulse on the side away from the cup. The pulses will arrive at the center at the same time. The rightward pulse will add to the leftward pulse and cancel it out. The sum of the waves will be zero. The waves will miss the cup, and the cup will remain standing.

What's Going On?

The pulses on the cord simply add together as they pass through each other.

Just like the waves on the cord, two sound waves can add together to make a sound get louder, or they can cancel each other out to make sounds recede. Sounds that cancel out other sounds are called anti-sound.

BEE HUMMER

Make a stick, rubber band, and index card sound like a swarm of bees.

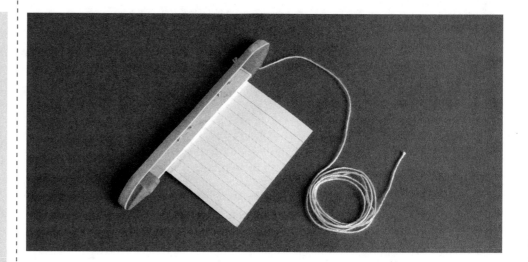

Introduction

When you spin it around, this toy sounds like a swarm of buzzing bees.

Assembly

(15 minutes or more)

1. Put a cap eraser on each end of the craft stick.

2. Trim an index card so it fits in the space between the two erasers on the stick.

3. Staple the card to the craft stick. It should stick out about 2 inches (5 cm) from one side of the stick.

4. Cut enough string (about 2 feet [60 cm]) to safely swing the Bee Hummer. Then tie the string next to one of the erasers, making several knots so it's secure.

5. Once the string is tied to your Bee Hummer, stretch the rubber band around the craft stick from one eraser to the other, and make sure it's snugly in place.

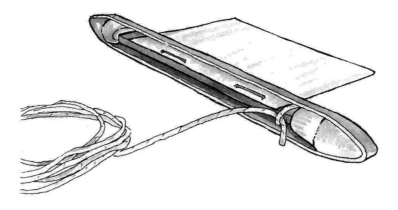

Etcetera

Experiment by changing how the Bee Hummer is made and used. What happens when the index card is slit, curved, or folded? How does the sound change if you change the size of the rubber band? If you spin your Bee Hummer faster or slower? Use a longer or shorter length of string? You can also modify the materials: Try using balls of clay on each end instead of erasers, or several thin rubber bands instead of one thick one.

To Do and Notice

(5 minutes or more)

Make sure the area is clear. Then hold the end of the string and swing your Bee Hummer in a circle. You should hear a sound like bees buzzing.

What's Going On?

When you spin your Hummer, moving air makes the rubber band vibrate. The air flowing over the rubber band makes it vibrate the same way that wind blowing over a flag makes it wave.

Sound is produced by those vibrations, in the same way that vibrating strings on a guitar or violin produce sound. The index card amplifies the sound.

If your Bee Hummer doesn't seem to be working, check to be sure that the rubber band isn't twisted, and that the string isn't touching the rubber band. Either of these things could stop the sound.

COFFEE-CAN CUICA
A homemade version of a traditional instrument.

Materials

- An empty metal can (like a coffee can) with a plastic lid (any size will work; different-sized cans will make different-sounding instruments)
- Can opener
- Electrical or duct tape
- A small nail
- Bamboo skewer
- String
- Scissors
- Hot-glue gun
- A small square of cotton cloth (material from an old T-shirt, for example) moistened in a little water

Introduction

In this activity, you'll build a cuica ("kwee-ka"), an instrument that originated in Africa but which is commonly played during Carnival festivities in Brazil.

Assembly
(30 minutes or less)

1. Remove the plastic lid from the coffee can and set it aside. Using a can opener, cut out the bottom of the can to make an open cylinder. Use tape to cover any sharp edges. Set the can aside.

2. Use the nail to poke a small hole in the middle of the can's plastic lid. The hole should be just large enough for your bamboo skewer to fit through, but not so large that the skewer can slip through easily.

3. Push the skewer through the hole in the lid so that a little bit (about 1/2 inch [1.25 cm]) is sticking out the top. (See drawings below.)

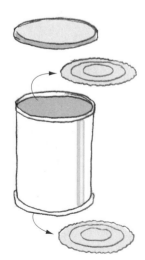

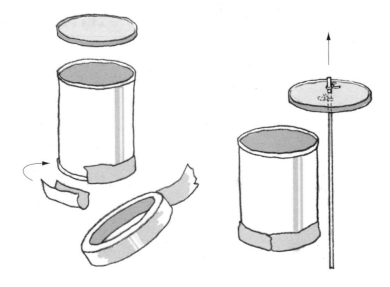

4. Cut two pieces of string a few inches long and knot one just above the plastic lid, and one just below it, at the short end of the skewer. Hot-glue the knots in place to keep the skewer from slipping through the lid, and clip off the pointy end of the skewer.

5. Fit the skewer-and-lid assembly back on the can. The lid should fit tightly. If it doesn't, you may want to add a few drops of hot glue to keep it attached.

To Do and Notice

(15 minutes or more)

To play your cuica, take the moistened cotton cloth in your hand, reach in through the open end of the instrument, and rub the cloth up and down along the long end of the bamboo skewer. Depending on how hard and fast you rub the skewer, you can make everything from low-pitched croaks to high-pitched squeaks and squeals. Try pressing gently in different places on the plastic lid to see if it changes the sound. What else can you do to make it sound different?

Etcetera
The "stick-and-slip" vibrations that make the cuica play are also responsible for the familiar sounds of chalk squeaking on a blackboard!

What's Going On?

Sound is a traveling vibration. When you strike a drum, for example, the drum starts to vibrate. These vibrations push and pull on the surrounding air, causing the air to vibrate. The vibrations travel through the air to reach your ear, where they cause a thin membrane—your eardrum—to vibrate. If the rate of vibration is within a certain range (from 20 to 20,000 vibrations per second), then you hear a sound.

When you rub the bamboo skewer of your cuica with a wet cloth, the cloth sticks and slides rhythmically along the length of the skewer, creating the vibrations you hear.

Although the vibrations begin in the bamboo skewer, the skewer isn't the only thing vibrating. As you play the cuica, its metal-can body and plastic-lid top are also vibrating. In addition, the open space inside the can acts like the inside of a drum, creating an air pocket in which sounds can vibrate and build.

In most instruments, there's a part that generates sound and a larger hollow space that amplifies it. In a saxophone, for example, a vibrating reed makes the sound vibrations that are amplified in the hollow, curved-tube body of the instrument. In a cuica, the skewer and lid together generate the sound, and the hollow metal can amplifies it.

You might also notice that larger cuicas make lower-pitched sounds than smaller cuicas. In fact, this rule is generally true for all instruments: Larger instruments make lower-pitched sounds than smaller ones. A giant tuba makes a lower-pitched sound than a tiny piccolo; a full-sized cello makes a lower-pitched sound than its smaller cousin, the violin. When sounds bounce back and forth across a larger space, the vibrations are slower, so the sound is lower.

CONVERSATION PIECE
A balloon acts as a lens to focus sound.

Materials

- Sturdy balloon, 12 to 16 inches (30 to 40 cm) in diameter
- A 1- or 2-L plastic soda bottle
- Coffee mug, or some other way to prop up your balloon
- Toy metal clicker or other noisemaker
- A way to fill the balloon with carbon dioxide (CO_2) just before use—either with a tank of carbon dioxide or by using crushed dry ice (available online and occasionally from party stores)
- Thick, lined leather gloves and tongs for handling the dry ice, if used

⚠ CAUTION
Use gloves and tongs when handling dry ice! Never touch dry ice with your bare skin.

Introduction

Sound energy spreads out as it travels away from a source, but a balloon filled with carbon dioxide gas can focus sound, acting like a lens to create a loud spot.

Assembly
(15 minutes or less)

1. Inflate the balloon with carbon dioxide just before you use it, because carbon dioxide leaks rather rapidly through rubber. If using dry ice as a source for your CO_2, put about 1/4 cup (60 mL) ice into the plastic bottle. *(Be sure you don't touch dry ice with your bare skin!)* Then fit the balloon securely over the top of the bottle. The balloon will slowly fill with carbon dioxide gas as the dry ice warms. Be patient: It usually takes 10 to 15 minutes. To inflate the balloon more quickly, put the bottle in some warm water while the balloon is filling.

2. When the balloon is full, remove it and tie it off. You now have a "lens" that will focus sound.

To Do and Notice
(15 minutes or more)

Put the mug on a table. Balance the balloon on top of the mug.

Have one person standing about 3 feet (1 m) away from the center of the balloon click the clicker or make sounds with another noisemaker. Have another person on the opposite side of the balloon move around to find the place where the sound is loudest.

Etcetera

A balloon full of helium does not focus sound. Helium is lighter than air, so the speed of sound in helium is faster than the speed of sound in air. A helium balloon causes sound waves to diverge, making sound spread out more quickly than it would in air.

NOTE

You need a high-frequency (short wavelength) sound source to do this activity. If the sound waves emitted by your noisemaker are longer than the radius of the balloon, they will diffract around the balloon. The "lens" works well only if the sound wavelength is less than the balloon's radius. To focus the low frequencies (long wavelengths) of human speech, you need a very large balloon.

The point where the sound is the loudest should be on a straight line from the sound source through the center of the balloon to about 18 inches (46 cm) away from the center. The exact distance will depend on the size of your balloon and the position of the sound source. When you find the loudest location, remove the balloon and listen to the clicker again. Notice that the sound is now quieter.

Put the balloon back on its coffee-mug stand. What happens if you change where you're standing? Change the position of the clicker and find the loudest point again. Notice that the loud point moves opposite the motion of the clicker. When the clicker moves up, the loud point moves down. When the clicker moves closer, the loud point moves farther away. (Note that if you move the clicker too close, there will be no loud point.)

Try moving farther and farther away. Find the loudest point for a distant sound (one that's more than 10 feet [3 meters] away). The distance from the center of the balloon to this point is the focal length of the balloon.

When you're done, drop the balloon and notice that it's heavier than air.

What's Going On?

Carbon dioxide (CO_2) molecules are more massive than the nitrogen, oxygen, and argon molecules that make up air (N_2, O_2, Ar), so the speed of sound in the carbon dioxide gas is slower than the speed of sound in air.

As sound waves enter the carbon-dioxide-filled balloon, they slow and bend, just as light waves slow down and bend when they pass from air into a glass lens. The sound waves that pass through different parts of the balloon bend by different amounts and then come together at one point on the other side of the balloon, creating a loud spot. The balloon focuses sound waves to create a loud spot much the way a magnifying glass focuses the sun's rays to create a hot spot.

DESIGNER EARS
Make "better" ears!

Materials
- Scissors
- Tape
- Glue
- Staplers
- A variety of construction materials including (but not limited to) construction paper, cardboard, plastic pieces, or Styrofoam, plastic containers and trays (clean yogurt cups and meat trays, for starters), craft sticks, and so on
- Pictures of animals' ears

Introduction
Why do animals' ears look different from yours? What would life be like if your ears were shaped differently? Make new ears for yourself and find out.

Assembly
(15 minutes or more)

Use your materials to fashion new outer ears, or pinnae, for yourself. Look at pictures of animal ears if you need ideas or inspiration. (Be careful not to cover the opening to your own ear when you make these new ear shapes—you want to collect sound in new ways, not block it!)

To Do and Notice
(15 minutes or less)

Compare your normal hearing with what you can hear when you wear the new ears you've made. What happens when you wear tall, thin ears like a horse's ears? What happens when you wear ears with flaps over them, like a basset hound's ears? Can you invent a shape you don't see in nature?

"Trade ears" with others to see how different shapes collect sound. What are the advantages and disadvantages of changing the shape of your ear? Does one design work better than the others? Do things sound different if you're wearing two different types of ears?

Etcetera

You might notice that your "designer ears" magnify a lot of background noise. Big pinnae funnel every sound to the ear—often a problem for people wearing hearing aids.

Look at the animal pictures again. You might have some clues now about why these animals have the kinds of ears they do.

What's Going On?

You'll probably find that ear designs that amplify sounds the best will be funnel-shaped and have large pinnae, or outer ear flaps. The pinnae of human ears (and most animal ears) act like funnels, collecting and directing sound into the inner ear, so our brains can detect and analyze what we hear.

Ears can also tell us about an animal's lifestyle. Some animals (such as dogs, elephants, and whales, for instance) can hear frequencies too high or low for us to hear. In some owls, one ear is set slightly higher than the other. This allows them to pinpoint the position of prey while in flight, assessing location in an up-and-down plane, in addition to left and right.

Animals that have very large ears (jackrabbits and foxes, for example), can generally hear very well, or at a great distance. Big ears can help animals locate prey, avoid predators, and find others of their kind.

Large ears can also provide extra surface area to radiate heat away from the body. In animals that cannot sweat as we do, having an expanse of blood vessels close to the skin's surface allows excess body heat to escape. In fact, ear shape is one way you can tell African elephants from Indian elephants: Elephants adapted to live in the hot African climate have bigger ears than Indian elephants have.

DOPPLER EFFECT

The Doppler effect causes the "neeeeeoowwm" sound of a speeding car passing by.

Materials

- Tennis ball or Wiffle ball
- Knife
- A 9-volt battery and connector
- A 9-volt buzzer (available at RadioShack; high-pitched works best)
- Scrap paper to pack inside the ball
- Heavy rubber bands or tape
- Strong string
- Optional: On/off switch (available at RadioShack or hardware stores)

Introduction

When a sound source moves in relation to you, its pitch changes. From this effect you can determine whether the source is moving toward or away from you, and you can estimate how fast it's going.

Assembly

(30 minutes or less)

1. Cut a slit halfway around the ball with a sharp knife.

2. Connect the wire from one terminal on the battery to the wire from one terminal on the buzzer. If the buzzer has a (+) and (–) terminal, be sure to connect the buzzer terminal to the matching battery terminal.

3. There will be a wire connected to the remaining terminal on the battery and another wire connected to the remaining terminal on the buzzer.

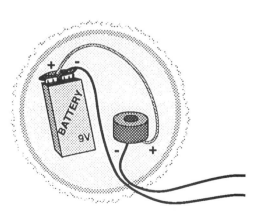

Place both battery and buzzer inside the ball, leaving the two unconnected wire ends protruding from the ball.

4. Pack the ball loosely with paper, leaving the buzzer near the outside.

5. Close the ball with tape or rubber bands, and twist the wires together to turn the buzzer on. You may want to wire a switch into your circuit so you can turn the buzzer on and off more conveniently.

To Do and Notice

(10 minutes or more)

Attach the ball to a string and twirl it around your head, or have some students toss the ball back and forth. Notice how the pitch of the buzzer changes as the ball approaches you or moves away from you.

What's Going On?

When an oscillator (the buzzer) moves toward you, in effect it is catching up slightly with its own sound waves. With each successive pulse of the buzzer, the sound source is a little closer to you. The result is that the waves are squeezed together, and more of them reach your ear each second than if the buzzer were standing still. Therefore, the pitch of the buzzer sounds higher. As the buzzer moves away from you, fewer waves reach your ear each second, so the resulting pitch sounds lower. The frequency of the buzzer itself does not change in either case.

For your ears to detect this effect—called the Doppler effect—the sound source has to be moving toward or away from you at a minimum speed of about 15 to 20 mph (24 to 32 kph). As the source moves faster, the effect becomes more pronounced.

If the buzzer has a frequency of 100 hertz, and it is moving toward you through still air at 35 meters per second, then the pitch you hear will be 110 hertz. This result comes from the equation

$$\text{pitch} = f/(1 - v/v_s)$$

where f is the frequency, v is the speed of the sources of the sound, and v_s is the speed of sound, 350 meters per second. If the object is moving away from you, simply replace the minus sign with a plus sign.

FALLING RHYTHM

Listen to the rhythm of the falling weights . . .

Materials

- Two pieces of heavy string or cord, each about 9 feet (3 m) long; we've found that parachute cord, 1/8 to 1/4 inch in diameter (3 to 6 mm), works well
- Ten weights to clip onto the strings—binder clips or 1/2-ounce (15 gram) fishing weights work well
- Metric ruler (to measure in centimeters)
- Marker (any color) to mark the strings
- Cookie sheet or other similar-sized square of metal or wood
- Optional: Step stool (if needed)

⚠ CAUTION

You may have to stand on a step stool to hold the string high enough off the floor. If so, be careful!

Introduction

You can space weights along a string so that they make a regular rhythm of beats when they strike the ground.

Assembly

(15 minutes or less)

1. On String 1, measure, mark, and then clip the weights at the following distances from the "bottom":

   50 cm, 100 cm, 150 cm, 200 cm, and 250 cm (the "top")

Etcetera

Notice that the distances 1, 4, 9, and 16 (the distances in centimeters between the weights on String 2) have the following interesting properties: they are all perfect squares, and the spacings between them are 3, 5, 7. Simply by starting at 1 and adding the odd integers one at a time, you produce the perfect squares.

2. On String 2, again measuring up from the "bottom," mark and then clip the weights at:

10 cm, 40 cm, 90 cm, 160 cm, and 250 cm (the "top")

3. Arrange the cookie sheet or square of metal or wood so that it sits at a 45-degree angle where you can drop the weights onto it. Besides increasing the sound as they hit the cookie sheet or board, the weights will slide off the angled surface to help smooth the descent of each weighted string.

To Do and Notice

(15 minutes or less)

Hold String 1 at the 250-cm point (closest to the "top" of the string, where you marked it), so the bottom of the string barely touches the cookie sheet.

Now drop the weighted string onto the angled piece of metal or wood and listen to the sound made by the falling weights. Notice that the rhythm gets faster and faster as the weights fall.

Now repeat with String 2. Hold it by the 250-cm point (closest to the "top" of the string, where you marked it), so the bottom of the string barely brushes the floor. Drop the weighted string onto the angled piece of metal or wood, as you did before, and listen for the rhythm. Notice that it has a constant beat: Even though the weights are not spaced evenly, they make a regular rhythm as they fall.

What's Going On?

The weights fall under gravity, accelerating downward—that is, both strings go faster and faster as they fall. Specifically, each weight falls a distance proportional to the square of the time that it falls. As a result, String 1, with its equally spaced weights, hits the floor with shorter and shorter time intervals between the weights.

In order to hit at equal time intervals, the weights must be spaced so that their distance from one another increases proportional to a square. If you look at where the weights were placed on String 2, you'll notice that the distances between the weights are proportional to the squares of the number of each weight: 1, 4, 9, 16, and so on.

The weights on String 1 are spaced at equal distances. Let them fall, and you can hear the way objects accelerate under gravity. The weights on String 2 are spaced to equalize the time it takes for each weight to hit the floor, so the rhythm of the weights hitting in free-fall is nice and even.

HEAD HARP
Learn a little string theory!

Material
→ A piece of string at least 3 feet (1 m) long

Introduction
Wrap a string around your head and pluck it to play music.

Assembly
None required.

To Do and Notice
(10 minutes or less)

Place the middle of the string behind your head, pull the string across your ears, and hold the two free ends together in front of your face. The string should cross over the opening in each ear. Pluck the string, and listen to the tone it makes.

You can hear your string, but the sounds are so quiet you will not disturb other people even if they are close to you.

How can you change the sound? Pull the string tighter, or make it looser, and listen to the change in pitch. Change the length of the string by sliding your hand along the string while keeping the tension as constant as possible. Then listen to the change in pitch.

BONUS!
If you want to go further, you can make a Two-Headed Harp! Make a large loop of string and wrap it around two heads. Pluck the strings and play music for two.

Etcetera

Many city bus services do not allow people to play loud music on buses. We find that if you wrap a string around your head and play music, not only will you abide by city laws, but you'll find yourself with more room as others move away from you.

What's Going On?

In this activity, you can actually hear how a string's frequency of vibration depends on its tension and length. When you pull the string tighter you increase the tension in the string and the pitch of the sound you hear increases. When you keep the tension constant and decrease the length of the string the pitch increases.

You're hearing the resonant frequencies of the string. The frequency is inversely proportional to the length of the string, and proportional to the square root of the tension in the string.

MAKE YOUR OWN RAINSTICK

Listen to the sound of a rainstorm—anytime, anywhere.

Materials

- Cardboard tube (a paper-towel roll is okay, but a long tube from gift-wrapping paper is even better; you can also take two or three paper-towel rolls and tape them together)
- Marker (any color)
- About forty 1-inch (2.5 cm) nails for each paper-towel tube you use
- Masking or packing tape
- Two index cards
- Scissors
- A few handfuls of raw rice or small dry beans, or a mix of such things

Introduction

The rainstick is a traditional instrument thought to have originated in Chile, where cactus spines are inserted into dried, hollowed-out cactus branches that are then filled with pebbles, raw rice, or dried beans.

Assembly

(30 minutes or less)

1. If you've chosen to use more than one paper tube, begin by taping them together.

2. Paper tubes have spiral seams. Use a marker to make dots about 1/2 inch (1.25 cm) apart all the way down the spiral seam of your tube.

3. Now poke a nail all the way in at each dot. (Make sure the nails don't poke through the other side of the tube.) You'll need about forty nails for each paper-towel tube.

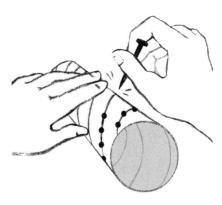

Etcetera

Instruments like these are found all over the world. In some places, including Australia and South America, legends say rainsticks were originally used as ceremonial instruments to call forth rain.

4. Wrap tape around the tube to hold the nails in place.

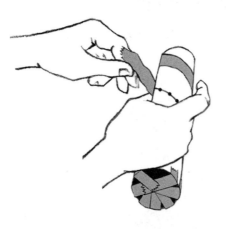

5. Cut two circles from the index cards just a little bigger than the ends of the tube. Tape one of the circles over one end of the tube. Cover the circle with tape so the whole end of the tube is sealed shut.

6. Put a handful or raw rice or beans into the open end of the tube. Cover the open end with your hand, and turn the tube over a few times, listening to the sound your rainstick makes. Add more rice or beans until you like what you hear. (Beans will make a harder sound; rice will make a softer sound.)

7. When you're ready, tip the tube up, put the second index-card circle over the open end, and seal it shut with tape.

To Do and Notice

(5 minutes or less)

Once your rainstick is complete, you can shake it like a rattle, use it as a percussive instrument, or gently tip it back and forth to make soothing environmental sounds.

What's Going On?

Each time a dry bean or grain of raw rice hits a nail it makes a tiny click. The nail carries the vibration of the clicking sound to the cardboard tube, which acts to convey the sound into the air, just like the soundboard on a piano.

The clicks happen at random as the rice falls through the tube, just as raindrops make sounds at random times as they fall onto a roof. This sound is called white noise. It is also the sound that AM radios make when they're not tuned to a station.

ORGAN PIPE
Bach to fundamentals!

Materials

- One large graduated cylinder (approximately 1-L capacity) or other clear, deep cylinder that can hold water (you can make your own by cementing a 2-foot length of 3-inch-diameter clear plastic pipe to a large, stable plastic base)
- One 3-foot (1 m) length of clear or opaque plastic pipe, approximately 2 inches (5 cm) in diameter (make sure the pipe can slide freely inside the cylinder noted above; thin-walled PVC pipe works well and is inexpensive)
- Tuning fork (one will do, but it is interesting to have others set to different frequencies)
- Water

Introduction

You can amplify a tuning fork by holding it over a pipe and changing the length of the pipe. At certain pipe lengths, the pitch made by the tuning fork sounds very loud as it resonates with the air column in the pipe.

Assembly

Stand the pipe on end in the cylinder and fill the cylinder with water.

To Do and Notice

(10 minutes or more)

Strike a tuning fork and hold it so that its tines, vibrating in a vertical plane, are above and very near the end of the pipe. While you hold the vibrating fork just above the end of the pipe, slide the pipe up and down in the cylinder until you find a place where the sound is louder. As the fork continues to vibrate (strike it again as needed), move the pipe upward to find other loud spots. Repeat the procedure with tuning forks of different frequencies and compare results.

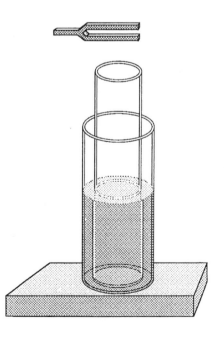

Here's another experiment you can do with this Snack: Try replacing the tuning fork with a speaker driven by an electronic oscillator (frequencies between 100 Hz and 700 Hz work well) or even with a tape recording of a tuning fork or oscillator. Or replace the tuning fork with an aluminum rod about 1/2 inch (1.25 cm) in diameter and at least 1 yard (1 m) long. Hold the rod at its center, strike one end with a hammer, and hold it vertically over the organ pipe. The aluminum rod will produce a loud, clear tone that will last for a long time.

You can also find the resonant frequencies of flexible pipe or hose. Listen with one end of the hose to your ear while you hum different frequencies (pitches) into the other end.

What's Going On?

As the tuning fork bends outward in its vibration, it squeezes together the air molecules in its path (see diagram). These molecules, in turn, squeeze the molecules next to them, and so on. In a sort of domino effect, a pulse of compression (a sound wave) travels down into the tube. The compression wave reflects off the surface of the water, at the bottom of the tube and then travels back up the tube.

When the compression wave reaches the mouth of the tube, it expands outward into the air. But the expansion of the air doesn't stop when it reaches the end of the tube. The air molecules overshoot and suck air from the tube. This produces a wave of expanded air that travels back down the tube, bounces off the water, and returns to the end of the tube. Air rushes into this expansion to create a compression. This process repeats over and over again.

If the tuning fork creates a new compression at the same time an existing compression reaches the top of the tube, the two compressions combine and the sound gets louder. This is known as resonance.

When you change the length of the tube, you change how long it takes for a sound wave to travel down and back up the tube. The sound wave is only synchronized with the tuning fork at certain pipe lengths.

For higher frequencies, the tube needs to be shorter to resonate. The sound wave has to bounce to the water and return sooner to be in sync with the tuning fork. All sound waves travel at the same speed in air (about 350 meters per second), so the only way to get the sound wave back to the tuning fork sooner is to make the tube shorter.

A pulse that starts at the tuning fork as a compression makes four complete transits of the tube (down as a compression, up as a compression, down as an expansion, up as an expansion) before it returns to the tuning fork as a compression. This means that one transit of the tube takes one-quarter of a tuning-fork cycle, or that one-quarter of a wavelength of sound will fit into the tube length. That means if you multiply the length of the tube by four, you will get the wavelength of the sound made by your tuning fork.

Be aware, though, that for a particular tuning fork, there are other resonances of the tube at tube lengths of 3/4 wavelength, 5/4 wavelength, and so on. Search for the shortest length of the tube that produces resonance: This will be 1/4 wavelength.

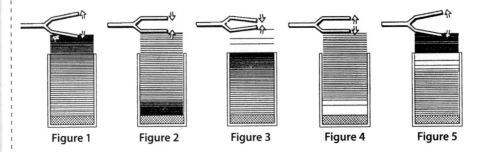

Figure 1   Figure 2   Figure 3   Figure 4   Figure 5

1. As the tuning fork vibrates, it compresses the air at the mouth of the tube.

2. The compressed air moves down the tube and bounces off the bottom.

3. The compressed air moves back up to the mouth of the tube. As it exits the tube, it begins to expand. The expansion is amplified by the vibration of the tuning fork.

4. The expanding air moves down the tube and bounces off the bottom.

5. The expanding air becomes a compression as it leaves the tube. The compression arrives at the vibrating tuning fork just in time to be further compressed.

PIPES OF PAN

When you hold a seashell to your ear, you can hear a steady roar.

Introduction

This simple construction allows you to separate the hum of background noise that surrounds us into some of its different frequencies.

Assembly

(15 minutes or more)

1. Cut six tubes to varying lengths. For example, you could make them 0.5 foot, 1 foot, 1.5 feet, 2 feet, 2.5 feet, and 3 feet long (15 cm, 30 cm, 45 cm, 60 cm, 90 cm).

2. Using tape or glue, attach the tubes to the board horizontally, near one end. Arrange them in order of length, so they look like a big xylophone.

To Do and Notice

(10 minutes or less)

Listen through each tube and compare the sounds you hear.

The background noise in a room is a mixture of many sounds with different pitches. Normally, these pitches blend, but you can separate them by listening through different tubes. Notice that you hear high-pitched sounds in the shorter tubes and low-pitched sounds in the longer tubes. Which tubes give the loudest sounds? Which give the softest sounds?

Listen to how the sounds change as you move your ear up against the end of the pipe, so that the end is actually sealed off by your ear.

Pan pipes—the ancient musical instrument used worldwide—also consist of an array of tubes of different lengths. The air inside these pipes is set into motion by blowing into the pipes, instead of by nearby sound sources. (Otherwise they wouldn't play very loudly!) The Exploratorium's full-sized Pipes of Pan exhibit could also be played this way—but only by a 30-foot-tall piper!

Organ pipes are also an array of different-sized tubes. Air is blown into these pipes, causing them to produce sounds. All aerophones (woodwinds and brass instruments) operate on the same principle: They are single tubes whose length can be changed by a musician using valves, slides, or keys.

Your ear contains a resonant tube, as well—open on the outside and closed on the inside by the eardrum. The resonances of this tube affect the range of sounds you can hear.

What's Going On?

Most of the sounds we hear are mixtures of many different frequencies. For example, at any one time, you may be hearing the sounds of voices, traffic, pigeons, wind, machinery, and your own footsteps. Each of these sources itself consists of a range of frequencies.

Pipes of Pan uses the principle of resonance to separate sound into individual frequency components. Any object has a frequency or set of frequencies, called its natural frequencies, at which it "likes" to vibrate. For example, a pendulum swinging by itself, with no pushing, will always oscillate at the same frequency. You can change this natural frequency by changing the length of the pendulum. In fact, an object's natural frequency, in general, depends on its size: The bigger it is, the more slowly it tends to vibrate.

In this Snack, the "object" that's vibrating is the air inside the tubes. The longer this column of air, the more slowly it tends to vibrate. Because each tube has a different length, it selects out a different set of frequencies from the mishmash of background noise, and ignores the other frequencies. When you put your ear to the longest tube, you hear the lowest frequencies; when you listen to the shortest tube, you hear the highest frequencies, and so on.

When you close off one end of the tube with your ear, the resonant frequencies become even lower. The lowest resonant frequency of a tube closed at one end is half that of the same-length tube open at both ends. An explanation of why this is so is beyond the scope of what we can reasonably include here, but it is commonly covered in many high school and college physics texts.

RADIOHEAD
An unconventional way to listen to the radio.

Materials

- A source of sound with a built-in speaker you can easily reach, such as a radio or wind-up music box (for this Snack, sound makers such as boom boxes, with separated speakers, don't always work well)
- Earplugs
- Sturdy plastic toothbrush with a solid plastic handle

Introduction

Most of the time, we hear sounds transmitted through the air, but that's not the only way to hear things.

Assembly

None needed.

To Do and Notice

(5 minutes or more)

Turn on the radio (or other sound source), and then put earplugs in your ears and adjust the volume low enough that you can't hear it.

Clasp one end of the toothbrush between your front teeth and touch the other end of the toothbrush to the radio near the vibrating speaker. You should be able to hear the radio again—but through your body instead of through the air!

Etcetera

In the late eighteenth century, when German composer Ludwig van Beethoven began to lose his hearing, he tried listening to his piano by clasping a wooden stick in his teeth and touching it to the piano. Two hundred years later, joggers could buy "Bone Fones," personal stereo systems that hung around the neck, giving the listener "breathtaking sound" directly through the bones of the neck and head.

What's Going On?

When you hear sounds through the toothbrush, you're actually hearing with your whole body. Vibrations from the sound source are transmitted through the hard plastic of the toothbrush into your teeth and jaw, then through the bones of your skull to the bones of your ear, and finally to the auditory nerve.

This works because bone is a relatively efficient conductor of sound, and so offers an alternate pathway for sound perception. People who have outer- or middle-ear problems may have trouble accessing and processing airborne sound vibrations, but for those whose auditory nerves can still process sound, devices that channel vibrations directly through the bones of the head can sometimes compensate for some hearing loss.

SOUND SANDWICH

Make beautiful music with sticks, straws, and rubber bands.

Materials

- Two jumbo craft sticks
- A straw
- One wide rubber band (#64 size)
- Two smaller, narrower rubber bands
- Scissors

Introduction

By making simple adjustments to a noisemaker called a "Sound Sandwich," you'll be able to raise or lower its pitch and make different kinds of sounds.

Assembly

(15 minutes or more)

1. Stretch a wide rubber band lengthwise over one of the craft sticks.

2. Cut two small pieces of straw, each about 1 inch to 1½ inches (2.5 to 3.8 cm) in length. Put one of the small straw pieces under the wide rubber band, about a third of the way up from one end of the stick.

3. Take the second craft stick and place it on top of the first one.

4. Wrap one of the smaller rubber bands around the end of the stick a few times, about 1/2 inch (1.25 cm) from the end, on the same side where you placed the straw. Make sure the rubber band pinches the two sticks tightly together.

① CAUTION

Not for unsettled nerves! A room full of Sound Sandwiches can create quite a cacophony!

Etcetera

Like the rubber band in the Sound Sandwich, your vocal cords also vibrate when you speak or sing. The more tension they're under, the faster they vibrate and the higher the sound they make.

5. Take the second small piece of straw and place it between the two craft sticks, at the opposite end. This time, though, place the straw on top of the thick rubber band, so it sits just under the top craft stick.

6. Wrap the second small rubber band around the loose end of the stick, about 1/2 inch (1.25 cm) from the end. When you're done, both ends should be pinched together and there should be a small space between the two craft sticks (created by the pieces of straw).

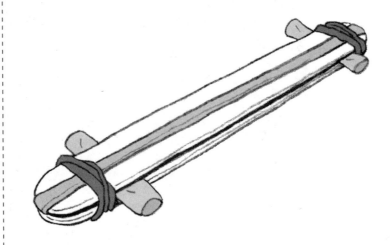

To Do and Notice

(5 minutes or more)

When your Sound Sandwich is complete, just put your mouth in the middle, as if you were playing a harmonica, and blow! (Remember to blow through the sticks, not the straws.) Notice that you can make different sounds by blowing through different areas of the instrument, blowing harder or softer, or by moving the straws closer together or farther apart. Experiment to find out how many different sounds the Sound Sandwich will make.

What's Going On?

When you blow into the Sound Sandwich, you make the large rubber band vibrate, and that vibration produces sound. Long, massive objects vibrate slowly and produce low-pitched sounds; shorter, less-massive objects vibrate quickly and produce high-pitched sounds. The tension of a rubber band also will change its pitch: Higher tensions lead to higher-pitched resonances. When you move the straws closer together, you shorten the part of the rubber band that can vibrate, so the pitch gets higher than the original sound. You may also have played with this effect if you've ever stretched a blade of grass between your fingers and blown into the gap to make the grass vibrate and buzz.

SPEAKER

Make a speaker that turns changing electric current into sound.

Materials

- About 8 feet (2.5 m) or more of 24-gauge or higher (thinner) magnet wire
- Piece of sandpaper, a few inches square
- C or D cell battery (it can be dead; it's just used to wind the coil)
- A mini mono-phono plug (you can either buy the plug or you can cut the headgear off an old pair of broken or unused headphones; you just need the wire with the plug on it that fits into a radio or other amplified audio device)
- Two alligator-clip connectors
- Scotch tape or masking tape
- Wire cutter/strippers or scissors
- One or two donut magnets about 1 inch (2.5 cm) in diameter and 1/4-inch (6.4 mm) thick
- Paper cup
- Working radio with headphone plug

Introduction

Wind up a coil of wire, attach it to the bottom of a paper cup, hold a magnet nearby, and listen to the radio! You've made your own speaker.

Assembly

(30 minutes or less)

1. Sand the enamel off the end of the last 2 inches (5 cm) of the magnet wire until the bare wire gleams at both ends.

2. Wind the magnet wire around the battery, leaving 4 inches (10 cm) free of the coil at each end.

3. Slide the wire off the battery and wrap the free ends around the coil to keep the arrangement in place. Leave a few inches of wire sticking out at each end.

4. Tape the coil to the outside bottom of the paper cup.

5. Attach one end of each alligator clip to the two protruding ends of the wire coil (see diagram).

6. With scissors or wire strippers, strip off the end of the mini mono-phono plug wire and separate the two strands (if there's a third ground wire in there, just bundle it with one of the other strands).

Etcetera

Paper cups make handy speakers because they fit easily over the ear, but you can use just about anything to vibrate the air. Attach the coil to other objects, hold them near your ear, and hear what happens.

7. Attach the free ends of the alligator clips to the two strands of wire on the mini mono-phono plug.

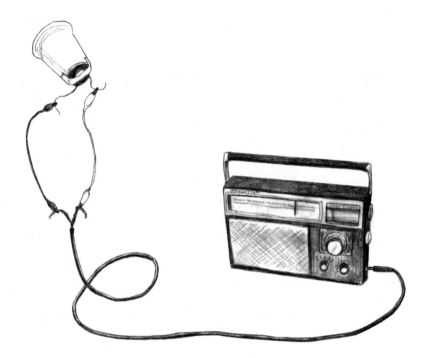

To Do and Notice

(10 minutes or more)

Plug the mini mono-phono plug into the radio and then turn the radio on (you may have to turn it up a bit louder than you normally would). With one hand, hold the cup to your ear. With your other hand, bring a magnet closer and closer to the coil of wire until you can hear the sound produced by your homemade speaker.

If you have two magnets, you can put one inside the bottom of the cup and the other next to the coil, on the outside of the cup (so the two magnets hold each other on) to keep the sound going.

What's Going On?

Look down at the loop of wire. When electric current goes around the loop clockwise as you look at the loop, there is a south magnetic pole nearest you. When the current reverses there is a north magnetic pole nearest you.

When the south magnetic pole of a magnet is near the coil of wire it will attract a north pole and repel a south pole of the coil electromagnet. The coil will move toward and away from the magnet, depending on the direction of the electric current. Because the coil is attached to the cup, the cup will also move toward and away from the magnet.

The cup pushes air back and forth, creating a sound that travels to your ear. The bare wire itself does not move much air, so it does not make much sound. However, if the coil is attached to a large, low-mass material, it will vibrate that material which, in turn, will vibrate the air, making a louder sound.

Inside almost every speaker there will be a magnet, a coil of wire, and a thin material to convey the sound into the air. The invention of strong rare-earth magnets allows speakers to create more sound using less electric current.

STEREO SOUND

Locating the source of a sound is mostly a matter of timing.

Materials

- One 3-foot (1 m) length of hose measuring 1 inch (2.5 cm) or more in diameter (vacuum-cleaner hose works well)
- Two 10-inch (25 cm) lengths of wood measuring 1 × 2 inches (2.5 × 5 cm)
- Wood for a base, measuring 2 × 4 × 6 inches (5 × 10 × 15 cm)
- One 2-foot (60 cm) length of wire
- Glue, nails, or screws
- A friend

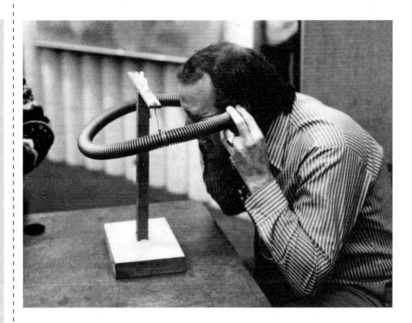

Introduction

Normally, sound from a given source must travel slightly different distances to reach each of your two ears. Consequently, each ear hears the sound at a slightly different time. This difference in timing lets you determine where a sound source is located.

Assembly

(10 minutes or less)

1. Fasten the 1 inch × 2 inch pieces so they form a T. Fasten the bottom of the T to the 2 × 4 × 6-inch wood base. (If you'd rather, devise a similar-sized stand from PVC pipe instead.)

2. Use the wire to hang the hose from the T's crossbar. The hose should be balanced and hang freely from the T (see photo at the beginning of this Snack).

To Do and Notice

(10 minutes or less)

Sit facing away from the hose (or sit facing the hose and close your eyes). Hold the hose so that one end covers each ear.

Have a friend tap the hose with a pencil. Can you tell whether the tapping is closer to your right ear or left ear? Try this several times while your friend varies the location of the tapping.

Try to guess when your friend is tapping in the center of the hose, midway between your ears. How far does the tapping have to move from this midpoint before you can hear that it's closer to one ear?

Try listening with only one ear. Can you locate the source of the sound with one ear?

Etcetera

An animal's hearing ability is related to its habitat. Humans are descended from tree-dwelling anthropoids. These animals had cup-shaped ears on the sides of their heads, which allowed the animals to locate sound sources in three dimensions. Plains-dwelling animals usually have pointed ears located on the top of their head. This arrangement is better for locating sound in a horizontal plane.

Just as you use the difference in arrival time to locate a sound, seismologists use the different arrival times of seismic waves at two or more receivers to calculate the locations of earthquakes. After all, seismic waves are just sound waves traveling through the ground.

What's Going On?

If your friend taps the hose to the left of center while you are listening with both ears, the sound will reach your left ear slightly before it reaches your right ear. For example, if your friend taps the hose 3 inches (7.6 cm) to the left of center, the sound will reach your left ear 1/2,000 of a second before it reaches your right ear.

Sound travels at about 1,000 feet/second (350 m/s). When your friend moves the pencil by 3 inches (7.6 cm), the path to your left ear becomes 3 inches (7.6 cm) shorter and the path to your right ear becomes 3 inches (7.6 cm) longer. The difference in path length is 6 inches (15.2 cm), or half a foot, which sound covers in half a millisecond. Your brain uses this difference in arrival time to determine whether the sound source is closer to your right ear or your left ear.

When you use two ears, you compare differences in the properties of intensity (volume), arrival time, phase, and frequency of a sound. If both ears hear a sound equally, you perceive a sound source as being directly in front of you or directly behind you. Your ears and brain use relative differences in the sound to locate it at some point away from center.

If you listen to the tube with only one ear, you will not be able to detect whether the tapping is slightly to one side or the other of the middle of the tube. However, you may be able to detect when the tapping is close to your ear and when it is far away.

Using one ear to locate a sound source is comparable to using one eye to locate an object. You can locate an object using one eye, but not as readily, and your view lacks depth. In the case of the ear, some direction can be detected by a single human ear because of its pinna—the cup-shaped, fleshy part of your outer ear. But, compared to our sophisticated ability to locate a sound source in space using two ears, the ability to locate a sound source using only one ear is very limited.

STRAW OBOE
Two lips make sound.

Materials
- Soda straws
- Scissors
- Optional: Poster paper, tape, soldering iron

Introduction

By cutting two "lips" into the flattened end of a soda straw and blowing with just the right pressure, you can make sounds resonate in the straw.

Assembly

(10 minutes or less)

1. Flatten one end of your soda straw by sticking the end in your mouth, biting down with your teeth, and pulling it out. Do this several times to make a flexible, flat-ended straw.

2. Cut equal pieces from each side of the flattened end (as shown), so that the straw has two "lips" at the end.

To Do and Notice

(5 minutes or more)

Put the straw in your mouth and bite down on it gently with your front teeth, just beyond the lips of the straw. Then blow into the straw. You'll probably have to experiment with blowing harder and softer while biting down with different amounts of pressure until you make the straw sing.

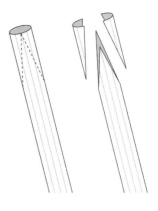

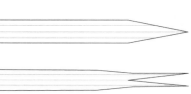

Etcetera

There are many ways to experiment with your straw oboe. Slide a slightly larger straw onto the end and use it like a trombone. Melt fingering-holes into the straw with a soldering iron. Snip the straw shorter and shorter with scissors to increase its pitch, or devise a "bell" with paper and tape to make your instrument louder. Experiment with new ways to change the sound.

What's Going On?

The beveled "lips" you cut into the squashed end of the straw act as a reed for your instrument. When you blow into the reed and get it vibrating, you send pulses of compressed air down the straw, causing the air in the tube to start vibrating, too. Affected by the length of the tube, this vibrating air in turn affects the reed's vibrations. When the reed vibrates at just the right frequency, the air in the straw vibrates powerfully, and you hear a loud, buzzing note, sort of like an oboe.

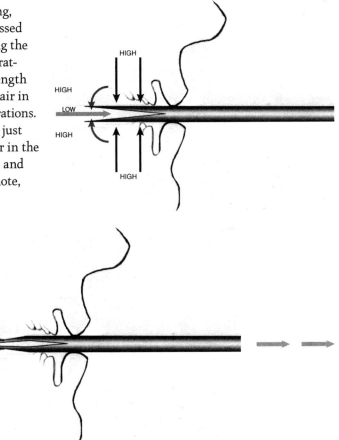

When you blow through the straw, there is a high pressure in your mouth. As air rushes through the straw, the pressure in the straw drops. The high pressure outside the straw pushes the sides of the reed inward, closing off the flow. The pressure then builds inside the straw and pops the reed open again.

The sound from your straw oboe is an example of a phenomenon called resonance. Every object has a natural frequency, a tendency to vibrate at a particular rate. When you vibrate something at its natural frequency, it resonates, meaning that the vibrations build and grow more and more extreme. Other examples of resonance include a car that shudders at certain speeds, a child swinging higher and higher on a swing, and a glass shattered by the high notes of a soprano.

The straw oboe resonates when the sound waves bouncing back and forth inside make a special pattern called a standing wave. Standing waves occur when waves going one way overlap with waves going the opposite way, creating a set of peaks and valleys that seem to stand still. You can't see the standing waves in your straw, but you can hear them.

The exact note that you hear when you blow your straw oboe depends on the length of the straw. In a shorter straw, the standing wave inside the straw will be shorter, too, causing the pitch to be higher. In a longer straw, the standing wave will be longer, and the note you hear will be lower.

WATER-BOTTLE MEMBRANOPHONE

This surprising instrument is fun to make—and even more fun to play.

Materials

- A clean, empty plastic water bottle, any size (bottles with ridges are best)
- Scissors (for children) or utility knife (for adults only)
- Latex, rubber, or vinyl gloves (or a balloon, though it's harder to work with)
- Rubber band
- Hole punch
- A straw
- Construction paper (acetate or card stock works too)

Introduction

Here, a water bottle and a paper tube make a membranophone—an instrument that produces sound from a vibrating stretched membrane. Kazoos and drums are both examples of membranophones. This one sounds a little like a cross between a saxophone and a clarinet.

Assembly

(30 minutes or less)

1. Leave the cap on the bottle, but peel the label off.

2. Count down about 3 ridges (3 inches [7.5 cm]) from the top of the bottle. Using scissors (or a utility knife, if an adult is doing this), cut along the ridge. Make sure you cut evenly along the edge. Trim off any bumpy spots.

3. Put the bottom of the bottle away; you'll just be working with the top half.

4. Take your hole punch and punch a hole near the cut edge of the remaining piece of the bottle, as far up as you can get it. Put the straw through the hole to test it for size. It should be a tight fit. If the hole isn't large enough for the diameter of the straw, repunch in nearly the same spot to widen the hole a bit.

5. Cut the fingers and thumb off the glove as a unit. The rest of the glove should now look like a wide tube. Cut the tube open to form a sheet of pliable material—a membrane.

6. Stretch the membrane over the hand-cut opening of the bottle, making sure that the hole you punched in the side doesn't get hidden by excess material.

7. Attach the membrane to the bottle with a rubber band. Wrap the rubber band around the bottle several times, making sure that the membrane is taut.

8. Twist the cap off the bottle and set it aside.

9. Roll a piece of construction paper into a tube, making it as tight and straight as possible. Put the rolled-up tube into the neck of the bottle, where the cap had been. Let go of the tube when it barely touches the bottom of the membrane. It should fit securely in the hole. Tape it to the neck of the bottle so it stays in place.

10. Insert the straw into the punched hole on the side of the bottle, and you're ready to play!

To Do and Notice

(5 minutes or more)

Now that your instrument is complete, simply blow into the straw on the side of the bottle, and your Water-Bottle Membranophone should play!

To make different sounds, you can add finger holes. To do this, pinch the paper tube slightly and cut out a diamond shape. Repeat to make more finger holes.

What's Going On?

Membranophones are instruments that make sound from the vibrations of stretched skins or membranes. Drums, tambourines, and some gongs are common examples of membranophones.

In this Snack, as you blow into the straw, you create pressure in the space between the outer wall of the construction-paper tube and the inner wall of the water bottle. That pressure forces the membrane to rise, allowing air to flow into the top of the tube and escape out the bottom.

As the air escapes, the membrane returns to its initial position. But as you continue blowing air into the instrument, you force the membrane to rapidly rise and fall, over and over again. If you place your finger over the top of the membrane, you can feel it vibrate. These vibrations produce sound.

Opening or covering the finger holes changes the pitch of the sound. That's because opening a hole has the same effect as shortening the length of the "pipe" (the rolled-up construction paper). The shorter the pipe, the higher the pitch of the sound.

WIRE-HANGER CONCERTO

A dramatic (and surprisingly melodic) demonstration of how well vibrations travel through metal.

Materials

- Unpainted metal clothes hanger
- String
- Scissors
- Optional: Cookie-cooling rack, metal salad tongs

Introduction

Did you ever see the bad guy in an old Western put his ear to the ground to hear the hoofbeats of the fast-approaching sheriff and his posse? Or perhaps you remember Aragorn with his ear to the ground, listening for the approach of the dreaded Orcs in the *Lord of the Rings: The Two Towers*. This activity shows why the trick works so well.

Assembly

(5 minutes or less)

1. Cut two lengths of string, each about 2 feet (0.6 m) long.

2. Tie the strings to each side of a metal hanger. Make finger loops in the free ends of the strings and hang the loops from one finger on each hand.

3. Place your fingers (with hanger assembly attached) gently into your ears. Swing the hanger so that it bangs lightly against something hard, like the edge of a desk or a doorframe, and then let the hanger hang free. As the hanger vibrates, you should hear the resulting sound ring through the strings like chimes.

4. To go further, try using different materials and see how well they work. Instead of using a metal hanger, for instance, try a cookie-cooling rack or a pair of metal salad tongs.

Etcetera

Sound is an organized motion. Heat is a random motion. Some materials, including lead, rapidly turn sound into heat. Others, such as quartz crystal, very slowly turn sound into heat.

What's Going On?

Although most of the sounds we hear are transmitted through the air, air is not the only carrier of sound waves—nor is it the best. A ticking clock can be heard through the air if you're close enough, but put your ear to the table with the clock on it and the ticking will sound much louder.

When something vibrates, the strength of the vibration and the length of time the vibrations continue can vary quite a bit, depending on the materials involved. Hit a piece of wood with a stick and the sound lasts for just an instant. Hit a metal gong with the same stick, and the sound may continue for many seconds. Water is another good transmitter of sound. Put your ear into a pan of water and listen to two rocks clacking together.

Why the difference? In some materials, the molecules are tightly packed together; in other materials, the molecules are more loosely arranged. How close the molecules are to one another can affect how easily they can bump into each other to start a vibration moving along.

About the Exploratorium and the Exploratorium Teacher Institute

The Exploratorium is a hands-on museum of science, art, and human perception dedicated to exploration and discovery. Founded in San Francisco in 1969 by noted physicist and educator Frank Oppenheimer, the museum has grown to become an internationally acclaimed science center. Its hundreds of interactive exhibits stimulate learning and richly illustrate scientific concepts and natural phenomena.

Since 1984, the Teacher Institute has provided workshops for science and math teachers of Grades 6 through 12. The Institute offers a discover-by-doing approach to science learning: museum exhibits, classroom activities, and a variety of new media are used to explore concepts and models of science and math using inquiry-based pedagogy. The Institute offers programs for both new and experienced teachers and welcomes graduates to its active community of more than three thousand teachers across the country.

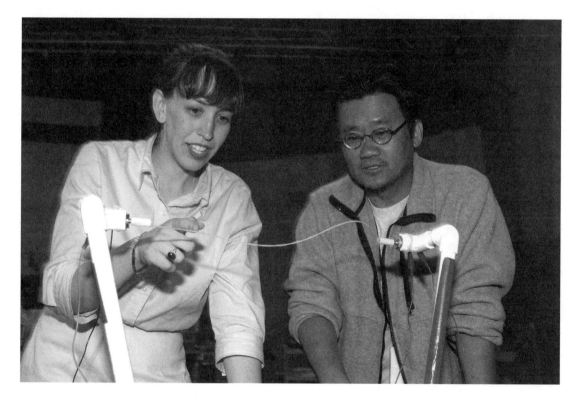

Contributors

At the Exploratorium, no one works alone. The *Exploratorium Science Snackbook* would not have been possible without the creativity and support of the Teacher Institute and the many museum staff members who contributed to its creation and development, including those listed here:

Leon Aksionczyk

Vivian Altmann

Larry Antila

Annette Anzalone

Rod Baird

David Barker

Maurice Bazin

Donald B. Beck

Judith Brand

Diane Bredt

Ruth Brown

Megan Bury

Cassie Byrd

Ray Canziani

Charles Carlson

Rilla Chaney

Darry Chinn

Yvonne Chong

Judith Christensen

Gary Crounse

Rosemary Davidson

Christopher de Latour

Pablo Dela Cruz

Paul Doherty

Shirley Dominic

Robert Draper

Vincent A. Dunn

Raleigh Ellisen

Gabe Espinda

Rose Falanga

Kurt Feichtmeir

Jane Ferguson

Jonathan Frank

Curt Gabrielson

Tricia Garlock

Cappy Greene

Winston Hall

Stephen Herrick

Charles Hibbard

Ron Hipschman

Gloriane Hirata

Steve Honett

Lori Hytrek

Laura Jacoby

Donald Jones

Michael Kamen

Karen Kalumuck

Tayeko Kaufman

Bob Keeble

Norman Keeve

Eric Kielich

Jad King

Arthur Koch

Esther Kutnick

Jennifer Lambdin

Lin Kim Lennie Lee

Sandy Lin

Elizabeth Looney

Alisa Lowden

Nance McChesney

Linda McCone

Grant Mellor

Karen Mendelow
Steve Miller
John Miron
Brenda Mitchell
Eric Muller
Fred Muller
Carol Murphy
Pat Murphy
Beth Napier
Erainya Neirro
Peter Olguin
Lorraine Perry
Tanya Phillips
James Ramberg
Don Rathjen
Madeleine Reiter
Charles Reynes
Charles Rhodes
John Rocky
Susan Schwartzenberg

Suzanne Shimek
Linda Shore
Sanford (Sandy) Siegel
Allen Sinor
Kevin Smith
Amy Snyder
Jeff Steinert
Modesto Tamez
John Teamer
Pearl Tesler
Guillermo Trejo-Mejilla
John Valentine
Joan Venticinque
Julie Walker
John Wherry
Thurston Williams
Jimmy Wong
Wilton Wong
Barbara Ziegenhals

We also want to thank Exploratorium Executive Director Dennis Bartels and Executive Associate Director Rob Semper for providing the institutional support necessary to make this project a reality.

National Science Education Standards

In 1996, the National Research Council, a division of the National Academy of Sciences, published the *National Science Education Standards,* which outlines outcomes of science learning that will lead to a scientifically literate society. The *Standards* presents a new vision of teaching and learning, with a strong emphasis on inquiry.

The grids on pages 280 through 289 show correlations between the Snacks and the standards for grades 5–8 and 9–12, based on the primary concepts covered. You may be able to modify any Snack so that it correlates to additional standards.

Note that a few of the Snacks—marked with an asterisk (*)—have no standards checked off for a particular grid. In those cases, the primary concepts in the activity do not correlate with the standards for that grade level. We've also included a math category. Although math is not one of the science education standards, some teachers might find this useful.

National Science Education Standards[0] — Grades 5–8	Science as Inquiry	Properties & changes of properties in matter	Motions & forces	Transfer of energy	Structure & function in living systems	Reproduction & heredity	Regulation & behavior	Populations & ecosystems	Diversity & adaptations of organisms	Structure of the earth's system	Earth's history	Earth in the solar system	Science & Technology	Science in Personal & Social Perspectives	History & Nature of Science	Math
THE CHESHIRE CAT AND OTHER EYE-POPPING EXPLORATIONS OF HOW WE SEE THE WORLD																
Afterimage	X			X	X		X						X			
Anti-Gravity Mirror	X			X									X			
Benham's Disk	X			X	X											
Bird in the Cage	X			X	X											
Blind Spot	X			X	X											X
Bronx Cheer Bulb	X			X	X											
Cardboard Tube Syllabus	X			X	X		X						X			
Cheshire Cat	X			X	X		X									
Color Contrast	X			X	X		X									
Depth Spinner	X				X											
Disappearing Act	X	X		X	X				X							
Everyone Is You and Me	X			X	X											
Fading Dot	X			X	X		X									
Far-Out Corners	X			X	X											X
Gray Step	X			X	X		X									
Jacques Cousteau in Seashells	X				X		X		X							
Mirrorly a Window	X				X		X									
Moiré Patterns*																
Peripheral Vision	X			X	X		X		X							
Persistence of Vision	X			X	X		X									
Pupil	X			X	X		X		X							
Size and Distance	X			X	X		X									
Squirming Palm	X			X	X											
Thread the Needle	X			X	X		X									X
Vanna	X				X		X									
Whirling Watcher	X			X	X		X						X			
THE COOL HOT ROD AND OTHER ELECTRIFYING EXPLORATIONS OF ENERGY AND MATTER																
Charge and Carry	X	X	X	X												
Circles of Magnetism I	X	X	X	X						X						
Circles of Magnetism II	X	X	X	X												

National Science Education Standards[0] — Grades 5–8	Science as Inquiry	Physical Science — Properties & changes of properties in matter	Motions & forces	Transfer of energy	Life Science — Structure & function in living systems	Reproduction & heredity	Regulation & behavior	Populations & ecosystems	Diversity & adaptations of organisms	Earth & Space Science — Structure of the earth's system	Earth's history	Earth in the solar system	Science & Technology	Science in Personal & Social Perspectives	History & Nature of Science	Math
Cold Metal	X			X	X		X									
Convection Currents	X	X		X						X	X					
Cool Hot Rod	X	X		X						X			X			X
Curie Point*																
Eddy Currents*																
Electrical Fleas	X	X	X	X												
Electroscope	X	X	X	X												
Fog Chamber	X	X		X						X						
Gas Model	X	X		X						X						
Give and Take	X	X		X						X						
Hand Battery	X	X		X												
Hot Spot	X	X		X												X
Magnetic Lines of Force	X	X	X	X						X		X	X			
Magnetic Suction	X		X	X									X			
Motor Effect	X		X	X									X			
Radioactive Decay Model				X						X			X			X
Short Circuit	X	X		X									X			
Stripped-Down Motor	X		X	X									X			
THE MAGIC WAND AND OTHER BRIGHT EXPLORATIONS OF LIGHT AND COLOR																
Blue Sky	X			X						X		X				
Bone Stress	X		X	X	X								X	X		
Bridge Light*																
Color Table	X			X	X								X			
Colored Shadows	X			X									X	X		
Corner Reflector	X			X									X			
Critical Angle	X			X									X			X
Cylindrical Mirror	X			X									X			X
Diffraction*																
Disappearing Glass Rods	X			X												
Duck-Into Kaleidoscope	X			X									X			
Giant Lens	X															

National Science Education Standards[0] / Grades 5–8	Science as Inquiry	Physical Science			Life Science					Earth & Space Science			Science & Technology	Science in Personal & Social Perspectives	History & Nature of Science	Math
		Properties & changes of properties in matter	Motions & forces	Transfer of energy	Structure & function in living systems	Reproduction & heredity	Regulation & behavior	Populations & ecosystems	Diversity & adaptations of organisms	Structure of the earth's system	Earth's history	Earth in the solar system				
Inverse-Square Law	X			X												X
Look into Infinity	X			X												X
Magic Wand	X			X	X								X			X
Parabolas	X			X									X			X
Pinhole Magnifier	X			X	X								X			X
Polarized Light Mosaic	X			X												
Polarized Sunglasses	X			X									X			X
Rotating Light*	X															
Soap Film Painting	X			X	X							X				
Spectra	X			X								X	X		X	X
Spherical Reflections	X			X												X
Touch the Spring	X			X												X
Water Sphere Lens	X			X									X			X
THE SPINNING BLACKBOARD AND OTHER DYNAMIC EXPLORATIONS OF FORCE AND MOTION																
Balancing Ball	X		X													
Balancing Stick	X		X													
Bernoulli Levitator	X		X										X			
Bicycle Wheel Gyro	X		X										X		X	
Bubble Suspension	X		X		X											
Bubble Tray	X		X		X											
Center of Gravity	X		X													
Coupled Resonant Pendulums	X		X													
Descartes Diver	X		X										X			
Downhill Race	X		X										X			
Drawing Board	X		X							X						
Momentum Machine	X		X													X
Non-Round Rollers	X		X													
Resonant Pendulum	X		X	X												
Resonant Rings	X		X	X						X						
Resonator	X			X												
Soap Bubbles	X	X			X								X			X
Spinning Blackboard	X		X							X					X	X

National Science Education Standards⁰ — Grades 5–8	Science as Inquiry	Physical Science: Properties & changes of properties in matter	Motions & forces	Transfer of energy	Life Science: Structure & function in living systems	Reproduction & heredity	Regulation & behavior	Populations & ecosystems	Diversity & adaptations of organisms	Earth & Space Science: Structure of the earth's system	Earth's history	Earth in the solar system	Science & Technology	Science in Personal & Social Perspectives	History & Nature of Science	Math
Strange Attractor	x		x	x												
Take It from the Top	x		x	x									x		x	
Vortex	x	x	x							x						
Water Spinner*	x	x										x				x
THE WIRE-HANGER CONCERTO AND OTHER EAR-SPLITTING EXPLORATIONS OF HOW WE HEAR THE WORLD																
Anti-Sound Spring	x		x	x												
Bee Hummer	x		x	x									x			
Coffee-Can Cuica	x			x	x											
Conversation Piece	x			x	x								x			
Designer Ears	x			x	x				x				x			
Doppler Effect	x			x	x			x					x			
Falling Rhythm	x		x	x	x							x				
Head Harp	x			x	x								x			x
Make Your Own Rainstick	x			x									x			
Organ Pipe	x		x	x	x											
Pipes of Pan	x			x												
Radiohead	x		x	x	x								x			
Sound Sandwich	x			x	x					x			x	x		
Speaker*																
Stereo Sound	x			x	x				x	x			x			
Straw Oboe	x		x	x	x								x			
Water-Bottle Membranophone	x			x	x											
Wire-Hanger Concerto	x		x	x	x								x			

National Science Education Standards	Science as Inquiry	Physical Science						Life Science	
Grades 9–12		Structure of atoms	Structure & properties of matter	Chemical reactions	Motions & forces	Conservation of energy & increase in disorder	Interactions of energy & matter	The cell	Molecular basis of heredity
THE CHESHIRE CAT AND OTHER EYE-POPPING EXPLORATIONS OF HOW WE SEE THE WORLD									
Afterimage	X					X			
Anti-Gravity Mirror	X		X			X			
Benham's Disk	X					X			
Bird in the Cage	X					X			
Blind Spot	X								
Bronx Cheer Bulb	X					X			
Cardboard Tube Syllabus	X					X			
Cheshire Cat	X					X			
Color Contrast	X								
Depth Spinner	X								
Disappearing Act	X								
Everyone Is You and Me	X					X			
Fading Dot	X					X			
Far-Out Corners	X								
Gray Step	X								
Jacques Cousteau in Seashells	X								
Mirrorly a Window	X					X			
Moiré Patterns	X								
Peripheral Vision	X								
Persistence of Vision	X								
Pupil	X								
Size and Distance	X								
Squirming Palm	X								
Thread the Needle	X								
Vanna	X								
Whirling Watcher	X					X			
THE COOL HOT ROD AND OTHER ELECTRIFYING EXPLORATIONS OF ENERGY AND MATTER									
Charge and Carry	X	X	X		X		X		
Circles of Magnetism I	X		X		X		X		
Circles of Magnetism II	X		X		X		X		
Cold Metal	X					X	X		
Convection Currents					X	X			
Cool Hot Rod	X				X	X	X		
Curie Point	X		X		X	X			
Eddy Currents	X		X		X		X		
Electrical Fleas	X	X	X		X	X	X		
Electroscope	X	X			X	X	X		
Fog Chamber	X		X		X	X	X		
Gas Model			X	X	X	X			
Give and Take	X				X				
Hand Battery	X		X	X	X				
Hot Spot	X					X	X		
Magnetic Lines of Force	X				X				
Magnetic Suction	X				X	X	X		
Motor Effect	X				X	X	X		
Radioactive Decay Model		X					X		

Life Science (continued)				Earth & Space Science				Science & Technology	Science in Personal & Social Perspectives	History & Nature of Science	Math
Biological evolution	Inter-dependence of organisms	Matter, energy, & organization in living systems	Behavior of organisms	Energy in the earth's system	Geo-chemical cycles	Origin & evolution of the earth's system	Origin & evolution of the universe				
			X								
			X					X			
			X								
			X								
			X								X
			X								
			X								
			X								
			X								
X			X								
			X								
			X								
		X									X
			X								
			X								
			X								
			X								
			X								
			X								
			X								
			X								X
			X								
			X					X			
				X							
			X								
				X	Geo						
								X			X
				X							
				X							
				X							
			X	X				X			
				X							X

National Science Education Standards	Science as Inquiry	Physical Science						Life Science	
Grades 9–12		Structure of atoms	Structure & properties of matter	Chemical reactions	Motions & forces	Conservation of energy & increase in disorder	Interactions of energy & matter	The cell	Molecular basis of heredity
Short Circuit	X					X			
Stripped-Down Motor					X	X			
THE MAGIC WAND AND OTHER BRIGHT EXPLORATIONS OF LIGHT AND COLOR									
Blue Sky	X					X	X		
Bone Stress	X						X		
Bridge Light							X		
Color Table	X						X		
Colored Shadows	X						X		
Corner Reflector	X					X	X		
Critical Angle	X						X		
Cylindrical Mirror	X						X		
Diffraction	X						X		
Disappearing Glass Rods	X		X				X		
Duck-Into Kaleidoscope	X					X	X		
Giant Lens	X						X		
Inverse-Square Law	X					X	X		
Look into Infinity	X						X		
Magic Wand	X						X		
Parabolas	X						X		
Pinhole Magnifier	X						X		
Polarized Light Mosaic	X					X	X		
Polarized Sunglasses	X					X	X		
Rotating Light	X		X				X		
Soap Film Painting	X						X	X	
Spectra	X						X		
Spherical Reflections	X					X	X		
Touch the Spring	X					X			
Water Sphere Lens	X					X			
THE SPINNING BLACKBOARD AND OTHER DYNAMIC EXPLORATIONS OF FORCE AND MOTION									
Balancing Ball	X				X				
Balancing Stick	X				X	X			
Bernoulli Levitator	X				X	X			
Bicycle Wheel Gyro	X				X	X			
Bubble Suspension	X		X		X		X	X	
Bubble Tray	X		X		X	X	X	X	
Center of Gravity	X				X				
Coupled Resonant Pendulums	X				X	X			
Descartes Diver	X				X				
Downhill Race	X				X	X			
Drawing Board	X				X	X			
Momentum Machine	X				X	X			
Non-Round Rollers	X				X				
Resonant Pendulum	X				X	X			
Resonant Rings	X				X	X			
Resonator	X				X	X			
Soap Bubbles	X		X		X	X		X	
Spinning Blackboard	X				X				

Life Science (continued)				Earth & Space Science				Science & Technology	Science in Personal & Social Perspectives	History & Nature of Science	Math
Biological evolution	Inter-dependence of organisms	Matter, energy, & organization in living systems	Behavior of organisms	Energy in the earth's system	Geo-chemical cycles	Origin & evolution of the earth's system	Origin & evolution of the universe				
								x			
				x							
								x	x		
								x			x
								x			
								x			
								x			x
								x			x
								x			x
				x			x				x
											x
								x			x
								x			x
				x				x			x
											x
			x					x			
			x					x			x
			x					x			
								x			
								x			x
								x			
x		x	x					x			
				x			x	x			
							x				
								x			
								x			
								x			
								x			
											x
								x			
								x			
								x			
								x			x
								x			
				x				x			
x								x			x
				x							x

National Science Education Standards	Science as Inquiry	Physical Science						Life Science	
Grades 9–12		Structure of atoms	Structure & properties of matter	Chemical reactions	Motions & forces	Conservation of energy & increase in disorder	Interactions of energy & matter	The cell	Molecular basis of heredity
Strange Attractor	x				x	x			
Take It from the Top	x				x				
Vortex	x		x		x	x			
Water Spinner	x				x				
THE WIRE-HANGER CONCERTO AND OTHER EAR-SPLITTING EXPLORATIONS OF HOW WE HEAR THE WORLD									
Anti-Sound Spring	x				x		x		
Bee Hummer	x				x		x		
Coffee-Can Cuica	x				x		x		
Conversation Piece	x				x	x	x		
Designer Ears	x				x	x	x		
Doppler Effect	x				x	x	x		
Falling Rhythm	x				x		x		
Head Harp	x				x	x			
Make Your Own Rainstick*									
Organ Pipe	x				x	x			
Pipes of Pan	x				x	x			
Radiohead	x								
Sound Sandwich	x				x				
Speaker	x				x		x		
Stereo Sound	x				x				
Straw Oboe	x				x				
Water-Bottle Membranophone	x				x	x			
Wire-Hanger Concerto	x				x	x			

Life Science (continued)				Earth & Space Science				Science & Technology	Science in Personal & Social Perspectives	History & Nature of Science	Math
Biological evolution	Inter-dependence of organisms	Matter, energy, & organization in living systems	Behavior of organisms	Energy in the earth's system	Geo-chemical cycles	Origin & evolution of the earth's system	Origin & evolution of the universe				
								X		X	
				X		X	X				
											X
				X				X			
								X			
								X			
			X				X	X			X
				X				X		X	X
								X			X
			X					X			
			X								
			X					X			
								X			
			X								
			X								
			X					X			
			X					X			

Concept Index

The index on pages 292 through 295 identifies the major science-related concepts covered by each of the Snacks in this book. Graphical icons representing these 17 concepts (see page x and below) are found at the beginning of each Snack, giving teachers a quick way to find activities that might be useful in the classroom.

By using the Concept Index, teachers can plan interesting ways to introduce their students to new ideas, or delve into familiar concepts in unexpected ways. The Non-Round Rollers Snack, for example, offers three ways to make "wheels" that roll, but aren't round. With it, students learn some interesting lessons in mechanics—while also being able to see the math involved. Bubble Suspension, which explores the behavior of fluids, introduces the idea of osmosis, giving teachers a way to address life sciences while their students play with bubbles.

Snacks be used in many ways to address many different concepts. For each of the activities in this book, the grid that follows offers some useful places to begin.

Chemistry   Color   Electricity   Fluids

Heat   Life Sciences   Light   Magnetism

Math   Mechanics   Perception   Polarization

Reflection   Refraction   Resonance   Sound

Waves

Light	Magnetism	Math	Mechanics	Perception	Polarization	Reflection	Refraction	Resonance	Sound	Waves
x				x						
x				x		x				
			x						x	x
			x							
			x							
									x	
x				x						
			x							
			x							
x				x						
		x		x						
x					x					x
x					x					
x										x
x				x						
x										
x										x
				x						
			x							
				x						
	x									
	x									
			x						x	
				x						
x				x						
x										
x				x						
x							x			
									x	x
x		x				x				
			x					x		
x						x	x			
	x									
x						x				
				x						
			x							
				x					x	
x										x
				x						
x						x	x			
									x	x
			x							
			x					x		
						x				
	x									
x				x		x				
				x						
		x	x						x	
				x						
x							x			
x										
x				x						

Light	Magnetism	Math	Mechanics	Perception	Polarization	Reflection	Refraction	Resonance	Sound	Waves
								X	X	
X						X				
X		X								
				X						
X						X				
X				X						
	X									
	X									
									X	
X						X				
X				X						
			X							
	X									
		X	X							
								X	X	X
X						X				
				X						
				X						
X				X						
								X	X	X
X					X					X
X					X					
X				X						
		X								
				X					X	
			X					X		
			X					X		
			X					X	X	
X					X					
				X						
X										X
X						X				X
									X	
	X								X	X
X										X
X						X				
		X	X							
				X						
									X	
	X									
								X	X	X
	X									
		X	X							
				X						
X						X				
				X						
X							X			
		X	X							
								X	X	X
				X						
									X	

References and Resources

This guide offers information on finding the materials and supplies you'll need to create the Snacks in this book, and ways to think about designing your own activities. It also includes a list of our favorite print resources, including books, manuals, and journals. Be creative when you're shopping, browsing through catalogs, or surfing the Web. You may find inspiration in the most unlikely places!

Materials and Supplies

Sources are listed alphabetically, including some specialty stores and suppliers you'll find online, and some types of stores you'll find in your neighborhood.

In your hunt for resources, we recommend you begin by looking all around you! Can you think of a way the offerings in your local grocery store, pharmacy, toy store, thrift shop, home-improvement center, or office-supply store might be of use in the classroom? Is there something you saw in a restaurant that could work as a great demonstration? Would that super-shiny bowl in the kitchen-supply store make a good concave mirror? Can you make a model from marshmallows and toothpicks instead of buying an expensive kit? This fascinating endeavor can result in some creative ideas for teaching science. In fact, the Exploratorium Teacher Institute actually offers an annual "Shopping for Science" field trip for its Beginning Teacher Program. Best of all, you can do it anytime, anywhere. Here are some more detailed ideas:

American Science and Surplus

www.sciplus.com

Useful science stuff (lab equipment, small motors, and so on), hardware odds and ends, and a wide range of unusual items for creative use. The array of available items changes over time.

Arbor Scientific

www.arborsci.com

Nice selection of interesting science materials.

Dowling Magnets

www.dowlingmagnets.com

Lots of different kinds of magnets, including neodymium and cow magnets, at reasonable cost.

Edmund Scientific Company

www.scientificsonline.com

A prime source for interesting science products, from moiré patterns and solar cells to liquid crystal and polarizing materials. A particularly good source for optics supplies.

Educational Innovations

www.teachersource.com

A wide variety of interesting science materials.

The Exploratorium Store

www.store.exploratorium.edu

Offers science books for adults and kids, science kits, puzzles, games, unique toys, and much more.

Feed Stores

Cow magnets—which you may be able to find at feed stores—work well for many science activities. Normally, these magnets are fed to cows so that any iron material eaten (nails, bits of wire, and so on) will remain in the animal's stomach and not pass through the digestive tract.

Flinn Scientific

www.flinnsci.com

In addition to being a chemical supply house, Flinn has an unmatched array of materials related to laboratory safety. It also offers a variety of activity ideas.

Forcefield

www.forcefieldmagnets.com/catalog

A source for strong magnets of all sizes, in addition to other products.

Frey Scientific

www.freyscientific.com

Large distributor of science supplies.

Grocery Stores

You can use cooking oil, corn syrup, or mineral oil for index of refraction investigations and demonstrations, sugar for making rock candy, antacids (such as Alka-Seltzer) for generating a gas, peanuts for calorimetry investigations, and bread for demonstrating density (before and after sitting on a loaf, for example).

Hardware and Home Improvement Stores

You can use pulleys and jacks for simple machines, flashlight bulbs, sockets, and knife switches for electricity activities, and mousetraps to power cars.

Kelvin

www.kelvin.com

Outstanding source for technology, electronics, and science materials, from motors to hydraulic syringes to plastic propellers.

Master Magnetics/The Magnet Source

www.magnetsource.com

A good source for magnets of all kinds.

Mouser Electronics

www.mouser.com

Electronics supplier with an extensive selection.

Office Supply Stores

You can use binder clips for mirror holders, colored stickers for afterimages, rubber bands for propulsion, paper clips in electric motor construction, and so much more!

Party Stores

At local party stores, you can find small novelties and toys that are suitable for science activities.

PITSCO

www.pitsco.com

Source for a wide range of technology, electronics, and project materials, including mousetrap cars and balsawood bridges.

Plastics Stores

You can get Plexi-mirror, clear and colored acrylic sheets (for static electricity demonstrations or colored filters), mirrored Mylar, and plastic tubes at plastics stores. Most will cut plastics to size (for a price), and many have bargain scrap bins for pieces by the pound.

RadioShack

www.radioshack.com

RadioShack stores are virtually everywhere and sell common electronic components such as resistors, alligator clips, buzzers, wire, LEDs, and more. Because of its easy accessibility, we've listed RadioShack as a source for many of the electronic components used in this book, but these materials are also available from Kelvin, Mouser, and other sellers of electronics.

Sargent-Welch

www.sargentwelch.com

Large distributor of science supplies.

Science First

www.sciencefirst.com

A source of efficient holographic diffraction gratings, along with many other products for teaching science.

Science Museum Stores

Check in your area for unique resources, including books, kits, and toys.

Steve Spangler Science

www.stevespanglerscience.com

Offers a potpourri of science materials including science kits, toys, and videos.

Tap Plastics

www.tapplastics.com

A large distributor of plastics and plastics products. There's an online store as well as brick-and-mortar stores on the West Coast.

Thrift Shops

Stores such as Goodwill, the Salvation Army, and St. Vincent de Paul, along with local thrift shops, can sometimes provide useful items at bargain prices. For example, we found a working hair dryer for $1.00 (for Balancing Ball), a working turntable for $5.00 (for Spinning Blackboard), and a bowling ball for $5.00 (which we used as the pendulum in Resonant Pendulum). Just use your imagination!

Toy Stores

You can use foam dart guns to investigate projectile motion, wind-up toys for energy transformations, and toy cars of various types to explore velocity and acceleration.

U.S. Toy Co.

www.ustoy.com

An online party store that carries pull-back cars, plastic and metal Slinky-type springs, magnifiers, and more. You can purchase many items by the dozen fairly inexpensively.

Recommended Books, Manuals, and Journals

Listed alphabetically by author. Note that textbooks tend to be revised fairly frequently, so it's worth checking to see if you can find editions later than those listed here. Book titles followed by an asterisk (*) may be difficult to locate, but they're worth the effort. Amazon and eBay are potential sources of used copies.

The Physics Teacher, American Association of Physics Teachers (AAPT); www.aapt.org

An excellent peer-reviewed monthly journal for physics teachers. Each issue presents a valuable array of activities, labs, articles, reviews, and columns.

ChemMatters, American Chemical Society; www.acs.org

An outstanding and affordable quarterly magazine for high school chemistry students. Each issue includes a Teacher's Guide containing hands-on activities and other resources.

How Things Work: The Physics of Everyday Life (4th ed.), by Louis Bloomfield, Wiley, 2009; www.wiley.com

Approaches physics through commonly encountered applications and devices, including lightbulbs, microwave ovens, CD players, cars, vacuum cleaners, and more. A unique and outstanding addition to your reference library.

Clouds in a Glass of Beer: Simple Experiments in Atmospheric Physics, by Craig F. Bohren, Dover Publications, 2001; www.doverpublications.com

Discussions and activities concerning atmospheric physics.

What Light Through Yonder Window Breaks? More Experiments in Atmospheric Physics, by Craig F. Bohren, Dover Publications, 2006; www.doverpublications.com

Discussions and activities concerning atmospheric physics.

Physics: A Window on Our World (7th ed.), by Jay Boleman, Ink Press, 2005

An excellent addition to your reference library.

A Potpourri of Physics Teaching Ideas, edited by Donna Berry Connor, American Association of Physics Teachers (AAPT); www.aapt.org

Large collection of outstanding experiments, activities, and demonstrations from *The Physics Teacher.*

How Things Work, by Richard Crane, American Association of Physics Teachers (AAPT), 1992; www.aapt.org

Collection of explanations of how many interesting things work, from the author's column in *The Physics Teacher.*

Physics (5th ed.), by John Cutnell and Kenneth Johnson, Wiley, 2009

Excellent addition to a reference library.

String and Sticky Tape Experiments, by Ronald Edge, American Association of Physics Teachers (AAPT), 1987; www.aapt.org

Extensive collection of simple experiments, activities, and demonstrations from the author's column in *The Physics Teacher.*

Turning the World Inside Out & 174 Other Simple Physics Demonstrations, by Robert Ehrlich, Princeton University Press, 1990; http://press.princeton.edu

A collection of demonstrations using low-cost materials to illustrate major physics concepts in simple and playful ways.

Why Toast Falls Jelly-Side Down: Zen and the Art of Physics Demonstrations, by Robert Ehrlich, Princeton University Press, 1997; http://press.princeton.edu

This collection of demonstrations, using low-tech and inexpensive materials from everyday life, makes key principles of physics easy to understand.

Thinking Physics (3rd ed.), by Lewis Carroll Epstein, Insight Press, 2002

Illustrated multiple-choice conceptual physics problems related to the real world (includes solutions).

Seeing the Light, by David Falk, Dieter Brill, and David Stork, Wiley, 1986; www.wiley.com

A unique and outstanding text covering virtually all aspects of light, vision, and color. Though essentially a college text, it is largely qualitative rather than mathematical. It also has many activities that are quite doable by students. For any science teacher teaching the topic of light.

A Demonstration Handbook for Physics, by G. D. Frier and F. J. Anderson, American Association of Physics Teachers (AAPT), 1981; www.aapt.org

Brief descriptions and diagrams for many physics demonstrations.

Physics (6th ed.), by Douglas Giancoli, Addison-Wesley, 2009; www.pearsonhighered.com

A fine addition to your reference library.

Conceptual Physical Science (4th ed.), by Paul G. Hewitt, John Suchocki, and Leslie Hewitt, Addison-Wesley, 2008; www.pearsonhighered.com

Excellent conceptual treatment of physical science.

Conceptual Physics Media Update (10th ed.), by Paul G. Hewitt, Addison Wesley, 2009; www.pearsonhighered.com

This package contains the tenth edition of the classic *Conceptual Physics* textbook—an outstanding example of a readable, qualitative approach to the concepts of physics that's a must for your reference library. It also includes the *Media Workbook,* which relates to interactive tutorials on *The Physics Place* Web site, and the *Practicing Physics* workbook.

[Prentice Hall] Conceptual Physics (A High School Physics Program), by Paul G. Hewitt, Prentice Hall, 2009; www.pearsonschool.com

A Teacher's Guide and an extensive range of ancillary materials are available.

*Making Simple Musical Instruments,** by Bart Hopkin, Lark Books, 1995

Instructions for making a variety of musical instruments. Complete materials lists, instructions, and discussions. A fairly sophisticated approach that requires some use of power tools, but not at the master-craftsman level.

Musical Instrument Design, by Bart Hopkin, See Sharp Press, 1996

Ideas and information for making and understanding musical instruments. A wonderful reference that is both sophisticated and understandable.

GEMS (Great Explorations in Math and Science), Lawrence Hall of Science, University of California at Berkeley; www.lhs.berkeley.edu/gems

A series of activity-based publications covering everything from bubbles to fingerprinting.

Invitations to Scientific Inquiry (2nd ed.),* by Tik L. Liem, Science Inquiry Enterprises, 1991; jmkris@scienceinquiry.com

A great collection of simple demonstrations and activities: a high-priority acquisition.

Apparatus for Teaching Physics, edited by Karl C. Mamola, American Association of Physics Teachers (AAPT); www.aapt.org

A collection of 150 columns from *The Physics Teacher,* with an emphasis on apparatus that's useful in introductory physics courses. The collection is divided into five topics: mechanics, waves and sound, thermal physics, electricity and magnetism, and light and color.

The Role of Toys in Teaching Physics, by Jodi McCullough and Roy McCullough, American Association of Physics Teachers (AAPT), 2000; www.aapt.org

An AAPT/PTRA Workshop Manual. Ideas for using a wide variety of toys in labs, demonstrations, displays, contests, and more. Includes sources for toys, concepts covered, questions, and other useful items.

Getting Started in Electronics (3rd ed.), by Forest M. Mims III, Master Publishing, 2003; www.masterpublishing.com

A good introduction to basic electronics. Includes theory and practical applications, and lots of stuff to build with relatively inexpensive parts.

*The Dick and Rae Physics Demo Notebook,** by Richard B. Minnix and D. Rae Carpenter Jr., Dick and Rae, Inc., 1993

Physics demonstrations from two decades of workshops at Virginia Military Institute.

NSTA Recommends, National Science Teachers Association (NSTA); www.nsta.org/recommends

A catalog of science-teaching materials. Available online only.

The Science Teacher, Science Scope, and *Science and Children,* National Science Teachers Association (NSTA); www.nsta.org

Three useful peer-reviewed journals designed for high school, middle school, and elementary school teachers, respectively. (Available to NSTA members only.)

The Science of Sound (3rd ed.), by Thomas D. Rossing, Richard F. Moore, and Paul A. Wheeler, Addison-Wesley, 2002

A well-known college text that provides an excellent introduction to acoustics.

Chemical Magic from the Grocery Store, by Andy S. W. Sae, Kendall/Hunt, 1996

An excellent collection of activities and demonstrations using common, easily obtainable materials.

Teaching Chemistry with Toys: Activities for Grades K–9, by Jerry L. Sarquis, Mickey Sarquis, and John P. Williams, Terrific Science Press, 1995; www.terrificscience.com/sciencestore

An excellent collection of chemistry activities based on toys.

Conceptual Chemistry (3rd ed.), by John Suchocki, Prentice Hall, 2007; www.pearsonhighered.com

A very readable qualitative approach to chemistry with many examples of how chemistry relates to everyday life. The book comes with *Conceptual Chemistry Alive,* an engaging DVD.

Demonstration Experiments in Physics, by Richard Sutton, American Association of Physics Teachers (AAPT), 2003; www.aapt.org

This is a reprint of the 1938 classic work.

Teaching Physics with Toys: Activities for Grades K–9, by Beverly Taylor, Dwight Portman, and Susan Gertz, Terrific Science Press, 2006; www.terrificscience.com/sciencestore

An excellent collection of physics activities based on toys.

TOPS Task Cards, TOPS Learning Systems; www.topscience.org/site_pages/flavors.html#1

Activity cards for physical science projects using everyday materials. An extremely valuable resource for teaching low-budget, hands-on science without elaborate facilities. The activities cover an amazingly wide range of content.

The Flying Circus of Physics (2nd ed.), by Jearl Walker, Wiley, 2006; www.wiley.com

An extensive, fascinating collection of problems and questions about the real world, with answers included.

College Physics (7th ed.), by Jerry Wilson and Anthony Buffa, Addison-Wesley, 2009; www.pearsonhighered.com

An excellent addition to any reference library.

Resources from the Exploratorium

A selection of books and posters available from the Exploratorium Store, www.store.exploratorium.edu.

The Ball Makes the Game, by the Exploratorium staff; illustrated by David Barker

There's a reason people don't play golf with basketballs. This poster shows how different balls spin, bounce, and move through the air.

Explorabook: A Kid's Science Museum in a Book, by John Cassidy and the Exploratorium, Klutz Press, 1991

Tools and ideas to inspire scientific exploration, written in the inimitable Klutz style.

Exploratopia, by Pat Murphy, Ellen Macaulay, and the staff of the Exploratorium; illustrated by Jason Gorski, Little, Brown, 2006

An award-winning, family-friendly book filled with astounding ideas, hands-on activities, fascinating facts, and eye-popping photos.

The Exploratorium Guide to Scale and Structure, by Barry Kluger-Bell and the School in the Exploratorium, Heinemann, 1995

These inquiry-based activities explore the physics and mathematics of structure as well as the effects of scale on structure.

How Does a Muscle Work? by the Exploratorium staff; scientific illustrations by David Goodsell, Exploratorium, 2003

This award-winning poster shows the molecular changes that make your muscles move. Detailed images include magnifications more than 1.5 million times life size.

Human Body Explorations (2nd ed.), by Karen E. Kalumuck and the Exploratorium Teacher Institute, Kendall/Hunt, 2005

The activities in this book lead to a better understanding of many of the intriguing and mysterious aspects of the human body, both macroscopic and microscopic.

Math and Science Across Cultures, by Maurice Bazin, Modesto Tamez, and the Exploratorium Teacher Institute, New Press, 2002

These inquiry-based activities highlight the science and math contributions of many of the world's cultures, both ancient and modern.

The Math Explorer, by Pat Murphy, Lori Lambertson, Pearl Tesler, and the staff of Exploratorium; illustrated by Jason Gorski, Key Curriculum Press, 2003

Games, puzzles, and other fun activities help kids develop math skills.

The Science Explorer, by Pat Murphy, Ellen Klages, Linda Shore, and the staff of the Exploratorium; illustrated by Jason Gorski, Exploratorium, 2002

Science activities that are fun to do and require little or no preparation encourage children's curiosity and eagerness to explore.

Square Wheels, by Don Rathjen, Paul Doherty, and the Exploratorium Teacher Institute; illustrated by Esther Kutnick, Exploratorium, 2002

Contains instructions for building thirty-one inexpensive activities, demonstrations, and classroom-sized science exhibits.

Exploratorium Web Site; www.exploratorium.edu

Multimedia sites that explore diverse science topics such as climate change, polar science, human origins, earthquakes, gardening, music, and much, much more, along with hands-on activities and interactive exhibits. Also available is information on the Exploratorium's teacher programs and opportunities for professional development.

Content Index